DISCOVER
the *Bible*
for YOURSELF

KAY ARTHUR

HARVEST HOUSE PUBLISHERS

EUGENE, OREGON

Cover by Koechel Peterson & Associates, Inc., Minneapolis, Minnesota

DISCOVER THE BIBLE FOR YOURSELF

Copyright © 2000 by Precept Ministries International
Published by Harvest House Publishers
Eugene, Oregon 97402
www.harvesthousepublishers.com

Library of Congress Cataloging-in-Publication Data
Arthur, Kay, 1933-
    Discover the Bible for yourself / Kay Arthur.
      p. cm.
    ISBN-13: 978-0-7369-1068-2
    ISBN-10: 0-7369-1068-9 (pbk.)
    1. Bible—Study and teaching. 2. Bible—Criticism, interpretation, etc.   I. Title.
    BS600.3.A78 2005
    220'.071—dc22   2005003380

WELCOME TO THE ADVENTURE OF INDUCTIVE BIBLE STUDY!

*o you long to know God? Do you yearn for a deep and abiding relationship with Him? Do you want to live the Christian life faithfully—and to know what He requires of you? Do you long to know how to understand God's Word?

God reveals Himself through His Word. Through it, He shows us how to live. Jesus made it clear: "Man shall not live on bread alone, but on every word that proceeds out of the mouth of God" (Matthew 4:4). And where do we find this divine bread? In the Scriptures.

As you study your Bible with the help of the Holy Spirit, and live out the truths that God reveals to you, you will discover new stability, strength, and confidence. You will be able to say with the prophet Jeremiah: "Your words were found and I ate them, and Your words became for me a joy and the delight of my heart" (Jeremiah 15:16).

Today, many people are convinced they cannot know truth for themselves. A babble of voices surrounds us claiming to know and interpret God's truth for us. Which voices are right? Which are wrong? How can we discern the true from the counterfeit unless we spend time with God and His Word?

Most Christians have been encouraged to study the Word of God, yet many have never been shown how. Others even feel inadequate to do so because they are not ministers or seminary students or scholars. Nothing could be further from the truth.

The most effective way to do this is through the inductive approach. The inductive approach means that you begin with the Word of God itself. In fact, if you want to satisfy your hunger and thirst to know God and His Word in a deeper way, you must do more than merely read Scripture and study what someone else has said about it. Just as no one else can eat and digest your food for you, so no one else can feed on God's Word for you. You must interact with the text yourself, absorbing its truths and letting God engrave His truth on your heart and mind and life.

That is the very heart of inductive study: seeing truth for yourself, discerning what it means, and applying that truth to your life. In His inspired Word, God has given us everything we need to know about life and godliness. But He doesn't stop there. He gives every believer a resident teacher—the Holy Spirit—who guides us into His truth.

The Bible is unlike any other book. It is supernatural. It is complete in itself. The Bible needs no other books or truths to supplement it. In inductive study the Bible becomes its own commentary, and any believer can see and understand what God has given us in His Word and how it applies to us today.

As you use this book you'll need a Bible, preferably one with margins to write in, a notebook to record your insights, and a good collection of maps. Enjoy your adventure in understanding God's Word!

How to Study the Bible Inductively

ை௳௳௳

If you know there is more to the Word of God than you have discovered so far...

- ☙ If you sense there must be concrete answers to the complexities of life...
- ☙ If you want a bedrock faith that keeps you from being tossed around by conflicting philosophies in the world and the church...
- ☙ If you want to be able to face the uncertainties of the future without fear...

...then inductive Bible study is designed for you.

God's eternal, infallible Word is your guidebook for all of life, and inductive study gives you the key to understanding that guide.

Inductive study, a method that brings you directly to the Word of God apart from another's understanding or interpretation of the text, involves three skills: *observation, interpretation,* and *application.*

OBSERVATION
Discover What It Says!

Observation teaches you to see precisely what the passage says. It is the basis for accurate interpretation and correct application. Observation answers the question: What does the passage say?

INTERPRETATION
Discover What It Means!

Interpretation answers the question: What does the passage mean?

APPLICATION
Discover How It Works!

Application answers the question: What does it mean to me personally? What truths can I put into practice? What changes should I make in my life?

When you know what God says, what He means, and how to put His truths into practice, you will be equipped for every circumstance of life. Ultimately, the goal of personal Bible study is a transformed life and a deep and abiding relationship with Jesus Christ.

The following ten steps provide the basis for inductive study. As you take these steps, observation, interpretation, and application will sometimes happen simultaneously. God can give you insight at any point in your study, so be sensitive to His leading. When words or passages make an impression on you, stop for a moment and meditate on what God has shown you. Record your personal notes and insights in the margin of your Bible so that you can remember what you've learned.

As you study the Bible chapter by chapter and book by book, you will grow in your ability to comprehend the whole counsel of God. In the future, you will be able to refer to your notes again and again as you study portions of Scripture and grow in your knowledge of Him.

OBSERVATION

Discover What It Says!

STEP ONE

BEGIN WITH PRAYER

Prayer is often the missing element in Bible study. You are about to learn the single most effective method of Bible study. Yet apart from the work of the Holy Spirit, that's all it will be—a method. It is the indwelling Holy Spirit who guides us into all truth, who takes the things of God and reveals them to us. Always ask God to teach you as you open the Scriptures.

STEP TWO

ASK THE "5 W'S AND AN H"

As you study any passage of Scripture, any book of the Bible, train yourself to constantly ask: *Who? What? When? Where? Why? How?* These questions are the building blocks of precise observation, which is essential for accurate interpretation. Many times Scripture is misinterpreted because the context isn't carefully observed. Asking these questions will help you to stay in the context of the passage.

When we rush into interpretation without laying the vital foundation of observation, our understanding becomes colored by our presuppositions—what we think, what we feel, or what other people have said. We must be careful not to distort the Scriptures to our own destruction (2 Peter 3:16).

Accurate answers to the following questions will help assure correct interpretation.

Who *is speaking? Who is this about? Who are the main characters?* For example, look at the sample passage from 1 Peter 5 (see page 11). In this chapter, "I" is speaking. Verse 1 tells us that "I" is a fellow elder, a witness of the sufferings of Christ, and a partaker of the glory to follow. From reading this and previous chapters (the context), you recognize that the "I" is Peter, the author of this epistle. You'll want to mark the author in a special color (such as blue) to help you with your study.

And ***to whom*** *is he speaking?* Verse 1 refers to "the elders," verse 5 to "you younger men," and verse 6 to "yourselves" (the recipients of the epistle). You'll find it helpful to mark the recipients in another color.

What *is the subject or event covered in the chapter? What do you learn about the people, the event, or the teaching from the text? What instructions are given?* In 1 Peter 5:2, Peter instructs the elders to shepherd the flock and exercise oversight.

When *do or will the events occur? When did or will something happen to a particular person, people, or nation? When* is a key question in determining the progression of events. In

1 Peter 5:4, we learn that "when the Chief Shepherd appears," the elders will receive their "unfading crown of glory." Mark references to time (such as "when") with a clock 🕐.

Where *did or will this happen? Where was it said?* In 1 Peter 5, the only reference to a place is in verse 13, where there is a greeting from "she who is in Babylon." Mark geographical locations by double-underlining them in green.

Why *is something being said or mentioned? Why would or will this happen? Why at this time? Why this person?* First Peter 5:12 explains why and how Peter wrote this epistle, establishing the book's purpose: to exhort and testify that this is the true grace of God, that they may stand firm in it.

How *will it happen? How is it to be done? How is it illustrated?* In 1 Peter 5:2, note *how* the elders are to exercise oversight: voluntarily and eagerly, according to the will of God.

Every time you study a passage of the Bible, you should keep the "5 W's and an H" in mind. Don't be concerned if you can't find the answer to each question every time. Remember, there are many types of literature in the Bible and not all the questions will apply. As you ask *who, what, when, where, why,* and *how,* make notes in the margin of your Bible. Meditate on the truths God reveals to you. Think how they apply to you. This will keep your study from becoming an intellectual pursuit of knowledge for its own sake.

STEP *T*HREE

MARK KEY WORDS AND PHRASES

A key word is one that is essential to the text. It might be a noun, a descriptive word, or an action that plays a part in conveying the author's message. A key word or phrase is one which, when removed, leaves the passage devoid of meaning. Often key words and phrases are repeated in order to convey the author's point or purpose for writing. They may be repeated throughout a chapter, a segment of a book, or the book as a whole. For example, notice that some form of the word *suffering* is used three times in 1 Peter 5.

The key words we have suggested are taken from the New American Standard Bible. If you are using the New International Version or King James Version, look at appendix seven at the back of this book. It lists many of the New American Standard Bible's key words and the words the New International Version and King James Version use.

As you mark key words, ask the same *who, what, when, where, why,* and *how* questions of them as you did of the passage as a whole. For example, *Who* suffers? *What* caused the suffering? etc.

Key words can be marked in several ways:

༄ *Through the use of colors.* Colored pencils or Micron pens work best.

༄ *Through symbols or a combination of colors and symbols.*

10

THE INDUCTIVE MARKING APPROACH

1 PETER 5 ∾ SAMPLE A

IN THE EPISTLES, MARK EVERY REFERENCE TO THE AUTHOR IN ONE COLOR AND EVERY REFERENCE TO THE RECIPIENTS IN ANOTHER

IDENTIFY SIMPLE LISTS

Chapter 5 Theme

5 [a]Therefore, I exhort the elders among you, as *your* [b]fellow elder and [c]witness of the sufferings of Christ, and a [d]partaker also of the glory that is to be revealed,

2 shepherd [a]the flock of God among you, exercising oversight [b]not under compulsion, but voluntarily according to *the will of God*; and [c]not for sordid gain, but with eagerness;

3 [c]nor yet as [a]lording it over [1]those allotted to your charge, but [2]proving to be [b]examples to the flock.

4 And when the Chief [a]Shepherd appears, you will receive the [b]unfading [1c]crown of glory.

5 [a]You younger men, likewise, [b]be subject to *your* elders; and all of you, clothe yourselves with [c]humility toward one another, for [d]GOD IS OPPOSED TO THE PROUD, BUT GIVES GRACE TO THE HUMBLE.

MARK KEY WORDS AND SYNONYMS, SUCH AS GOD, CHRIST, DEVIL, SUFFERING

6 Therefore [a]humble yourselves under the mighty hand of God, that He may exalt you at the proper time,

7 casting all your [a]anxiety on Him, because He cares for you.

8 [a]Be of sober *spirit*, [b]be on the alert. Your adversary, [c]the devil, prowls around like a roaring [d]lion, seeking someone to devour.

9 [1a]But resist him, [b]firm in *your* faith, knowing that [c]the same experiences of suffering are being accomplished by your [2]brethren who are in the world.

10 After you have suffered [a]for a little while, the [b]God of all grace, who [c]called you to His [d]eternal glory in Christ, will Himself [e]perfect, [f]confirm, strengthen *and* establish you.

11 [a]To Him *be* dominion forever and ever. Amen.

12 Through [a]Silvanus, our faithful brother [1](for so I regard *him)*, [b]I have written to you briefly, exhorting and testifying that this is [c]the true grace of God. [d]Stand firm in it!

DOUBLE-UNDERLINE IN GREEN ALL GEOGRAPHICAL LOCATIONS

13 She who is in Babylon, chosen together with you, sends you greetings, and *so does* my son, [a]Mark.

14 [a]Greet one another with a kiss of love.
[b]Peace be to you all who are in Christ.

Suffering:
1. Christ Suffered.

2. Brethren are suffering.

3. You will suffer.

4. But God perfects, confirms, strengthens, and establishes those who suffer!

MAKE LISTS FROM KEY WORDS

11

Always mark each key word the same way every time you observe it. Then, in future study, the visual impact of your marks will help you track key subjects and quickly identify significant truths throughout Scripture. To be sure that you are consistent, list key words, symbols, and color codes on an index card and use it as a bookmark in your Bible.

Be sure to mark pronouns (*I, you, he, she, it, we, they,* and so on), synonyms (words that have the same meaning in the context), and other closely related words the same way you mark the words to which they refer. For example, a synonym for the devil in 1 Peter 5:8 is *adversary.* The pronoun *him* in verse 9 also refers to the devil. Notice how marking the synonym *adversary* for the devil gives additional insight into his nature.

STEP FOUR

LOOK FOR LISTS

Making lists can be one of the most enlightening things you do as you study a section of Scripture. Lists reveal truths and highlight important concepts. The best way to discover lists in the text is to observe how a key word is described, note what is said about someone or something, or group related thoughts or instructions together. (Develop lists on a separate piece of paper or in a notebook.)

1 Peter 5:2-3, for example, contains a *simple list* instructing the elders how to shepherd their flock. You can number simple lists within the text for easy reference.

Topical lists capture a truth, quality, or characteristic of a specific subject throughout a passage. One way to discover a topical list is to follow a key word through a chapter and note what the text says about the word each time it is used. (You may want to develop your lists on a worksheet.) See sample A for how a list could be made for the key word *suffering.*

As you write your observations on suffering, you will begin to have a better and broader understanding of God's thoughts on this subject. You will learn that:

- ❧ Christ suffered
- ❧ the brethren in the world are suffering
- ❧ the recipients of the letter may also endure suffering

You will also discover that God does several things in the lives of those who suffer:

- ❧ perfects
- ❧ strengthens
- ❧ confirms
- ❧ establishes

The application value of lists such as these is immeasurable. The next time you endure suffering, you will be able to recall these truths more quickly:

- ❧ Christ suffered
- ❧ others are suffering
- ❧ ultimately God will use suffering to strengthen your own life

Discovering truths that apply to your daily life is what makes lists such an important part of the inductive method.

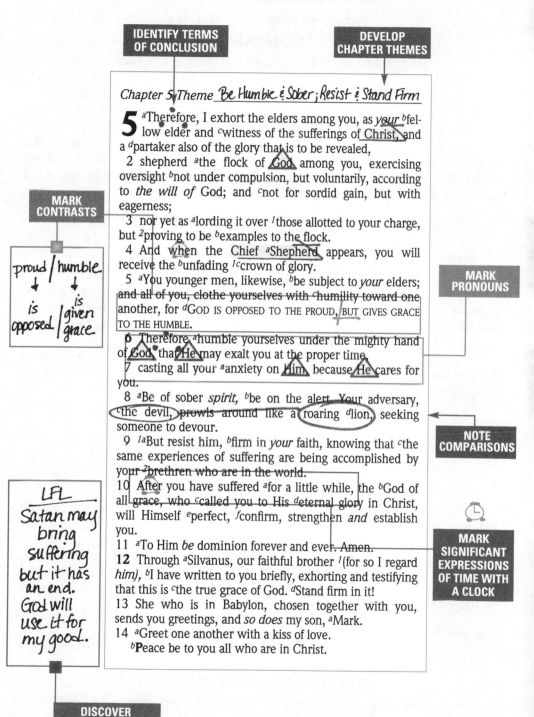

IDENTIFY TERMS OF CONCLUSION

DEVELOP CHAPTER THEMES

Chapter 5 Theme _Be Humble & Sober; Resist & Stand Firm_

5 [a]Therefore, I exhort the elders among you, as _your_ [b]fellow elder and [c]witness of the sufferings of Christ, and a [d]partaker also of the glory that is to be revealed,

2 shepherd [a]the flock of God among you, exercising oversight [b]not under compulsion, but voluntarily, according to _the will of_ God; and [c]not for sordid gain, but with eagerness;

3 nor yet as [a]lording it over [1]those allotted to your charge, but [2]proving to be [b]examples to the flock.

4 And when the Chief [a]Shepherd appears, you will receive the [b]unfading [1c]crown of glory.

5 [a]You younger men, likewise, [b]be subject to _your_ elders; and all of you, clothe yourselves with [c]humility toward one another, for [d]GOD IS OPPOSED TO THE PROUD, BUT GIVES GRACE TO THE HUMBLE.

6 Therefore [a]humble yourselves under the mighty hand of God that He may exalt you at the proper time,

7 casting all your [a]anxiety on Him, because He cares for you.

8 [a]Be of sober _spirit,_ [b]be on the alert. Your adversary, [c]the devil, prowls around like a roaring [d]lion, seeking someone to devour.

9 [1a]But resist him, [b]firm in _your_ faith, knowing that [c]the same experiences of suffering are being accomplished by your [2]brethren who are in the world.

10 After you have suffered [a]for a little while, the [b]God of all grace, who [c]called you to His [d]eternal glory in Christ, will Himself [e]perfect, [f]confirm, strengthen _and_ establish you.

11 [a]To Him _be_ dominion forever and ever. Amen.

12 Through [a]Silvanus, our faithful brother [1](for so I regard _him),_ [b]I have written to you briefly, exhorting and testifying that this is [c]the true grace of God. [d]Stand firm in it!

13 She who is in Babylon, chosen together with you, sends you greetings, and _so does_ my son, [a]Mark.

14 [a]Greet one another with a kiss of love.
[b]Peace be to you all who are in Christ.

MARK CONTRASTS

proud / humble
↓ ↓
is / is
opposed / given grace

MARK PRONOUNS

NOTE COMPARISONS

MARK SIGNIFICANT EXPRESSIONS OF TIME WITH A CLOCK

LFL
Satan may bring suffering but it has an end. God will use it for my good.

DISCOVER LESSONS FOR LIFE

13

WATCH FOR CONTRASTS AND COMPARISONS

Contrasts and comparisons use highly descriptive language to drive home significant truths and vital lessons. The word pictures they paint make it easier to remember what you've learned.

A *contrast* shows how things are different or opposite, such as light/darkness or proud/humble. The word *but* often signifies a contrast is being made. You may want to note contrasts in the text or the margin of your Bible.

A *comparison* points out similarities and is often indicated by the use of words such as *like, as,* and *as it were.* For example, Peter says in 1 Peter 5:8: "Your adversary, the devil, prowls around *like* a roaring lion." You may want to highlight comparisons in a distinctive way so you will recognize them quickly when you return to the passage in the future.

NOTE EXPRESSIONS OF TIME

The relationship of events in time often sheds light on the true meaning of the text. The timing of something can be observed in exact statements such as "on the tenth day of the eleventh month" or "at the feast of Booths." These phrases can be indicated in the margin by drawing a simple clock ⏱ in a specific color, such as green.

Time is also indicated by words such as *until, then, when,* and *after.* These words show the relationship of one statement or event to another. Marking them will help you see the sequence of events and lead to accurate interpretation of Scripture.

IDENTIFY TERMS OF CONCLUSION

Terms of conclusion usually follow an important sequence of thought and include words such as *wherefore, therefore, for this reason,* and *finally.* As the saying goes, when you see a *therefore* (or any term of conclusion), note what it is there for. You should be able to look through the preceding verses and summarize the message. For example, 1 Peter 5:6 says, *"Therefore* humble yourselves...." If you will look, you will discover that you should humble yourself under the hand of God because God "is opposed to the proud, but gives grace to the humble."

STEP EIGHT

DEVELOP CHAPTER THEMES

The theme of a chapter will center on the main person, event, teaching, or subject of that section of Scripture. Themes are often revealed by reviewing the key words and lists you developed. Try to express the theme as briefly as possible, using words found in the text.

For example, possible themes for 1 Peter 5 might be *Exhortations to Elders, Younger Men, and the Suffering,* or *God Gives Grace to the Humble.* The point of observation is to answer the question: What does the passage say? The theme summarizes the answer. Although many Bibles give chapter or paragraph themes, you may want to record the chapter theme as you understand it near the beginning of the chapter. (The NISB has a line for this at the beginning of each chapter.) If needed, record the themes in pencil so you can adjust them as your study deepens.

STEP NINE

DISCOVER LESSONS FOR LIFE

In the process of observing the text and seeing how God instructed people and dealt with various individuals, the Holy Spirit will bring to your attention truths that God wants you to be aware of and live by in your own life. These "Lessons for Life" can be noted in the margin under the abbreviation "LFL," or you may wish to create a distinctive symbol to mark your Lessons for Life throughout your Bible.

Recording these will add a "devotional" element to your Bible and serve as a good reminder (or legacy) of what God has spoken to your heart when you or others read it.

STEP TEN

COMPLETE THE
AT A GLANCE CHART

The AT A GLANCE charts provide a compact visual summary of each book. See a sample AT A GLANCE chart on the following page.

∾ **Record the author of the book.** If the author is not mentioned by name, leave this space blank.

∾ **Record the date the book was written** if the date of writing is known.

∾ **Record the key words.** If the key words are not already listed on the AT A GLANCE chart, you will find them listed in the THINGS TO DO section at the beginning of each book. As we mentioned earlier, the key words we have suggested are taken from the New American Standard Bible. If you are using the New International Version or King James Version, look at appendix seven at the back of this book. It lists many of the New American Standard Bible's key words and the words the New International Version and King James Version use.

In order to notice subjects that run throughout the entire Bible, there are some key words or phrases you will want to consistently mark in a distinctive manner. Write these on a card, color-code them in the way you intend to mark them throughout your Bible, and use the card as a bookmark.

A sample list of key words to mark (already colored) appears on page 19.

∾ **Copy the chapter themes** that you recorded at the beginning of each chapter. Because chapter divisions were added much later than the Bible was originally written, they do not always fall naturally in the text. Occasionally you will find a chapter with more than one theme. If this is true, record both themes.

15

1 PETER AT A GLANCE

Theme of 1 Peter: Suffering and Glory

SEGMENT
DIVISIONS

	CHAPTER THEMES
1	Trials Prove Your Faith – Be Holy
2	You're Chosen: Follow Christ's Example – Submit
3	
4	
5	

Author:
Peter
Date:
63 or 64 A.D.
Purpose:
To exhort
to stand firm
in true grace
(5:12)

Key Words:
suffering, trials
(and all
synonyms)
grace
glory
salvation
any reference
to Jesus' future
revelation
love
Holy Spirit
called
chosen
holy

Complete the AT A GLANCE charts throughout the Bible as you discover book and chapter themes

∾ **Look for and record segment divisions.** See if any of the chapters can be grouped under a common theme or a common event. This is called a *segment division*. Segment divisions help you see the framework of a book.

The number and types of segment divisions will vary. A book might be divided according to dates, geographical locations, reigns of kings, major characters or events, topics, or doctrines.

When you gain a broad view of a book through its segment divisions, it is easier to understand its content and purpose. The AT A GLANCE chart for the Gospel of John (sample D) shows a number of ways this book could be divided. For example, on the last line under "Segment Divisions," you will notice "Structure of Book." This shows you how John presents his material to achieve his purpose for writing this Gospel.

∾ **Record the purpose of the book.** Discerning the author's purpose for writing and then keeping this purpose in mind while you study the text will help you handle the Word of God accurately. Unless the author specifically states his purpose for writing, as in 1 Peter 5:12 and John 20:31, you will have to discover it by other means:

1. Look for the main subjects covered in the book. These can often be recognized as you study the key repeated words.
2. Watch for any problems that are addressed. It may be that the author's purpose in writing was to deal with these problems.
3. Note exhortations and warnings that are given. These may be the reason for the book.
4. Observe what the author did *not* cover in his writing. When you know what the author covered and what was left unsaid, you are better able to narrow down the real purpose of the book.

∾ **Record the main theme of the book.** Once you have listed the theme for each chapter, evaluated the author's purpose for writing, and observed the content of the book chapter by chapter and segment by segment, you will be prepared to determine the theme of the book. What one statement best describes the book as a whole?

☙❧❧❧❧❧

Once you have completed the ten steps of observation, you are ready to move into interpretation and application.

THE AT A GLANCE CHARTS
GOSPEL OF JOHN ∽ SAMPLE D

JOHN AT A GLANCE

Theme of John: Eternal life through Jesus Christ, Son of God

SEGMENT DIVISIONS

Author: **John**

Date: about **A.D. 85**

Purpose: that his readers would believe that Jesus is the Christ, God's Son, and thus have eternal life

Key Words: (including synonyms)
signs / miracles
believe
life
judge
judgment
witness
sin
true, truth
king
kingdom
love
works
commandments
fruit
abide
ask
truth, truly, true
devil (Satan, ruler of this world)

Structure of Book	Written	Signs and Miracles	Ministry	Chapter	Chapter Themes
Introduces Jesus as Christ, Son of God	That you may believe Jesus is the Christ, Son of God	Water to wine	To Israel	1	Prologue – The Word / John the Baptist / calling disciples
				2	wedding Cana / cleansing temple
Gives signs that prove Jesus is Christ, Son of God		Heals noble-man's son / Heals lame man / Feeds 5,000 / walks on water		3	born again
				4	woman at well / royal official
				5	father / son
				6	bread / feeding 5,000
				7	feast of tabernacles / thirst-drink
		Heals blind man		8	adulterous woman / truth sets free
				9	blind man
		Raises Lazarus from dead		10	sheep / shepherd
				11	raising Lazarus
	Decision time	Hour has come	To Disciples	12	dinner at Bethany / King on donkey
Life that belongs to those who believe God	That you may have life			13	last supper / washing-disciples
				14	Father's house / hearts be troubled
				15	abide / vine and branches
				16	Holy Spirit / another helper
				17	Lord's prayer / high-priestly prayer
	Obtaining of that life – by death and resurrection		To All Mankind	18	arrest and trial
				19	crucifixion
		Resurrection appearances		20	resurrection
Purpose of life: love and follow			To Disciples	21	do you love Me?

18

A System for Marking Key Words Including Synonyms and Pronouns Throughout Your Bible

❧ Color-coding key words with various color combinations is very helpful, as using too many symbols can clutter the text.

❧ In an epistle, color *the author* in one color (e.g. blue) and *the recipient(s)* another (e.g. orange).

❧ As you mark, choose certain colors to represent various things. For example, blue could be your color for Israel, and anything connected with Israel would always have blue in the color combination. Yellow could be your color for God, anything connected with redemption could be red, and so on.

❧ When you mark a key word such as *circumcised,* mark the negative variation, *uncircumcised,* with a line through it like this: ⟋

❧ Mark references to time with a green clock like this: 🕐

❧ Double-underline in green all geographical locations like this: ══

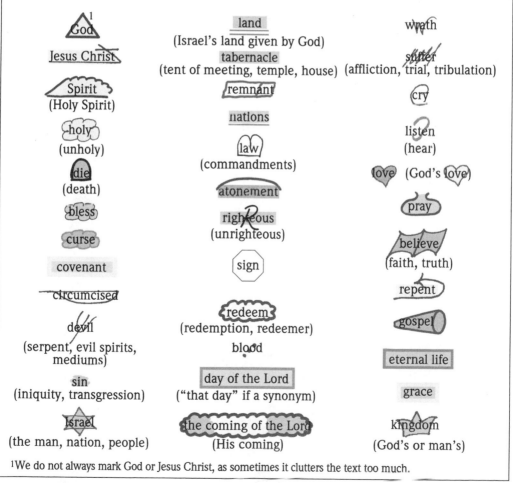

God[1]

Jesus Christ

Spirit
(Holy Spirit)

-holy-
(unholy)

die
(death)

bless

curse

covenant

circumcised

devil
(serpent, evil spirits, mediums)

sin
(iniquity, transgression)

Israel
(the man, nation, people)

land
(Israel's land given by God)

tabernacle
(tent of meeting, temple, house)

remnant

nations

law
(commandments)

atonement

righteous
(unrighteous)

sign

redeem
(redemption, redeemer)

blood

day of the Lord
("that day" if a synonym)

the coming of the Lord
(His coming)

wrath

suffer
(affliction, trial, tribulation)

cry

listen
(hear)

love (God's love)

pray

believe
(faith, truth)

repent

gospel

eternal life

grace

kingdom
(God's or man's)

[1]We do not always mark God or Jesus Christ, as sometimes it clutters the text too much.

19

INTERPRETATION

Discover What It Means!

While observation leads to an accurate understanding of what the Word of God *says*, interpretation goes a step further and helps you understand what it *means*. When you accurately interpret the Word of God, you will be able to confidently put its truths into practice in your daily life.

Like many other people, you may have been taught a system of beliefs before you ever studied God's Word for yourself. Or you may have formed opinions of what the Bible teaches before you carefully examined the Scriptures. As you learn to handle God's Word accurately, you will be able to discern if what you believe is in agreement with Scripture. If this is your desire and you come to the Word of God with a teachable spirit, God will lead you and guide you into all truth.

As you seek to interpret the Bible accurately, the following guidelines will be helpful.

1. Remember that context rules.

The word *context* means "that which goes with the text." To understand the context you must be familiar with the Word of God. If you lay the solid foundation of observation, you will be prepared to consider each verse in the light of:

- ∽ the surrounding verses
- ∽ the book in which it is found
- ∽ the entire Word of God

As you study, ask yourself: Is my interpretation of a particular section of Scripture consistent with the theme, purpose, and structure of the book in which it is found? Is it consistent with other Scripture about the same subject, or is there a glaring difference? Am I considering the historic and cultural context of what is being said? Never take a Scripture out of its context to make it say what you want it to say. Discover what the author is saying; don't add to his meaning.

2. Always seek the full counsel of the Word of God.

When you know God's Word thoroughly, you will not accept a teaching simply because someone has used one or two isolated verses to support it. Those verses may have been taken out of context, or other important passages might have been overlooked or ignored that would have led to a different understanding. As you read the Bible regularly and extensively, and as you become more familiar with the whole counsel of God's Word, you will be able to discern whether a teaching is biblical or not.

Saturate yourself in the Word of God; it is your safeguard against wrong doctrine.

3. Remember that Scripture will never contradict Scripture.

The best interpretation of Scripture is Scripture. Remember, all Scripture is inspired by God; it is God-breathed. Therefore, Scripture will never contradict itself.

The Bible contains all the truth you will ever need for any situation in life. Sometimes, however, you may find it difficult to reconcile two seemingly contradictory truths taught in Scripture. An example of this would be the sovereignty of God and the responsibility of man. When two or more truths that are clearly taught in the Word seem to be in conflict, remember that we as humans have finite minds. Don't take a teaching to an extreme that God doesn't. Simply humble your heart in faith and believe what God says, even if you can't fully understand or reconcile it at the moment.

4. Don't base your convictions on an obscure passage of Scripture.

An obscure passage is one in which the meaning is not easily understood. Because these passages are difficult to understand even when proper principles of interpretation are used, they should not be used as a basis for establishing doctrine.

5. Interpret Scripture literally.

The Bible is not a book of mysticism. God spoke to us that we might know truth. Therefore, take the Word of God at face value—in its natural, normal sense. Look first for the clear teaching of Scripture, not a hidden meaning. Understand and recognize figures of speech and interpret them accordingly.

Consider what is being said in the light of its literary style. For example, you will find more similes and metaphors in poetic and prophetic literature than in historical or biographical books. Interpret portions of Scripture according to their literary style.

Some literary styles in the Bible are:

- Historical—Acts
- Prophetic—Revelation
- Biographical—Luke
- Didactic (teaching)—Romans
- Poetic—Psalms
- Epistle (letter)—2 Timothy
- Proverbial—Proverbs

6. Look for the single meaning of the passage.

Always try to understand what the author had in mind when you interpret a portion of the Bible. Don't twist verses to support a meaning that is not clearly taught. Unless the author of a particular book indicates that there is another meaning to what he says, let the passage speak for itself.

APPLICATION
Discover How It Works!

Regardless of how much you know *about* God's Word, if you don't apply what you learn, Scripture will never benefit your life. To be a hearer of the Word and not a doer is to deceive yourself (James 1:22-25). This is why application is so vital. Observation and interpretation are the "hearing" of God's Word. With *application*, you will be transformed into Christ's image. Application is the embracing of the truth, the "doing" of God's Word. It is this process that allows God to work in your life.

Second Timothy 3:16-17 says: "All Scripture is inspired by God and profitable for teaching, for reproof, for correction, for training in righteousness, so that the man of God may be adequate, equipped for every good work." Here is the key to application: Apply Scripture in the light of its teaching, reproof, correction, and instructions on life.

Teaching (doctrine) is what the Word of God says on any particular subject. That teaching, whatever the subject, is always true. Therefore, everything that God says in His Word about any given subject is absolute truth.

The first step in application is to find out what the Word of God says on any particular subject through accurate observation and correct interpretation of the text. Once you understand what the Word of God teaches, you are then obligated before God to accept that truth and to live by it. When you have adjusted any false concepts or teaching you may have believed, and embraced the truth revealed in God's Word, then you have *applied* what you have learned.

Reproof exposes areas in your thinking and behavior that do not align with God's Word. Reproof is finding out where you have thought wrongly or have not been doing what God says is right. The application of reproof is to accept it and agree with God, acknowledging where you are wrong in thought or in behavior. This is how you are set free from unbelief, from sin.

Correction is the next step in application and often the most difficult. Many times we can see what is wrong, but we are reluctant to take the necessary steps to correct it. God has not left you without help or without answers in this step of correcting what is wrong. Sometimes the answers are difficult to find, but they are always there, and any child of God who wants to please his or her Father, and asks for help, will be shown by the Spirit of God how to do so.

Many times correction comes by simply confessing and forsaking what is wrong. Other times, God gives very definite steps to take. An example of this is in Matthew 18:15-17, in which God tells us how to approach a brother when he sins. When you apply correction to your actions and attitudes, God will work in you to do His good pleasure (Philippians 2:13). Joy will follow obedience.

Training in righteousness: Although God's Word is profitable for reproof and correction, the Bible was also given to us as a handbook for living. As we spend time studying His Word, God equips us through:

- ～ teachings
- ～ commands
- ～ promises
- ～ exhortations
- ～ warnings
- ～ and the lives of biblical characters and insights into God's character and dealings with man

Scripture has everything you need to meet any and all situations of life so that you "may be adequate, equipped for every good work." The most effective application takes place as you go before the Lord and talk with Him about those things that you have read, studied, seen, and heard.

INSIGHTS ON
APPLYING SCRIPTURE

In applying Scripture to your life, the following questions may be helpful:

1. **What does the passage teach?** Is it general or specific? Does it apply only to specific people? To a cultural problem of the day? To a certain time in history? Has it been superseded by a broader teaching? For example, in the Old Testament, Jews were not allowed to eat certain foods or to wear a certain combination of materials. Are those prohibitions applicable to Christians today?

2. **Does this section of Scripture expose any error in my beliefs or in my behavior?** Are there any commandments that I have not obeyed? Are there any wrong attitudes or motives in my life that the Scriptures bring to light?

3. **What is God's instruction to me as His child?** Are there any new truths to be believed? Are there any new commandments to be acted upon? Are there any new insights I am to pursue? Are there any promises I am to embrace?

4. **When applying Scripture, beware of the following:**
   - ～ Applying cultural standards rather than biblical standards
   - ～ Attempting to strengthen a legitimate truth by using a Scripture incorrectly
   - ～ Applying Scripture out of prejudice from past training or teaching

One of the apostle Paul's concerns for Timothy, his son in the faith, was that Timothy learn to handle God's Word in a way that would please the Lord (2 Timothy 2:15). Someday we too will want to give a good account of our stewardship of God's Word. Did we handle it accurately? Were we gentle and reasonable about our faith, giving honor to those whom God has called to lead us, while at the same time searching Scripture ourselves to understand its truths? Did we allow God's living and active Word to change our lives?

Observation, interpretation, and application lead to *transformation*. This is the goal of our study of the Word of God. Through it we are changed from glory to glory into the image of Jesus.

GETTING STARTED

With this basic understanding of the inductive process, you are ready to begin a lifetime of personal Bible study. Prayerfully choose one of the Bible's 66 books and then begin your study.

As you begin, quickly read through the THINGS TO DO section for an overview, but don't let the instructions overwhelm you. Taken one by one, chapter by chapter, and book by book, they become very manageable.

The THINGS TO THINK ABOUT section encourages you to get alone with God to consider how the truths of the book apply to you.

Many Old Testament historical and prophetic books have a HISTORICAL CHART to help you see where the book fits historically and chronologically. And many of the books in the New Testament contain an OBSERVATIONS CHART on which to record information you are instructed to look for in the THINGS TO DO section. You will want to keep many notes in a notebook.

Finally, each book of the Bible ends with an AT A GLANCE chart, as discussed earlier.

For added insights on particular topics relevant to your personal Bible study, you will find several appendixes at the end of this book.

When you begin studying the prophets, you'll see many references to the day of the Lord, the day of wrath, the day of God, and similar phrases. As you study, make a chart in your notebook titled DAY OF THE LORD with four headings: the biblical reference, how the day is described, what happens in nature, and signs of the beginning or end of the day.

As you study the Bible inductively, you will get to know God in a deep, exciting, and enlightening way—and "the people who know their God will display strength and take action" (Daniel 11:32b).

THE HISTORY OF ISRAEL—ADAM TO SOLOMON

| 5000 | 4000 | 3000 | 2000 | 1800 | 1600 | 1400 | 1200 | 1150 | 1100 | 1050 | 1000 | 950 |

*T*o truly appreciate and fully comprehend the totality of God's revelation to man in the Word of God, one needs a clear understanding of the whole counsel of God. Keeping events, revelations, truths, and peoples in perspective is essential. This easy-to-understand guide to Israel's history from the beginning to modern times is designed to help you place Scripture in its proper historical and chronological context. It is a tool which will make your inductive study even more rewarding and enlightening.

For a written history of the nation of Israel, see page 311.

PHARAOHS OF EGYPT

Thutmose III
Pharaoh of the
oppression
1483-1450

Amenhotep II
Pharaoh of
the Exodus
1450-1423

1 Chronicles   2 Chronicles
▼   ▼

HISTORICAL BOOKS OF THE BIBLE (with chapter numbers)

10   29 1

| Genesis | | Exodus | Judges | 1 Samuel | 2 Samuel |
| 1 | 12   37 50 | | | | 1 |

Leviticus ▲ ▲ Joshua
Numbers
Deuteronomy

1 Kings ▲

| Adam | Father ▼ Abraham | Israel in Egypt 1875 | Exodus 1445 Moses 1525 Aaron | Judges | Saul 1051-1011 ▼ | Solomon 971 ▼ |

David

1804   276 years between   1373   1020   1011 971

▲ Joseph   ▲ Joshua and elders
1914-1804   1405-1381

Israel	Prophets: Southern Kingdom	Babylon
Northern Kingdom (Israel)	Egypt	Medes and Persians
Prophets: Northern Kingdom	Aram/Damascus/Syria	Greece
Southern Kingdom (Judah)	Assyria	Rome
	Books of the Bible	

| 5000 | 4000 | 3000 | 2000 | 1800 | 1600 | 1400 | 1200 | 1150 | 1100 | 1050 | 1000 | 950 |

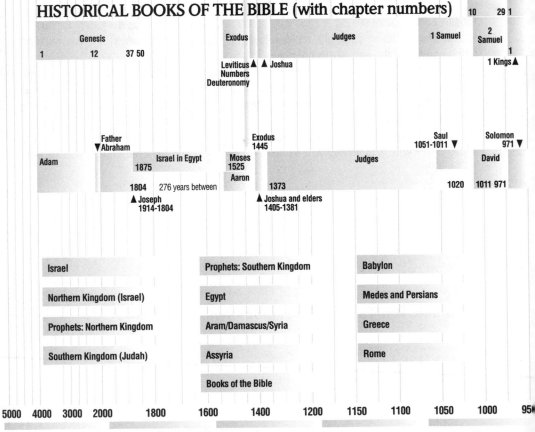

Scholars vary in the dating systems they use. The NISB generally follows John Whitcomb's system throughout for the sake of consistency.

THE HISTORY OF ISRAEL—THE DIVIDED KINGDOM

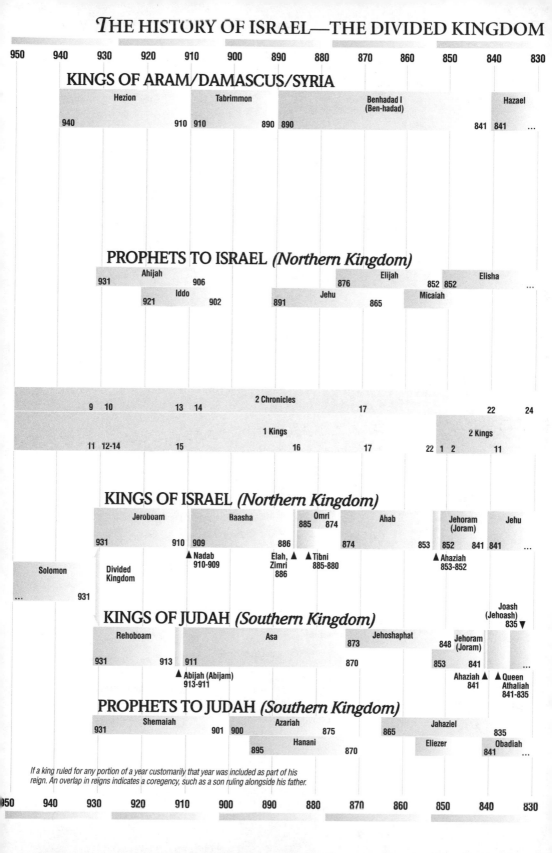

950 940 930 920 910 900 890 880 870 860 850 840 830

KINGS OF ARAM/DAMASCUS/SYRIA

Hezion · 940 · 910
Tabrimmon · 910 · 890
Benhadad I (Ben-hadad) · 890 · 841
Hazael · 841 ...

PROPHETS TO ISRAEL *(Northern Kingdom)*

Ahijah · 931 · 906
Iddo · 921 · 902
Elijah · 876 · 852
Jehu · 891 · 865
Micaiah · 852
Elisha · 852 ...

2 Chronicles
9 10 13 14 17 22 24

1 Kings
11 12-14 15 16 17 22 1 2 11

2 Kings

KINGS OF ISRAEL *(Northern Kingdom)*

Jeroboam · 931 · 910
Baasha · 909 · 886
Omri · 885 · 874
Ahab · 874 · 853
Jehoram (Joram) · 852 · 841
Jehu · 841 ...

▲ Nadab 910-909
Elah, ▲ Zimri 886
▲ Tibni 885-880
▲ Ahaziah 853-852

Solomon ... 931
Divided Kingdom

KINGS OF JUDAH *(Southern Kingdom)*

Rehoboam · 931 · 913
Asa · 911 · 870
Jehoshaphat · 873 · 848
Jehoram (Joram) · 853 · 841
Joash (Jehoash) 835 ▼

▲ Abijah (Abijam) 913-911
Ahaziah ▲ 841
▲ Queen Athaliah 841-835

PROPHETS TO JUDAH *(Southern Kingdom)*

Shemaiah · 931 · 901
Azariah · 900 · 875
Hanani · 895 · 870
Jahaziel · 865 · 835
Eliezer
Obadiah · 841 ...

If a king ruled for any portion of a year customarily that year was included as part of his reign. An overlap in reigns indicates a coregency, such as a son ruling alongside his father.

950 940 930 920 910 900 890 880 870 860 850 840 830

THE HISTORY OF ISRAEL—THE ASSYRIAN CAPTIVITY

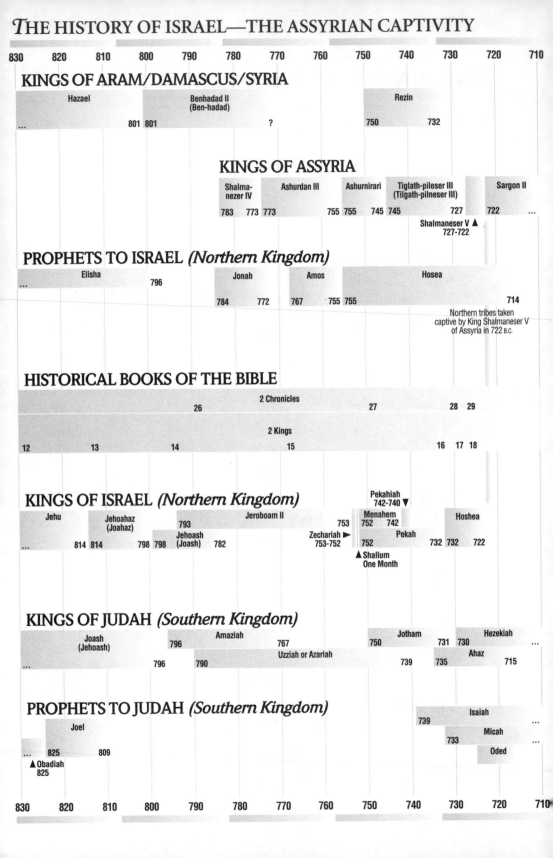

830   820   810   800   790   780   770   760   750   740   730   720   710

KINGS OF ARAM/DAMASCUS/SYRIA

Hazael
... 801
Benhadad II (Ben-hadad) 801   ?
Rezin 750   732

KINGS OF ASSYRIA

Shalma-nezer IV 783   773
Ashurdan III 773   755
Ashurnirari 755   745
Tiglath-pileser III (Tilgath-pilneser III) 745   727
Shalmaneser V ▲ 727-722
Sargon II 722   ...

PROPHETS TO ISRAEL *(Northern Kingdom)*

Elisha
... 796
Jonah 784   772
Amos 767   755
Hosea 755   714

Northern tribes taken captive by King Shalmaneser V of Assyria in 722 B.C.

HISTORICAL BOOKS OF THE BIBLE

2 Chronicles
26   27   28   29

2 Kings
12   13   14   15   16   17   18

KINGS OF ISRAEL *(Northern Kingdom)*

Jehu
... 814
Jehoahaz (Joahaz) 814   798
Jehoash (Joash) 798   782
793
Jeroboam II 753
Zechariah ▶ 753-752
▲ Shallum One Month
Pekahiah 742-740 ▼
Menahem 752   742
Pekah 752   732
Hoshea 732   722

KINGS OF JUDAH *(Southern Kingdom)*

Joash (Jehoash)
... 796
Amaziah 796   767
790
Uzziah or Azariah 790   739
Jotham 750   731
Ahaz 735   715
Hezekiah 730   ...

PROPHETS TO JUDAH *(Southern Kingdom)*

Joel
... 825   809
▲ Obadiah 825
Isaiah 739   ...
Micah 733   ...
Oded

830   820   810   800   790   780   770   760   750   740   730   720   710

THE HISTORY OF ISRAEL—THE BABYLONIAN CAPTIVITY

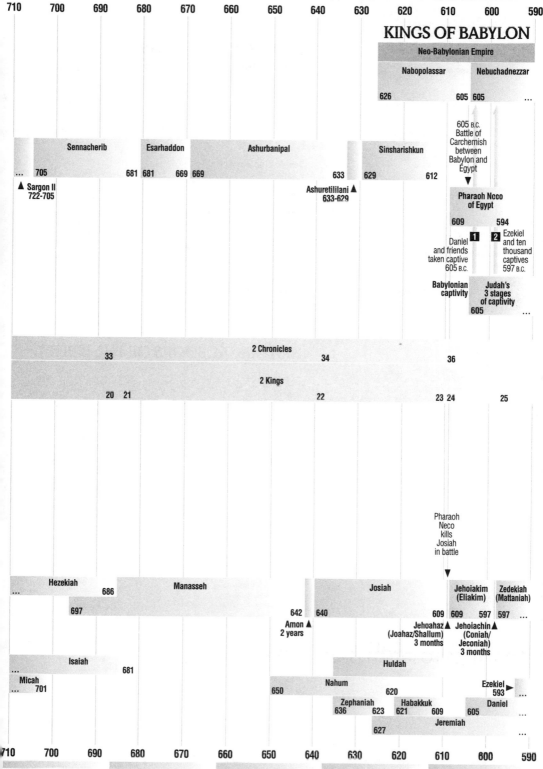

THE HISTORY OF ISRAEL—THE REBUILDING OF THE TEMPLE

| 590 | 580 | 570 | 560 | 550 | 540 | 530 | 520 | 510 | 500 | 490 | 480 | 470 |

KINGS OF BABYLON

Neo-Babylonian Empire

Nebuchadnezzar

KINGS OF MEDO-PERSIA

Nabonidus
556   539

Cyrus   Cambyses
539   530 530   521

Darius I
Hystaspes

Ahasuerus
(Xerxes)

Belshazzar
553   539

Darius the
539 Mede 525

562

521

486 486

...

Evil-Merodach ▲ ▲ ▲ Labashi
562-560   Marduk
                     556

▲ Smerdis
521

▲   ▲   ▲

Feast of   Feast
Xerxes   of
Queen Vashti Purim
deposed   473
483

Neriglissar
560-556

Fall
of
Babylon
538

Esther
crowned
queen
478

Destruction
of
Jerusalem
586

Decree of Cyrus to return
and rebuild Temple
538
1

Zerubbabel
returns, begins
TEMPLE
536

TEMPLE
work
resumed
520

Judah taken captive by
King Nebuchadnezzar
of Babylon in 586 B.C.
Jerusalem and Temple
destroyed

TEMPLE
work
stopped
▼▼▼ ▼ 534

TEMPLE
finished
▼ ▼ 516

Judah's
3 stages
of captivity
...

70-year Jewish captivity

Return of the
remnant to Israel

536 536

HISTORICAL BOOKS OF THE BIBLE

Ezra 1-6

536   516

Esther

483   473

3

◄ Zedekiah
(Mattaniah)
586
...

PROPHETS TO JUDAH *(Southern Kingdom)*

Ezekiel
...   559

Haggai
520   505

Daniel
...   536

Zechariah
520   489

Jeremiah
...   574

| 590 | 580 | 570 | 560 | 550 | 540 | 530 | 520 | 510 | 500 | 490 | 480 | 470 |

THE HISTORY OF ISRAEL—THE GREEK AND ROMAN PERIODS

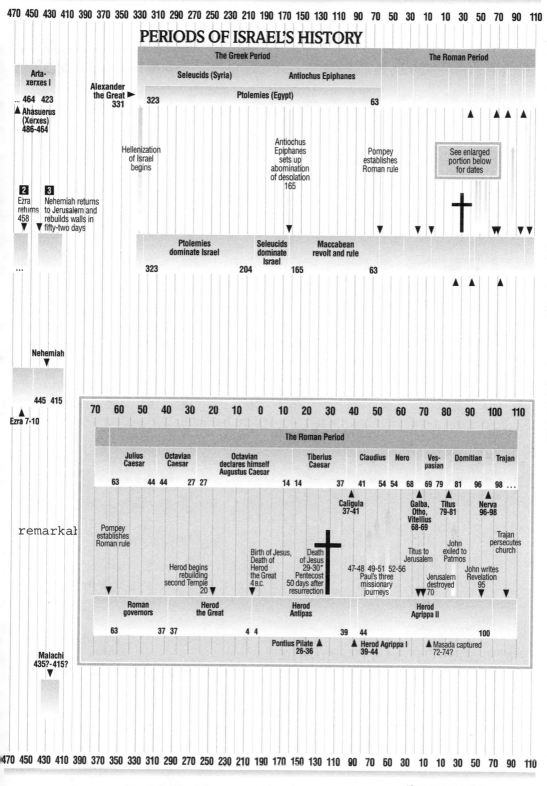

470 450 430 410 390 370 350 330 310 290 270 250 230 210 190 170 150 130 110 90 70 50 30 10 10 30 50 70 90 110

PERIODS OF ISRAEL'S HISTORY

The Greek Period

The Roman Period

Arta-xerxes I

... 464 423

▲ Ahasuerus (Xerxes) 486-464

Alexander the Great ▶ 331

Seleucids (Syria)

Antiochus Epiphanes

Ptolemies (Egypt)

323

63

Hellenization of Israel begins

Antiochus Epiphanes sets up abomination of desolation 165

Pompey establishes Roman rule

See enlarged portion below for dates

2 Ezra returns 458 ▼

3 Nehemiah returns to Jerusalem and rebuilds walls in fifty-two days ▼

...

Ptolemies dominate Israel

323

Seleucids dominate Israel

204

Maccabean revolt and rule

165

63

Nehemiah ▼

445 415

▲ Ezra 7-10

70 60 50 40 30 20 10 0 10 20 30 40 50 60 70 80 90 100 110

remarkab

The Roman Period

Julius Caesar	Octavian Caesar	Octavian declares himself Augustus Caesar	Tiberius Caesar	Claudius	Nero	Vespasian	Domitian	Trajan
63	44 44	27 27	14 14	41	54 54	69 79	96	98 ...

37

Caligula 37-41

Galba, Otho, Vitellius 68-69

Titus 79-81

Nerva 96-98

Pompey establishes Roman rule ▼

Herod begins rebuilding second Temple 20 ▼

Birth of Jesus, Death of Herod the Great 4 B.C. ▼

Death of Jesus 29-30* Pentecost 50 days after resurrection

47-48 49-51 52-56 Paul's three missionary journeys

Titus to Jerusalem

Jerusalem destroyed 70 ▼▼

John exiled to Patmos

John writes Revelation 95 ▼

Trajan persecutes church

Roman governors	Herod the Great	Herod Antipas	Herod Agrippa II
63	37 37	4 4	39 44 100

Pontius Pilate ▲ 26-36

Herod Agrippa I 39-44

Masada captured 72-74?

Malachi 435?-415? ▼

470 450 430 410 390 370 350 330 310 290 270 250 230 210 190 170 150 130 110 90 70 50 30 10 10 30 50 70 90 110

*Some scholars say 33 A.D.

THE HISTORY OF ISRAEL—110 A.D. TO MODERN TIMES

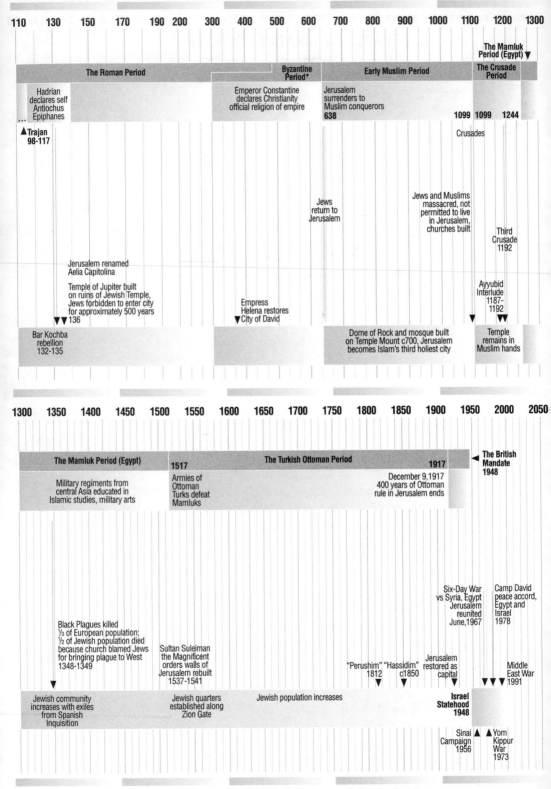

| 110 | 130 | 150 | 170 | 190 | 200 | 300 | 400 | 500 | 600 | 700 | 800 | 900 | 1000 | 1100 | 1200 | 1300 |

The Mamluk Period (Egypt) ▼

The Roman Period — **Byzantine Period*** — **Early Muslim Period** — **The Crusade Period**

Hadrian declares self Antiochus Epiphanes

Emperor Constantine declares Christianity official religion of empire

Jerusalem surrenders to Muslim conquerors **638**

▲ Trajan 98-117

1099 | **1099** | **1244**

Crusades

Jews return to Jerusalem

Jews and Muslims massacred, not permitted to live in Jerusalem, churches built

Third Crusade 1192

Jerusalem renamed Aelia Capitolina

Temple of Jupiter built on ruins of Jewish Temple, Jews forbidden to enter city for approximately 500 years
▼ ▼ 136

Empress Helena restores ▼ City of David

Ayyubid Interlude 1187-1192

Bar Kochba rebellion 132-135

Dome of Rock and mosque built on Temple Mount c700, Jerusalem becomes Islam's third holiest city

Temple remains in Muslim hands

| 1300 | 1350 | 1400 | 1450 | 1500 | 1550 | 1600 | 1650 | 1700 | 1750 | 1800 | 1850 | 1900 | 1950 | 2000 | 2050 |

The Mamluk Period (Egypt) | **1517** | **The Turkish Ottoman Period** | **1917** | **The British Mandate 1948**

Military regiments from central Asia educated in Islamic studies, military arts

Armies of Ottoman Turks defeat Mamluks

December 9,1917 400 years of Ottoman rule in Jerusalem ends

Six-Day War vs Syria, Egypt Jerusalem reunited June,1967

Camp David peace accord, Egypt and Israel 1978

Black Plagues killed ⅓ of European population; ½ of Jewish population died because church blamed Jews for bringing plague to West 1348-1349

Sultan Suleiman the Magnificent orders walls of Jerusalem rebuilt 1537-1541

"Perushim" "Hassidim" 1812 c1850 ▼ ▼

Jerusalem restored as capital ▼

Middle East War ▼ ▼ ▼ 1991

Jewish community increases with exiles from Spanish Inquisition

Jewish quarters established along Zion Gate

Jewish population increases

Israel Statehood 1948

Sinai Campaign 1956 ▲

▲ Yom Kippur War 1973

** The dates from the Byzantine Period are taken from **The Tower of David**, Museum of the History of Jerusalem.*

GENESIS בראשית
B'RESHIT

*W*hen there was nothing, there was God. Then God spoke.

THINGS TO DO

General Instructions

Genesis falls into two segments. The first, chapters 1 through 11, covers four major events. The second segment, chapters 12 through 50, covers the lives of four major characters. The instructions on how to study this book will be divided according to these two segments.

1. As you read chapter by chapter, ask the "5 W's and an H" about the text: Who? What? When? Where? Why? and How? Ask questions such as: Who is speaking? What is happening? When is it happening? Where will it happen? Why was this said or done and what were the consequences? How did it happen? How was it to be done? etc.

2. Mark in a distinctive way any repeated words or phrases that are key to understanding the content of the chapter. There are several key words you should look for throughout the book of Genesis. These are listed on the GENESIS AT A GLANCE chart. Write these on an index card and use it as a bookmark while you study Genesis.

3. The timing and location of events can be very important. Mark time phrases with a clock ⏱, and double-underline every geographical location in green.

4. In the margin of your Bible, summarize the main things that occur in the chapter. List them in the order in which they occur. You may want to number them. For example, in Genesis 1 you could summarize what happens on each of the six days of creation.

5. If you learn something significant about God or His ways, you may want to put a triangle like this △ in the margin and color it yellow. This will act as an indicator of an important truth you've learned about God.

6. Look for the theme (the main subject) of each chapter. Record it on GENESIS AT A GLANCE. Also record the theme at the beginning of each chapter in your Bible.

7. Genesis is often referred to as the book of beginnings; it is the seedbed of truth. This is because the Word of God is a progressive revelation. *Progressive revelation* means that truth is unveiled over a period of time throughout various books of the Bible. God doesn't say everything He has to say about a particular subject at one time or in one place. Rather, He will introduce a truth and then reveal more and more about it.

Since Genesis is the book of beginnings, when you come to the "first" of anything, record it in the chapter margin in a special way or color so you can spot it easily. For example, next to Genesis 1:26-27 you could write: "First man and woman."

8. Watch for the origins of various people groups.

Chapters 1–11

1. Genesis 1–2

   a. Note what is created on each day. Notice when a day begins and ends.

   b. There are a number of key repeated phrases in Genesis 1. Mark each in a distinctive color.

   c. Chapter 2 gives a detailed explanation of the creation of mankind. Note the order of events and the man's relationship and responsibilities to God and to the woman.

2. Genesis 3–5

   a. In chapter 3 list all you learn about the serpent and his tactics: how he tempts Eve, what he says. Then note what happens to Satan because he deceives Eve.

   b. Note Eve's progression into sin. List what happens before and after she sins.

   c. Watch what happens to Adam and Eve's relationship with God. Note the consequence of Adam's disobedience.

   d. In chapters 3 through 5 note the consequences of sin's entrance into the world. Genesis 3:15 is the first promise of a Redeemer. Also, in chapter 4, observe the occupations and abilities of the people.

   e. When you read chapter 5, you'll find the chart "The Overlapping of the Patriarchs' Lives" on page 36 very helpful.

3. Genesis 6–9

   a. As you study these chapters observe the reasons for the flood, how and when it came, who was affected and how.

   b. Watch the timing of events. Mark time phrases with a clock or record them in the margin; e.g., "Rains forty days and nights."

   c. Mark the word *covenant* and list all you learn from the text about covenant.

4. Genesis 10–11

   a. Observe who was separated, why and how they were separated, when and where this occurred, and what happened as a result.

   b. Babylon plays an intermittently prominent role throughout the Bible, and of course its roots are in Genesis. Therefore whenever you come to any mention of Babel or Babylon you need to make a note of what you learn.

5. When you finish reading Genesis 11, look at GENESIS AT A GLANCE. Next to "Chapter Themes" you will find a place for segment divisions. Fill in the four main events covered in Genesis 1 through 11. The chapter divisions are noted on the chart.

Chapters 12–50

1. Genesis 12 through 50 covers the biographical segment of Genesis, which focuses on the lives of four main characters: Abraham, Isaac, Jacob (also called Israel), and Joseph. When you read:

   a. Follow the "General Instructions" for studying each chapter (see page 33).

   b. Watch for and mark every reference to time in the life of each of the major characters (including their wives and children) in these chapters. God will often tell how old the person was when certain events occurred in his or her life.

   c. The word *covenant* is more prominent in this last segment. Mark each occurrence of this word and then list all you learn about covenant from observing the text. Read the insight about covenant on page 35.

   d. Note any insights or lessons you learned from the way these people lived. Note how and why God deals with these men, their families, and their associates, and what happens as a result.

2. Watch when the focus of a chapter moves from Abraham to Isaac, then to Jacob, and then to Joseph. Then on GENESIS AT A GLANCE, on the line where you recorded the four major events of Genesis 1 through 11, divide the chapters into segments that cover the lives of Abraham, Isaac, Jacob, and Joseph. Look at the chapter themes to see where

the focus moves from one of these men to the other.

3. When you finish reading Genesis 50, record on GENESIS AT A GLANCE the theme of Genesis. Under Segment Divisions, record the "firsts" that you marked throughout Genesis. (There is a blank line for any other segment divisions you might want to note.)

THINGS TO THINK ABOUT

1. What have you learned about God—His character, His attributes, and the ways He moves in the lives of men and nations? Since God never changes, can you trust Him? Can you rely on what the Word of God reveals about Him even though you may not fully understand His ways?

2. What can you learn from the lives of those mentioned in Genesis? Romans 15:4 says the things written in the Old Testament were written for our instruction, that through perseverance and the encouragement of Scripture we might have hope. What are the blessings of obedience and the consequences of disobedience?

3. Jesus took the book of Genesis at face value and attributed its authorship to Moses. As you study the Gospels, you will see that Jesus referred to the creation of Adam and Eve, to the flood, and to the destruction of Sodom and Gomorrah. He even referred to Satan as a murderer from the beginning. Jesus never contradicted the teachings of Genesis; He only affirmed them. Are you going to take God's Word at face value and believe as Jesus did, or are you going to listen to the philosophies of men? Are you going to follow men with finite minds who critique God and His Word, or are you going to accept the Bible as the Word of God and then think and live accordingly?

INSIGHT

Beriyth, the Hebrew word for covenant, is a solemn binding agreement made by passing through pieces of flesh. The Greek word for covenant, *diatheke*, means a testament or an agreement. The Bible is divided into the Old and New Testaments—or covenants. Everything God does is based on covenant. For example, see Exodus 2:23-24; 32:9-14; Jeremiah 34:12-21.

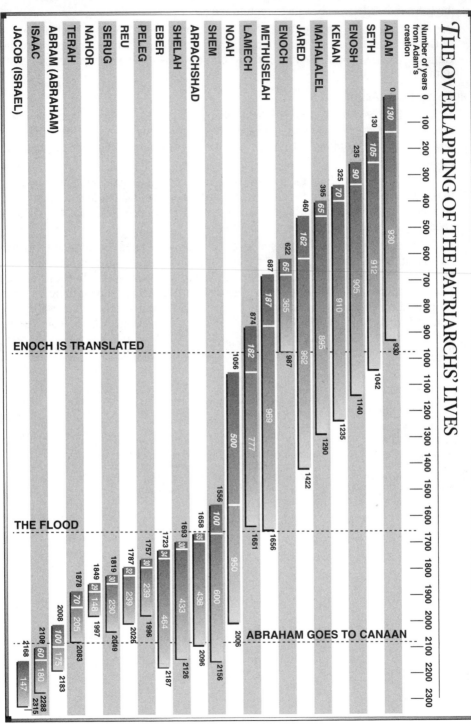

THE OVERLAPPING OF THE PATRIARCHS' LIVES

ENOCH IS TRANSLATED

THE FLOOD

ABRAHAM GOES TO CANAAN

Number of years from Adam's creation
0 100 200 300 400 500 600 700 800 900 1000 1100 1200 1300 1400 1500 1600 1700 1800 1900 2000 2100 2200 2300

ADAM — 0 / 130 / 930
SETH — 130 / 105 / 912
ENOSH — 235 / 90 / 905
KENAN — 325 / 70 / 910
MAHALALEL — 395 / 65 / 895
JARED — 460 / 162 / 962
ENOCH — 622 / 65 / 365 / 987
METHUSELAH — 687 / 187 / 969
LAMECH — 874 / 182 / 777
NOAH — 1056 / 500 / 950
SHEM — 1556 / 100 / 600
ARPACHSHAD — 1658 / 35 / 438
SHELAH — 1693 / 30 / 433
EBER — 1723 / 34 / 464
PELEG — 1757 / 30 / 239
REU — 1787 / 32 / 239
SERUG — 1819 / 30 / 230
NAHOR — 1849 / 29 / 148
TERAH — 1878 / 70 / 205
ABRAM (ABRAHAM) — 2008 / 100 / 175
ISAAC — 2108 / 60 / 180
JACOB (ISRAEL) — 2168 / 147

930
1042
1140
1235
1290
1422
1651
1656
2006
2156
2096
2126
2187
1996
2026
2049
1997
2083
2183
2288 / 2315

KEY: The first number inside the block is the man's age when his son (whose name is in the next line below) was born. The second number in the block is the number of years the man lived. The numbers preceding and following each block are the number of years from Adam's creation.

36

GENESIS AT A GLANCE

Theme of Genesis:

Author:
Moses
(Luke 24:27)

Date:

Purpose:

Key Words:
(include synonyms)

God said
(or commanded)

the generations of
(now these are the
generations of . . .)

covenant (oath)

altar

land (when it
refers to the land
promised to
Abraham, Isaac,
and Jacob)

circumcised

Abram
(or Abraham)

bless (blessed,
blessing)

sin (do evil,
act wicked)

dream

died

SEGMENT DIVISIONS

THE FIRSTS		4 MAIN EVENTS/4 CHARACTERS	TIME SPANS	CHAPTER THEMES
MAN				1
MARRIAGE				2
	BEGINNINGS OF MAN		APPROXIMATELY 2080 YEARS	3
				4
				5
				6
				7
				8
				9
				10
				11
	BEGINNINGS OF ISRAEL *(CONTINUED NEXT PAGE)*		APPROXIMATELY 300 YEARS *(CONTINUED NEXT PAGE)*	12
				13
				14
				15
				16
				17
				18
				19
				20
				21
				22
				23
				24
				25

See appendix 7 for key words in the New International Version and King James Version.

37

SEGMENT DIVISIONS

THE FIRSTS		4 CHARACTERS	TIME SPANS	CHAPTER THEMES
				26
				27
				28
				29
				30
				31
	BEGINNINGS OF ISRAEL		APPROXIMATELY 300 YEARS	32
				33
				34
				35
				36
				37
				38
				39
				40
				41
				42
				43
				44
				45
				46
				47
				48
				49
				50

EXODUS שְׁמוֹת
SHMOT

$\mathcal{W}$hen Jacob and his family, a relatively small group, went into Egypt, they were welcomed and honored because they were relatives of Joseph. Four hundred and thirty years later the children of Israel were Egypt's slaves, a people so numerous it frightened the Egyptians.

The Israelites were God's covenant people, different from all the nations, a people of His own choosing. And because God is a covenant-keeping God, He could not leave Jacob's people in Egypt—they had to be redeemed by the blood of a lamb, a Passover lamb.

THINGS TO DO

General Instructions

1. As Genesis comes to a close, the children of Israel are living in Egypt rather than in Canaan, the land of promise. The book that began with the creation of man in Eden ends with the children of Israel looking into a coffin in Egypt—but not without a promise that someday they would leave Egypt. Read Genesis 50:22-26 and Exodus 1:1-7 and notice how the book of Exodus relates chronologically to the book of Genesis.

2. Exodus can be divided into three segments according to the location of the children of Israel. In Exodus 1 through 12 they are in Egypt. In Exodus 13 through 18 they journey to Sinai, and then in Exodus 19 through 40 they camp at Sinai. Record this information on the EXODUS AT A GLANCE chart on the first line for segment divisions. This division will be the basis of some of your instructions.

3. Read through Exodus one chapter at a time. As you read do the following:

   a. Remember that you are reading a historical account. As you read, ask the "5 W's and an H": Who? What? When? Where? Why? and How? Ask questions such as: Who are the main characters in this chapter? What is happening? When and where is it happening? What were the consequences of their actions? How and why did this occur?

   b. Mark key repeated words. Although a list of the key words for Exodus is recorded on EXODUS AT A GLANCE, remember that other words will be predominant in specific chapters. Don't miss these. Write the key words on an index card and use it as a bookmark.

   c. List insights you glean from the repeated use of a key word.

   d. Mark references to time with a clock. Geographical locations are very important in the Old Testament. Do not forget to double-underline them in green.

   e. List the main points or events covered in a particular chapter or group of chapters. This will give you a concise analysis of the content of the chapter.

   For example, Exodus 2 gives an account of Moses from his birth to the birth of his first son. In the margin you could list the major events in this chapter: Moses' birth, Moses' adoption by Pharaoh's daughter, Moses kills Egyptian, Moses flees to Midian, etc.

4. When you finish reading a chapter, record the main theme or subject of the chapter on EXODUS AT A GLANCE under "Chapter Themes." Also record it in your Bible at the beginning of the chapter.

Chapters 1–12

1. As you study these chapters, add *Pharaoh, heart, staff,* and *sign (miracle)* to your list of key words. Mark these words and their synonyms in a distinctive way.

2. You can gain insights into God's character, power, and dealings with mankind from these chapters. As you read each chapter, in the margin note what you learn about God. You may want to put a distinguishing mark such as this △ in the margin and then color it yellow so you can easily recognize it.

3. There are lessons to be learned from Moses' life in these chapters. Note these lessons in the margins.

4. As you read chapters 7 through 12, in the margin of your Bible list the plagues as they appear in the text, numbering each one in the order in which they appear.

5. When you come to Exodus 12, mark *Passover lamb.* Then list what you learn by asking the "5 W's and an H."

Chapters 13–18

1. As you read:
   a. Watch for the key words, including those you marked in the first segment. Add *first-born*, *test,* and *grumble*, along with their synonyms. In the margin note what the tests were and why the people grumbled. Also continue your list of insights on Pharaoh and on Moses' staff.

   b. Mark references to time with a symbol and note where events occur. Locate these places on a map.

2. Note what God is called in 15:26 and 17:15 and the circumstances in which these names are revealed.

3. In chapter 16, mark *bread* and *manna.* Make a list of all you learn from the text about manna and why it was given. When you finish you might compare this with Deuteronomy 8:1-3. Add *sabbath (seventh day)* to your list of key words.

4. In chapter 17 note the conditions under which Moses strikes the rock. Compare this with 1 Corinthians 10:1-4 and John 7:37-39.

Chapters 19–40

1. In chapters 19 through 24 God gives Moses the law. Watch for and mark key words.
   a. Chapter 20 presents the ten commandments. Number these within the text.

   b. In chapters 21–23, list the various ordinances in the margin for easy reference. Note what is to be done if these are violated.

   c. Chapter 24 is very important because it deals with the inauguration of the law, the old covenant. In the margin note the circumstances and procedure connected with its inauguration and how the people respond.

2. In chapters 25 through 31 God gives the pattern for the tabernacle and all that is necessary for the priests.
   a. Note in the margin the main points of these chapters.

   b. Watch for other key words that are predominant in specific chapters. Mark them.

   c. In chapter 31 list everything you learn about the sabbath from the text. Compare Exodus 35:1-3 with Numbers 15:32-36.

3. Chapters 32–34 are very significant. Mark every reference to the *calf (god).*
   a. Note how Moses deals with this situation.

   b. Read 2 Corinthians 3:12-18 for additional insights regarding the veil over Moses' face.

4. Chapters 35 through 40 are an account of the construction of the tabernacle and the making of the priests' garments. As you read, highlight or mark in a distinguishable way the first reference to each piece of furniture.

5. After you have recorded all the chapter themes on EXODUS AT A GLANCE, see if any of the chapters can be grouped according to main events. Record these segment divisions on the appropriate line next to the chapter themes. Then record the theme of Exodus on the chart.

THINGS TO THINK ABOUT

1. Daniel 11:32b says, "The people who know their God will display strength and take action." What have you learned about God, His character, and His ways? What have you seen of His power and sovereignty? When we speak of God as being sovereign, we mean He rules over all. How do you see God's sovereignty and power manifested in Exodus? Meditate on what you have learned and then make it a matter of prayer and application.

2. Since the Bible is a progressive revelation of truth, keep in mind what you have observed about redemption and the Passover. These are Old Testament pictures of the salvation to be offered through the Lord Jesus Christ; therefore, they are pictures of truths to be applied to your life (1 Corinthians 5:6-8). Are you a slave to sin? Jesus Christ has provided for your redemption from sin through His blood. Have you been redeemed?

3. What have you learned from Moses' life and his example as a leader? How did he deal with difficult situations and people? What was his overriding passion? What did you learn about Moses' relationship with God that you can apply to your own life today?

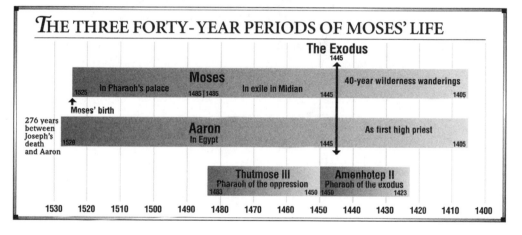

THE THREE FORTY-YEAR PERIODS OF MOSES' LIFE

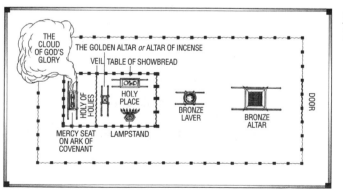

Inside the Tabernacle

41

Theme of Exodus:

Author:

Date:

Purpose:

Key Words:
(including synonyms)

slave(s)
(bondage)

cry

deliver
(delivered)

Mount Sinai
(Horeb,
Mountain of
God)

die (death)

holy

the Lord
commanded
(I commanded)

covenant

cloud

test(ed)

law

tabernacle
(tent, tent of
meeting)

SEGMENT DIVISIONS

CHAPTER THEMES

				Chapter Themes
			1	
			2	
			3	
			4	
			5	
			6	
			7	
			8	
			9	
			10	
			11	
			12	
			13	
			14	
			15	
			16	
			17	
			18	
			19	
			20	
			21	
			22	
			23	
			24	
			25	

See appendix 7 for key words in the New International Version and King James Version.

SEGMENT DIVISIONS

			CHAPTER THEMES
			26
			27
			28
			29
			30
			31
			32
			33
			34
			35
			36
			37
			38
			39
			40

LEVITICUS ויקרא
VAYIKRA

*I*n Genesis we see the ruin of man as a result of listening to the serpent rather than to God. The human race is condemned to sin's awful wage—death. Yet through the mercy and grace of God comes the promise of redemption through the seed of the woman, through the seed of Abraham, as God calls out a people for Himself. God makes a covenant with Abraham, which He confirms to Isaac and then to Jacob, later to be renamed Israel.

The book of Genesis begins with the creation of man in Eden and ends with the children of Israel looking into a coffin in Egypt, yet not without a promise that someday they would leave Egypt. As Genesis comes to a close, the children of Israel are living in Egypt rather than in Canaan, the land of promise.

Exodus plays out the drama of redemption as Israel is redeemed from slavery through the blood of the Passover lamb. After the descendants of Abraham were enslaved and oppressed for 400 years, just as God promised, they left Egypt with great possessions, and God went before them in His cloud of glory.

And what follows the redemption of ruined man? That is what the book of Leviticus is all about. Study it well, for Leviticus shows us in pictorial form what God expects from those who have been redeemed.

THINGS TO DO

General Instructions

1. As you read Leviticus watch for the verses that attribute the authorship of this book to Moses. When you come across those references, record them under "Author" on the LEVITICUS AT A GLANCE chart.

2. Read Exodus 40:17,32-38 and Leviticus 1:1-2 and note the uninterrupted transition from one book to the other. Then compare Numbers 1:1 with these verses. As you do this you will see that the book of Leviticus covers a period of one month.

3. As you read through Leviticus one chapter at a time, do the following:

   a. Ask the "5 W's and an H": Who? What? When? Where? Why? and How? For example: Who is to do what? When are they to do it? How are they to do it? Why? What if they didn't know why? Questions that interrogate the text help you see what is being said.

   b. Mark the key repeated words listed on LEVITICUS AT A GLANCE. You will find it helpful to list these key words on an index card that you can use as a bookmark while you study Leviticus. Also watch for any other key words that might be used in that particular chapter. If you gain insights from marking these words, list pertinent insights in your notebook.

   c. Record the main theme or subject of the chapter at the beginning of the chapter in your Bible. Then record it on LEVITICUS AT A GLANCE.

   d. You may want to summarize the main points or the order of events covered in the chapter. Record them in the margin.

   e. Record any new insights about the character and ways of God. You could identify your insights on God with this symbol △ and then color it yellow, which would make it easy to recognize.

Chapters 1–7

1. As you read chapters 1 through 7, which give instructions regarding the various sacrifices or offerings, mark the text as instructed under "General Instructions" and then record what you learn about each of the offerings on the chart THE OFFERINGS AND THEIR PURPOSES on page 46.

2. Watch what God says about unintentional sin, guilt, and restitution. Note what is to be done when a leader sins and when the congregation sins. Mark it in the text.

Chapters 8–10

This segment covers the consecration of Aaron and his sons. Add *ordination, eat, clean,* and *unclean* to your key word list. In chapter 10 note what happened, why it happened, and who was involved. Chapter 10 has the first reference in the Bible to God's holiness.

Chapters 11–15

This segment deals with laws of cleanliness. In the margin record what each law covers. For example: food, women, infections, etc. Mark *leprosy* and *discharge* as key words.

Chapters 16–17

These chapters cover the day of atonement and regulations regarding the blood of the sacrifice.

1. In the margin of chapter 16 or in your notebook carefully outline what is to be done on the day of atonement. Note what you learn about the scapegoat.

2. Note the regulations in chapter 17 regarding sacrifices and blood.

Chapters 18–27

This segment lays out statutes on issues regarding moral laws, the priests, the celebration of annual feasts, the land, etc.

1. As you read each chapter, in the margin list the main topics or situations.

2. If moral laws are given, note the consequences of breaking the laws and the reason for the consequences.

3. In chapter 23 note the feasts, when they are to be celebrated, and how. When you finish studying the chapter, consult the chart THE FEASTS OF ISRAEL on pages 48–49.

4. Give special attention to any mention of the land—its sabbath rest, principles of redemption, etc. Mark the words *redeem, redemption,* and any other related words. Record your insights in the margin.

5. When you finish reading through Leviticus, complete LEVITICUS AT A GLANCE.

   a. See if any of the chapters can be grouped categorically. If so, record this under "Segment Divisions" on the chart. Record any other possible segment divisions. For instance, you could do a segment division titled "Laws Regarding."

   b. Record the theme of Leviticus.

THINGS TO THINK ABOUT

1. What have you learned about God and His attitude toward sin? What happens when sin goes unpunished?

2. What have you learned about the occult and about the types of sexual sin? How severely were these sins to be dealt with? What does this tell you about how God feels regarding these sins and their consequences? What do you think would happen in your country if these sins were dealt with according to God's law? Read 1 Timothy 1:8-11.

3. Jesus told the Jews that the Scriptures—the Old Testament—testified of Him. Think about how Jesus Christ and His work are foreshadowed in Leviticus.

4. What have you learned about holiness from Leviticus? If you want to be holy, how will you live your life? Are there any changes you need to make? Are you willing? If not, why not?

The Jewish Calendar

Babylonian names (B) for the months are still used today for the Jewish calendar. Canaanite names (C) were used prior to the Babylonian captivity in 586 B.C. Four are mentioned in the Old Testament. **Adar-Sheni** is an intercalary month used every two to three years or seven times in 19 years.

1st month	2nd month	3rd month	4th month
Nisan (B) Abib (C) March-April	Iyyar (B) Ziv (C) April-May	Sivan (B) May-June	Tammuz (B) June-July
7th month	*8th month*	*9th month*	*10th month*
5th month	**6th month**	**7th month**	**8th month**
Ab (B) July-August	Elul (B) August-September	Tishri (B) Ethanim (C) September-October	Marcheshvan (B) Bul (C) October-November
11th month	*12th month*	*1st month*	*2nd month*
9th month	**10th month**	**11th month**	**12th month**
Chislev (B) November-December	Tebeth (B) December-January	Shebat (B) January-February	Adar (B) February-March
3rd month	*4th month*	*5th month*	*6th month*

Sacred calendar appears in black • Civil calendar appears in gray

THE OFFERINGS AND THEIR PURPOSES

THE OFFERING	CHAPTER/ VERSE	VOLUNTARY/ INVOLUNTARY	REASON/PURPOSE

Theme of Leviticus:

Author:

Date:

Purpose:

Key Words:
(including synonyms)

the Lord spoke
to Moses saying

offering

tabernacle
(tent of
meeting)

fat

law

restitution

sacrifice

anoint

sin (iniquity)

death (die)

blood

atonement

consecrate

holy

covenant

land (when it
refers to that
given by God)

sabbath

jubilee

SEGMENT DIVISIONS			CHAPTER THEMES
	LAWS REGARDING	MAIN DIVISION	
		WORSHIPING A HOLY GOD	1
			2
			3
			4
			5
			6
			7
			8
			9
			10
			11
			12
			13
			14
			15
			16
			17
		LIVING A HOLY LIFE	18
			19
			20
			21
			22
			23
			24
			25
			26
			27

See appendix 7 for key words in the New International Version and King James Version.

The Feasts of Israel

Slaves in Egypt	1st Month (Nisan) Festival of Passover (Pesach)				3rd Month (Sivan) Festival of Pentecost (Shavuot)
	Passover	**Unleavened Bread**	**First Fruits**		**Pentecost or Feast of Weeks**
	Kill lamb & put blood on doorpost Exodus 12:6-7	*Purging of all leaven* (symbol of sin)	*Wave offering of sheaf* (promise of harvest to come)		*Wave offering of two loaves of leavened bread*
	1st month, 14th day Leviticus 23:5	1st month, 15th day for 7 days Leviticus 23:6-8 *(1st and 7th days are Sabbath)*	Day after Sabbath Leviticus 23:9-14 *(It is a Sabbath)*		50 days after first fruits Leviticus 23:15-21 *(It is a Sabbath)*
Whosoever commits sin is the slave to sin	**Christ our Passover has been sacrificed**	**Clean out old leaven... just as you are in fact unleavened**	**Christ has been raised...the first fruits**	**Going away so Comforter can come** Mount of Olives	**Promise of the Spirit, mystery of church: Jews-Gentiles in one body**
John 8:34	1 Corinthians 5:7	1 Corinthians 5:7-8	1 Corinthians 15:20-23	John 16:7 Acts 1:9-12	Acts 2:1-47 1 Corinthians 12:13 Ephesians 2:11-22

Months: Nisan—*March, April* • **Sivan**—*May, June* • **Tishri**—*September, October*

	Feast of Trumpets	Day of Atonement	Feast of Booths or Tabernacles	
Interlude Between Festivals				
	Trumpet blown — a holy convocation	*Atonement shall be made to cleanse you* Leviticus 16:30	*Harvest celebration memorial of tabernacles in wilderness*	
	7th month, 1st day Leviticus 23:23-25 *(It is a Sabbath)*	7th month, 10th day Leviticus 23:26-32 *(It is a Sabbath)*	7th month, 15th day, for 7 days; 8th day, Holy Convocation Leviticus 23:33-44 *(The 1st and 8th days are Sabbaths)*	**New heaven and new earth**
	Regathering of Israel in preparation for final day of atonement Jeremiah 32:37-41	**Israel will repent and look to Messiah in one day** Zechariah 3:9-10; 12:10; 13:1; 14:9	**Families of the earth will come to Jerusalem to celebrate the Feast of Booths** Zechariah 14:16-19	**God tabernacles with men** Revelation 21:1-3
	Ezekiel 36:24	Ezekiel 36:25-27 Hebrews 9–10 Romans 11:25-29	Ezekiel 36:28	

Coming of Christ

Israel had two harvests each year—spring and autumn

NUMBERS במדבר
BAMIDBAR

*T*he Israelites cried out to God. The Lord heard their cry and raised up Moses to deliver the children of Israel out of the land of Egypt. They had lived in Egypt for 430 years, 400 of those years as slaves. After camping at Sinai, they were to go to Canaan, the land promised to Abraham, Isaac, and Jacob. At last they would see the land with their own eyes. And God would go with them in a pillar of cloud by day and a pillar of fire by night.

Soon the journey would begin, but first there must be a numbering of all the sons of Israel from 20 years of age on up.

THINGS TO DO

General Instructions

The book of Numbers can be divided into three segments according to the journeys and encampments of the children of Israel. In Numbers 1 through 10:10 they are encamped at Sinai. In Numbers 10:11 the cloud lifts and their journeying begins and does not end for about 39 years. In Numbers 22 Israel camps on the plains of Moab, opposite Jericho, as they prepare to enter the land of promise.

Chapters 1–10:10

1. The first five books of the Bible, Genesis through Deuteronomy, are closely related. They follow each other chronologically. To put Numbers into context:

   a. Read Exodus 40:1-2,17,33-38, which gives an account of the building of the tabernacle at Mount Sinai.

   b. Read Leviticus 1:1 and then 27:34. All of the book of Leviticus takes place at Mount Sinai.

   c. Compare where Leviticus ends and Numbers begins. Read Numbers 1:1-2.

   d. Look at Exodus 40:17 again and Numbers 1:1, and you will see one month elapsed between the close of Exodus and the beginning of Numbers. Leviticus covers a period of only one month.

2. Read through this first segment chapter by chapter. As you do, do not become discouraged and quit; Numbers becomes delightfully interesting and practical after this segment. As you read:

   a. Mark the key words listed on the NUMBERS AT A GLANCE chart. Also mark *number* or *census* and *of the sons of* (then underline whose sons they were). Write all the key words on an index card and use it as a bookmark as you study Numbers.

   b. Mark every reference to time with a clock ⏰, and double-underline all geographical locations in green.

   c. In the margin of each chapter make lists of key truths you want to be able to find with ease. For instance, next to 9:15 you might write: "Instructions re: Cloud" or simply "The Cloud."

   d. Note the theme of each chapter and record it on the NUMBERS AT A GLANCE chart and at the beginning of the chapter in your Bible.

Chapters 10:11–21:35

1. This segment covers about 39 years. As you study you will discover why it takes so long to cover such a relatively short distance. Do the following as you study chapter by chapter:

   a. Since much of what you will read in this segment is historical, you can learn a lot simply by asking the "5 W's and an H." Ask: Who are the main characters in this chapter? What is happening? Why is it happening? When and where is it happening? Why are they told to do something? What were the consequences of their actions? How and why did this occur?

      1) You might want to note in the margin when and where events occur.
      2) Follow the movements of the Israelites on a map.

   b. Mark key repeated words. Add *grumbled (complain)* and *anger* to your list. Watch for key words that are not on the list but will be significant in a particular chapter.

   c. Write on a piece of paper what you learn about the land the Israelites are to possess and what you learn about Korah and Balaam. (Balaam appears in Numbers 22.) These two men will be mentioned again, even in the New Testament, so it will be helpful to mark them in a distinctive color and then to summarize all you learn about them on the chart INSIGHTS FROM NUMBERS on page 53.

   d. There are lessons to be learned from Moses' life about leadership and about our relationship to God. You will also find it profitable to summarize what you learn by making a chart in your notebook called LESSONS FROM THE LIFE OF MOSES. When you record your insights, make sure you note the book, chapter, and verse from which you took your insight.

2. As you did before, record each chapter theme on NUMBERS AT A GLANCE and in the text.

Chapters 22–36

1. This final segment of Numbers is a mixture of historical events, instructions, and numberings. As you read each chapter, remember to ask the "5 W's and an H" and to record any pertinent insights in the margin.

2. To your list of key words add the following: *Moab* (Moab is first mentioned in Numbers 21, so go back and mark *Moab* in that chapter also), *Midian (Midianites), burnt offering,* and *sin offering*.

3. Balaam plays a major role in this last segment. Note all you learn about him on INSIGHTS FROM NUMBERS on page 53. As you near the end of Numbers you will read more about Balaam, so note in the margin where these final verses on Balaam can be found.

4. Record the main points or events of these chapters in the margin. In Numbers 35 mark every reference to *murderer* and *blood avenger*. See what you learn.

5. Record what you learn about Moses. Give special attention to Numbers 27:12-23 in the light of Numbers 20. Next to Numbers 20:1-13 you might want to write Numbers 27:12-23 as a cross-reference.

6. Record your chapter themes as you did before.

7. Record the predominant theme or event in each of the three segments of Numbers on NUMBERS AT A GLANCE. See if any of the chapters can be grouped according to the types of commands, ordinances, and/or events. In other words, do several chapters cover similar topics or events? For example, chapters 1 and 2 cover the census. Note these in the first column under "Segment Divisions" and complete the NUMBERS AT A GLANCE chart.

THINGS TO THINK ABOUT

1. Review all you learned from Moses' life and then pray about how it applies to your own life.

2. Remember, God is the same yesterday, today, and forever. His character did not change between the Old Testament and the New Testament. Think about what you have learned about God from the book of Numbers. Are you living according to His standard of righteousness?

3. Are you jealous because the children of Israel had a cloud to guide them? Have you realized that God's presence in the form of the indwelling Spirit is available to guide you? Do you seek and ask for His Spirit to lead and guide you just as surely as He led the children of Israel? What can you learn from the children of Israel so you won't make the same mistakes?

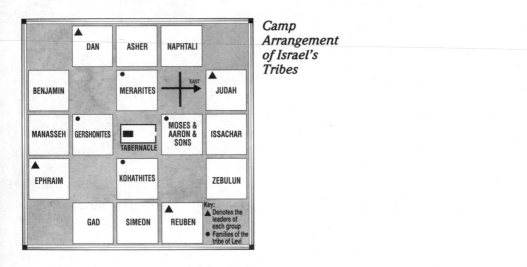

Camp Arrangement of Israel's Tribes

LAND OF CANAAN	BALAAM	KORAH

Theme of Numbers:

Segment Divisions

	Journeys/ Encampments	Chapter Themes
		1
		2
		3
		4
		5
		6
		7
		8
		9
		10
		11
		12
		13
		14
		15
		16
		17
		18
		19
		20
		21
		22
		23
		24
		25
		26
		27
		28
		29
		30
		31
		32
		33
		34
		35
		36

Author:

Date:

Purpose:

Key Words:

the Lord spoke to

service

cloud

wilderness

tent (tabernacle)

offering

atonement

Passover

sin (iniquity)

curse

covenant

holy

See appendix 7 for key words in the New International Version and King James Version.

DEUTERONOMY דברים

DVARIM

$\mathcal{D}$euteronomy is the crown jewel of the Pentateuch. It lays before us clearly what God expects from those whom He redeems: a life of uncompromising obedience.

God raised up Moses to deliver His people from the land of Egypt, the land of bondage. That had been accomplished. Now he stood at Pisgah, near the land of promise. He was 120 years old.

When Moses struck the rock a second time, he failed to respect God's holiness. Therefore, he could not enter the land of promise. But the people who survived and whom he had led so faithfully for the last 40 years would go in and possess it.

Moses had to do one more thing before God took him home: tell God's children how to live in the land that the God of their fathers was giving them.

THINGS TO DO

General Instructions

1. For the book's historical context, read Numbers 21:21–22:1; 36:13; Deuteronomy 1:1-5.

   a. Record the author, date, and geographical setting of the book on the DEUTERONOMY AT A GLANCE chart.

   b. When you study Deuteronomy, watch for any verses that confirm Moses' authorship. Although the last chapter tells of Moses' death, this doesn't negate the fact that Moses wrote the rest of the book. The last chapter would be an appropriate postscript after his death.

2. Read Romans 15:4 and 1 Corinthians 10:1-14 and keep these verses in mind as you study.

   a. As you study each chapter, note in the margin of your Bible (under the symbol △) insights you glean about the character of God and the ways He deals with His children and with unbelievers.

   b. Also note in the margin any specific instructions or admonitions that are to be followed in respect to God—for example, "Fear Him."

   c. Record in the margin any "Lessons for Life" you learn from the text under the heading "LFL."

3. There are insightful lessons to be learned from Moses' life about leadership and about our relationship to God. As you study Deuteronomy, note these in your notebook. When you record your insights, make sure you note the book, chapter, and verse from which they came.

4. Double-underline all geographical locations in green, and look them up on a map to see where the events took place.

Chapters 1–3

Moses rehearses what happened from the time they left Horeb (Mount Sinai) until they camped in the valley opposite Beth-peor at the foot of Mount Nebo (Pisgah).

1. As you read these three chapters:

   a. Ask the "5 W's and an H." Watch what happens in each chapter, where it happens and to whom, why it happens, and what the consequences or results are. Also note how things are accomplished.

   b. Mark every reference to time and every use of *then* so you can see the sequence of events.

2. In a distinctive way mark these key words and their synonyms: *covenant, fear, heart, command (commanded),* and *listen.* Write these on an index card to use as a bookmark while studying Deuteronomy.

3. Choose the theme of each chapter and record it at the beginning of the chapter and on DEUTERONOMY AT A GLANCE.

Chapters 4–11

Moses instructs the children of Israel regarding what they are to do when they enter the land.

1. Read this segment chapter by chapter, keeping in mind the "5 W's and an H." Words such as *when, then, watch, hear, listen, beware,* and *you shall therefore* will come to your attention. When you see the word "when," look and see if "then" eventually follows it. If so, circle each word and connect them with a line.

2. Mark the following key words when you come to them in the text: *observe (keep, do), love, remember, commandment (statutes), nations, blessing,* and *curse.*

3. Record the main points of each chapter in the margin or number them in the text.

4. Record the chapter themes as you did previously.

Chapters 12–26

Moses gives the people the statutes and the judgments they are to observe.

1. Make sure you mark every occurrence of the phrase *you shall purge (remove) the evil.* Also mark the words *life* and *death.* Mark every reference to the *feasts.*

2. As you read these chapters, note in the margin of the text what the people are to do and why.

3. Record the theme of the chapters on DEUTERONOMY AT A GLANCE and in your Bible.

Chapters 27–30

Moses tells the people about the necessity of obedience and that if they obey they will be blessed, but if they disobey they will be cursed.

1. Carefully mark the words on your key words list. Underline every reference to *the LORD will.* Think about what you observe from marking the text.

2. As you read these chapters, keep asking the "5 W's and an H." Note who Moses speaks to, who he's making a covenant with, and who or what will be affected by their obedience or disobedience. Also note everything that will happen if they obey or disobey.

3. Don't forget to note what you learn about God from these chapters and to record the theme of each chapter.

Chapters 31–34

This segment contains Moses' parting words, song, and blessing, as well as the account of his death.

1. Mark the key repeated words listed on your index card.

2. As Moses sings his song in chapter 32, he recounts Israel's relationship to God and God's dealings with them. *Jeshurun* in 32:15 is a reference to Israel.

   a. Pay attention to what you learn about Israel. Observe what leads to Israel's downfall and what the consequences are.

   b. Remember that although Moses begged God to change His mind and allow him to enter the promised land, God said no. Keep this in mind as you read these chapters and see Moses' heart and hear his words in respect to God. Take note of all you learn about God from these significant chapters. List what you learn about "the Rock" in your notebook.

3. Observe what Moses says will happen after his death and note this in the margin.

4. When you study chapter 33, mark the name of each of the tribes of Israel and carefully observe how they are described and what is said about each one of them. Underline every occurrence of *they shall* (NIV *he*) in 33:10.

5. Complete DEUTERONOMY AT A GLANCE.

THINGS TO THINK ABOUT

1. Since we are under the new covenant of grace, what is our relationship to the blessings and curses set forth in Deuteronomy? Read Hebrews 8–10.

2. What kind of allegiance does God call for from Israel? Do you think He expects anything less from the church, the body of the Lord Jesus Christ? Do you think grace allows us to continue in sin and disobedience without any consequences or chastening from the Father?

3. What have you learned regarding the long-suffering of God and His gracious ways with His covenant people?

4. How does a follower of God demonstrate his love for the Lord?

Theme of Deuteronomy:

SEGMENT DIVISIONS

			CHAPTER THEMES	Author:
		1		
		2		Date:
		3		
		4		Geographical
		5		Location:
		6		
		7		
		8		Purpose:
		9		
		10		
		11		Key Words:
		12		
		13		covenant
		14		fear
		15		heart
		16		command
		17		(commanded)
		18		listen
		19		observe (keep, do)
		20		love
		21		remember
		22		commandment
		23		(statutes)
		24		nations
		25		blessing
		26		curse
		27		you shall purge
		28		(remove) the evil
		29		life
		30		death
		31		the Lord will
		32		
		33		
		34		

See appendix 7 for key words in the New International Version and King James Version.

JOSHUA יהושע
YEHOSHUA

*F*or years Joshua had faithfully served Moses—and God. How well Joshua had come to understand the meaning of his name, "The Lord is salvation." All his contemporaries except Caleb had died in the wilderness because they had not believed God. But God had spared Joshua and Caleb because they had followed Him fully.

After Moses died, God appointed Joshua to lead the children of Israel into the land of promise. Their salvation from their enemies would not come from the east nor from the west but from the One who made the heaven and the earth!

God's encouragement rang in Joshua's heart: "Be strong and courageous."

THINGS TO DO

General Instructions

1. If you are not familiar with who Joshua is, before you begin studying the book, read Numbers 13; 14; 27:18-23; Deuteronomy 34:9.

2. As you study Joshua one chapter at a time, it will help you keep everything in context if you keep in mind that the book of Joshua falls into four segments. In chapters 1 through 5 the children of Israel prepare to enter the land. Chapters 6 through 12 describe the conquest of the land. Chapters 13 through 21 tell of the allocation of the land. In chapters 22 through 24 Joshua calls Israel to serve the Lord, who gave them the land.

3. As you read each chapter, ask the "5 W's and an H": Who? What? When? Where? Why? and How? For example, in a historical book such as Joshua, ask: What is this chapter about? Who are the main characters? What is taking place? Where is it happening and when? Who is involved? Why is this occurring, being said, or to be done? What are the consequences? How is it going to happen? How should it be done? Record the main points or events of the chapter in the margin of your Bible. Double-underline every geographical location in green.

4. Look on a map to find the various cities and places mentioned throughout this book. This will help you keep the book in its geographical context.

5. Mark every reference to time with a clock ◷. This will help you see when events occurred and the chronological relationship of one event to another.

6. After you finish studying each chapter, write the theme or event covered in that chapter at the beginning of the chapter in your Bible. Then record it on the JOSHUA AT A GLANCE chart.

Chapters 1–5

1. As you read these chapters, mark the following key words and their synonyms: *Joshua, land, strong, courageous, firm, command (commanded, as the Lord commanded, in accordance with the command of the Lord), possess, covenant, ark of the Lord (ark of the covenant)*, and *Israel*. Write these on an index card that you can use as a bookmark while studying this segment.

2. Watch how the events or the instructions prepare the Israelites to enter the land. Also note the procedure for entering the land and the requirements placed on them as they arrive in the land. You might list these in the margin under the heading "Possessing the Land."

3. If while reading chapter 5 you need a review of circumcision, read Genesis 17 and

Exodus 4:24-26.

4. Don't forget to record the theme of each chapter in your Bible and on JOSHUA AT A GLANCE.

Chapters 6–12

1. As you study this section keep in mind the general instructions above.

2. Although you will mark many of the same key words, make a new bookmark with the following key words: *God, Lord, Joshua, covenant, strong, courageous, land, fear, command (commanded), fight (fought), captured, ark of the Lord (of the covenant),* and *Israel.*

3. Carefully observe what God tells the people to do when they conquer a city. Read Genesis 15:7-21 and note that God told Abraham He would bring his descendants into Canaan when the iniquity of the Amorites was complete. Also recall the covenant God made with Abraham on that day. You might write "Genesis 15:7-21" in the margin of this section as a cross-reference.

4. As you read, watch what happens when the people fail to consult God or to obey His commands regarding the inhabitants of the land. Note this in the margin.

5. When you come to chapter 8, note where Mount Ebal and Mount Gerizim are located and what takes place there. Refer back to Deuteronomy 11:29 and Deuteronomy 27:11-14. Use a map to locate these places. Also mark all clues to time with a clock.

6. Record the theme of each chapter.

Chapters 13–21

1. Once again make a new bookmark and write the following key words on it, although some words will remain the same: *Israel, land, Joshua, Caleb, strong, fear, command (commanded, commandments), fought, captured, inheritance, possession, possessed* (also mark *possession* in chapter 12), and *promised.*

2. Double-underline the geographical locations in green, then locate them on a map. Also mark in the text the name of each tribe as it is allotted its portion of the land.

3. As you read, watch for any mention of Caleb. Remember what you read about Joshua and Caleb in Numbers 13 and 14. There are important lessons to be learned from their example.

4. Pay careful attention to chapter 20 and what you learn about the cities of refuge.

5. Also note the inheritance given to the Levites in Joshua 21.

6. Don't forget to record the chapter themes.

Chapters 22–24

1. Make one final bookmark for the key words you want to mark in the text: *land, possess (possession), covenant, strong, firm, fear, command (commandment, commanded), serve (served), Israel, Joshua, promised, fought,* and *inheritance.*

2. List God's instructions and what the people are to do in order to keep them. Also note the consequences of disobedience.

3. As you read Joshua 23, mark the word *cling.* Then read Jeremiah 13:1-11.

4. Complete JOSHUA AT A GLANCE. Fill in the four main segment divisions and any others you see.

5. Compare what Joshua tells the children of Israel in chapter 23 with God's word to Joshua in chapter 1. You might write "Joshua 1:7-9" in the margin of Joshua 23.

THINGS TO THINK ABOUT

1. Do you consult the Lord and His Word and then walk in obedience to what He says?

2. Joshua was admonished to be strong and courageous. What do you think this means? Read Revelation 21:8 and note what is said about the cowardly.

3. Have you decided whom you are going to follow? Have you counted the cost? What would cause you to compromise? Could you get away with compromise? What would it cost you? Would it be worth it?

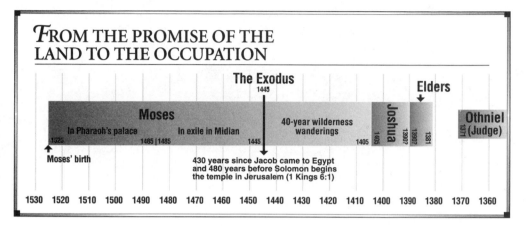

*F*ROM THE PROMISE OF THE LAND TO THE OCCUPATION

The Exodus 1445

Elders

Moses
In Pharaoh's palace 1525 1485 | 1485 In exile in Midian 1445

40-year wilderness wanderings 1405

Joshua 1405

Joshua 1390?

1381

Othniel 1371 (Judge)

Moses' birth

430 years since Jacob came to Egypt and 480 years before Solomon begins the temple in Jerusalem (1 Kings 6:1)

1530 1520 1510 1500 1490 1480 1470 1460 1450 1440 1430 1420 1410 1400 1390 1380 1370 1360

Theme of Joshua:

Author:

Date:

Purpose:

Key Words:

SEGMENT DIVISIONS

			CHAPTER THEMES
			1
			2
			3
			4
			5
			6
			7
			8
			9
			10
			11
			12
			13
			14
			15
			16
			17
			18
			19
			20
			21
			22
			23
			24

See appendix 7 for key words in the New International Version and King James Version.

JUDGES שופטים
SHOFTIM

*D*uring Joshua's leadership, Israel finally entered the land that had been promised to Abraham. There were giants in the land, but none who were greater than God. The Captain of the Host was able to subdue all Israel's enemies. In one battle, the sun stood still until the people of Israel had avenged themselves on their enemies.

Then there arose a generation that did not know war, nor did they know the Lord or the work He had done for His children. Israel went from victory to defeat, plunging into more than 300 years of darkness. These were the days of the judges, days from which we can learn valuable lessons.

THINGS TO DO

Chapters 1–2

1. Because the book of Judges is not strictly chronological, it is helpful to understand the setting of the book. Read chapters 1 and 2. Then go to the end of Judges and read Judges 17:6; 18:1; 19:1; 21:25 and look for the key repeated phrase. Mark this phrase in a distinctive way and record it on the JUDGES AT A GLANCE chart under "Key Words."

2. Now read chapters 1 and 2 again and do the following:

   a. Mark in the text the key words and phrases listed on JUDGES AT A GLANCE. Put these on an index card that you can use as a bookmark while you study Judges.

   b. Judges 1:21-33 contains an important key phrase that is not on this list because it is not used afterward. Look for that phrase and mark its repeated use in a distinctive way. Then look up Exodus 23:20-33, Deuteronomy 7:1-11,16, and Joshua 23:5-13. Record these references in the margin of chapter 1 for cross-references.

   c. As you read each chapter, question the text with the "5 W's and an H": Who? What? When? Where? Why? and How? You will not always find the answer to every question. As you read, make sure you note who does what and why. Watch for where events take place and when. Always ask how something was accomplished, happened, or is to be done.

   d. On a separate piece of paper, list everything you learn from chapter 2 about the sons of Israel, Joshua, the elders, and the judges.

3. When you finish your observations of chapter 2, review all you have learned, especially from verses 11 through 23. Notice the cycle of events. Make sure you record this in the margin; it sets the pattern for chapters 3 through 16.

4. Discern the themes of these chapters and record them on JUDGES AT A GLANCE and in your Bible next to the chapter number.

Chapters 3–16

1. Study chapters 3 through 16 the same way you did chapters 1 and 2: Mark key words, ask the "5 W's and an H," list your insights in the margin, and record the theme of each chapter in the appropriate places.

2. As you read Judges 3 through 16, note the names of the judges and record them in the chapter margin where they appear. Then record what you learn about them on a separate piece of paper or the AT A GLANCE chart. To understand when these judges ruled and what their relationship was to one another, carefully study the historical chart on the next page.

3. As you study each judge, note where the judge is from and write his or her name on a map next to the proper location.

Chapters 17–21

1. There is no indication that chapters 17 through 21 chronologically follow chapters 3 through 16. Rather, they give an overview of the moral setting of the time. Examine each chapter carefully as you have done the other chapters of Judges and note your insights. Watch the progression of events.

2. As you read these chapters, keep in mind the key phrase you marked when you began your study. Note how the result of this phrase is manifested in the way the people live.

3. Record the chapter themes as you have done previously on JUDGES AT A GLANCE. Also record the main theme of each segment division and any other segment division you may see. Finally, record the main theme of Judges.

THINGS TO THINK ABOUT

1. What have you learned from Judges about carefully listening to and obeying the commands of the Lord? What have you seen about the consequences of doing what is right in your own eyes? What parallels do you see between the sins committed in Judges 17 through 21 and today? What does this tell you?

2. Think about why the cycle of sin wasn't broken in the days of the judges. Are you caught in a cycle of sin in your own life? What will it take to break it?

3. What have you learned by studying the lives of the judges? Carefully review your AT A GLANCE chart and meditate on the lessons you can apply to your own life.

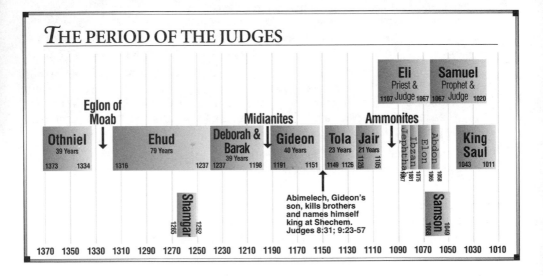

Theme of Judges:

Segment Divisions

Oppressor	Judge & Years Rulled	Chapter Themes
		1
		2
		3
		4
		5
		6
		7
		8
		9
		10
		11
		12
		13
		14
		15
		16
		17
		18
		19
		20
		21

Author:

Date:

Purpose:

Key Words:

covenant

sons of Israel did evil

sold (served)

sons of Israel cried

the Lord raised up a deliverer (or judge)

judge(s)

See appendix 7 for key words in the New International Version and King James Version.

RUTH   רות

*T*he events recorded in the book of Ruth take place during the dark years of the judges. This book offers encouragement and hope to those who decide to follow God. This story of love and dedication revolves around three people who determine in their hearts to walk in integrity, clinging to their God and His precepts—three people who know who their King is and who do what is right in His eyes.

THINGS TO DO

1. As you read Ruth one chapter at a time:

   a. First read each chapter simply to catch the flavor of the lives of these people.

   b. Then read each chapter again, focusing on the "who" and the "what." Look at the main characters mentioned in each chapter. Note the sequence of events and how each character confronts and deals with his or her situations. Note how chapter 1 gives you the historical context of Ruth.

   c. Watch for and mark the key repeated words listed on the RUTH AT A GLANCE chart. After you finish marking key words in a chapter, observe what you learn about each. If there is something significant you want to remember, write it in the margin.

2. Determine the theme of each chapter and record it on RUTH AT A GLANCE and at the beginning of each chapter in your Bible.

3. When you finish reading Ruth and marking every reference to *redeem, kinsman*, and *closest relative:*

   a. List everything you learn about the process of redeeming a close relative. Pay attention to the process in chapter 4.

   b. Look up the laws regarding redemption in Leviticus 25:23-28 and Deuteronomy 25:5-10. You may want to record these cross-references next to your insights on *redemption.*

4. Complete RUTH AT A GLANCE.

THINGS TO THINK ABOUT

1. What have you learned about loyalty from the story of Ruth? What does it mean to be loyal to God, to His people, to His precepts, and to trust God to do what He says He will do?

2. As you think of Boaz redeeming Ruth, remember that you have a Kinsman Redeemer, the Lord Jesus Christ. Think of how the Lord has acted on your behalf as your Kinsman Redeemer by becoming a man so He could break death's hold by paying for your sin (Hebrews 2:14-15). Remember that you were not redeemed from your empty way of life with silver or gold, but with the precious blood of the Lamb of God, a Lamb without spot or blemish (1 Peter 1:18-19).

3. The final verses of Ruth show us that Ruth was included in the genealogy of David and therefore in the human lineage of our Lord Jesus Christ. Not only did a sovereign God include Rahab the harlot in the genealogy of His Son, but He also chose a Gentile, Ruth. Both of these women chose to believe God when those around them didn't! Consider how their example might apply to your life.

4. In the book of Judges, Israel forsook the true God and turned to idols, while in Ruth we see the opposite. One Gentile woman turns from idols to serve the only true God. In which category do you find yourself?

Theme of Ruth:

Author:

Date:

Purpose:

Key Words:

redeem
(redemption)

relative
(closest relative,
kinsman)

Naomi

Ruth

Boaz

SEGMENT DIVISIONS	CHAPTER THEMES
1	
2	
3	
4	

See appendix 7 for key words in the New International Version and King James Version.

1 SAMUEL שמואל א

*T*he days of the judges were dark until God raised up Samuel as a prophet, priest, and judge. Samuel was committed to doing what was right in God's eyes. But the people weren't satisfied. They cried, "Now appoint a king for us to judge us like all the nations!" With that plea they rejected the Lord as their King. What would it be like to live under a monarchy rather than a theocracy? The children of Israel were soon to find out. The kingdom, at first united, eventually was divided because of the disobedience of the kings.

The books of 1 and 2 Samuel, 1 and 2 Kings, and 1 and 2 Chronicles record the days of the kings of Israel. God's children can learn many valuable lessons from these books. The lessons begin when God rejects Saul and chooses as king a man after His own heart. And what will such a man be like? Will he live a perfect life? Is this what will make him a man after God's own heart?

THINGS TO DO

General Instructions

As you study this book, never forget that these are actual people, frail but with access to God and His precepts and statutes of life. Observe the text prayerfully and carefully, and as you study, note in the margin God's lessons for life.

Chapters 1–7: Samuel, the Last Judge

1. As you observe these first seven chapters, mark the following words in a distinctive way and then record in the margin key insights that you want to remember.

   a. *Ark (of the Lord, of God, of the covenant), ephod, judge (judged), king, Ichabod,* and *Ebenezer.* The last three words are used only one time in these chapters but are significant. *Ephod* is used only twice in this segment but will have greater significance in the last segment of 1 Samuel. List these key words on 1 SAMUEL AT A GLANCE and on an index card you can use as a bookmark for this segment.

   b. Double-underline in green every geographical location. Then locate these places on a map.

2. Since 1 Samuel is a historical account, note the focus of each chapter. Who and/or what event does the chapter center on?

   a. You might want to list your insights about the main characters and what they do in the margin of each chapter.

   b. Read the insights on Nazirites and the ephod on page 71.

   c. Using an easily recognizable symbol such as △, note in the margin your insights about God and His ways. For instance, in chapter 1 God closes the womb and opens the womb.

3. Record the theme of each chapter next to each chapter number in your Bible and on the 1 SAMUEL AT A GLANCE chart.

Chapters 8–15: From Samuel to Saul, from Judge to King

1. As you observe this segment of 1 Samuel:

   a. Mark the following key words: *judge (judges), king* (don't include foreign kings), *sin (sins, sinned), evil, Spirit of God (of the Lord), ark of God,* and *ephod.* Put them on 1 SAMUEL AT A GLANCE and on an index card to use as a bookmark.

    b. List what you learn about Samuel, Saul, King Agag, and the Amalekites. See the chart "Saul's Family Tree" on page 71.

    c. Note all you learn about God and His ways.

    d. Mark the references to time (when Saul begins his reign, etc.) and geographical locations.

    e. There are no references to the ark in 1 Samuel after this segment. Review what you learned about the ark in this book and note in the margin where it is last mentioned and its location. Read "The Ark of the Covenant" on page 323.

2. Carefully observe all you learn from marking the word *king*. Watch for the following and record your insights in the margin:

    a. Why the people wanted a king, how they perceived the kingship, and what kind of king they wanted.

    b. How God responded to the people's request, what God desired in a kingship, and how the success or failure of a king was determined. Compare this with Deuteronomy 17:14-20.

3. Examine each chapter as you did in the previous segment, watching for and recording the main event of each chapter and any pertinent subpoints. Don't forget to record the chapter theme on 1 SAMUEL AT A GLANCE and in the text.

Chapters 16–31: The Preparation of Another King

1. In this segment:

    a. Make a new bookmark and mark the following key words: *king* (not foreign kings), *evil, evil spirit, sin (sinned), judge, covenant, inquire (inquired)*, and *ephod*. Don't forget to record what you are learning from marking *king* and *ephod*.

    b. Mark all references to time and to geographical locations as before.

2. Observe and record in the margin of each chapter the major points you learn about Samuel, Saul, and David. Observe all that happens to David and how he responds to God and to man. Watch for and note in the margin the "LFL" (Lessons for Life).

3. In the margin write "Covenant" and list what you have observed from the text. Ask the "5 W's and an H": Who makes the covenant? How is it made? What is done? What is promised? What are the conditions? When is it made? Where is it made? Why? Remember that you are in covenant with God if you are a child of God (Matthew 26:26-29); watch for any principles which might apply to you. Read the insights on covenants on page 35.

4. As you read each chapter, watch for insights about God, note the events of each chapter and the subpoints of the chapter, and record the chapter themes.

5. Complete 1 SAMUEL AT A GLANCE. Watch for any additional segment divisions in 1 Samuel. Look at the chapter themes and see if there is any other way 1 Samuel might be segmented: Can any chapters be grouped in respect to David's relationship to Saul, to Jonathan, to the Philistines, or to others? Or is there any geographical segmentation, such as where Samuel, Saul, and David spend their time?

6. Record the theme of 1 Samuel on 1 SAMUEL AT A GLANCE.

THINGS TO THINK ABOUT

1. What lessons did you learn from Eli's dealings with his sons? Do you see your accountability before God to discipline your children?

2. What do you learn from Samuel's, Saul's, and David's lives regarding seeking God, listening to Him, and obeying Him? Are there consequences when you don't?

3. Did you notice how much time has elapsed since David was anointed to be king? Still, as 1 Samuel comes to a close, David is not king over Israel. Think about all that transpired since Samuel anointed David. What can you learn from this about God's promises, His purpose, and His timing? Are you waiting patiently on God for the fulfillment of His promises to you?

4. Review the "Lessons for Life" you observed and the insights you recorded about God in the margins of 1 Samuel. Make these a matter of prayer.

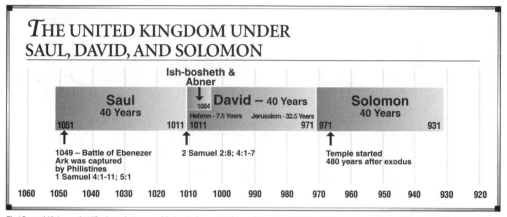

THE UNITED KINGDOM UNDER SAUL, DAVID, AND SOLOMON

Ish-bosheth & Abner

| Saul 40 Years | 1004 David – 40 Years | Solomon 40 Years |

Hebron – 7.5 Years   Jerusalem – 32.5 Years

1051   1011 1011   971 971   931

1049 – Battle of Ebenezer
Ark was captured
by Philistines
1 Samuel 4:1-11; 5:1

2 Samuel 2:8; 4:1-7

Temple started
480 years after exodus

1060 1050 1040 1030 1020 1010 1000 990 980 970 960 950 940 930 920

First Samuel 13:1 says that "Saul was *forty* years old when he began to reign, and he reigned *thirty*-two years over Israel." Acts 13:21 says that Saul was king for 40 years. In Hebrew the numbers are missing in 1 Samuel 13:1. In Hebrew, the word for years is plural when the number of years is 1-19, and is singular when the number of years is 20 and above. In this case the word for years is singular, so we know the missing number is 20 or more years. But this verse does not tell us how old Saul was when he began to reign or how long he reigned. Any number given in English is supplied or guessed. The first word of 1 Samuel 13:2 is a connector word that can be used in ten different ways. A better translation of 1 Samuel 13:1-2 would be "Saul was ... years old when he began to reign and he had reigned two years over Israel when he chose for himself...."

INSIGHT

A *Nazirite* (which means "consecration, devotion, and separation") was someone who was bound by a vow of consecration to God's service for either a specific period of time or for life. A Nazirite's devotion to God was evidenced outwardly by not cutting the hair, abstaining from wine and alcoholic drinks, and avoiding contact with the dead. Violation of these brought defilement and need of purification.

In 1 Samuel 1:11, when Hannah made her vow, she was making a Nazirite vow.

INSIGHT

The *ephod* was used to seek guidance from God. Described in Exodus 28, it was a linen garment worn by the priest and also by David when he was king (2 Samuel 6:14). The ephod was fastened on each shoulder by onyx clasps which had the names of six tribes engraved on one clasp and six tribes engraved on the other. The *breastpiece*, which was fastened to the ephod, had a linen pouch which held the *Urim* and *Thummim*, which may have been used as sacred lots to reveal God's will (1 Samuel 28:6).

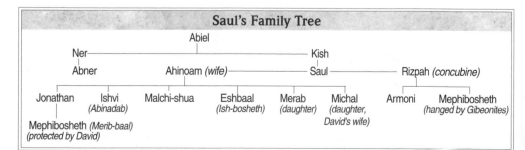

Saul's Family Tree

Abiel

Ner————————————————————Kish

Abner   Ahinoam *(wife)*————————Saul————————Rizpah *(concubine)*

Jonathan   Ishvi   Malchi-shua   Eshbaal   Merab   Michal   Armoni   Mephibosheth
            (Abinadab)   *(Ish-bosheth)* *(daughter)* *(daughter, David's wife)*   *(hanged by Gibeonites)*

Mephibosheth *(Merib-baal)*
(protected by David)

Theme of 1 Samuel:

SEGMENT DIVISIONS

		MAIN DIVISIONS	CHAPTER THEMES
		SAMUEL, THE LAST JUDGE	1
			2
			3
			4
			5
			6
			7
		FROM SAMUEL TO SAUL, FROM JUDGES TO KINGS	8
			9
			10
			11
			12
			13
			14
			15
		THE PREPARATION OF ANOTHER KING	16
			17
			18
			19
			20
			21
			22
			23
			24
			25
			26
			27
			28
			29
			30
			31

Author:

Date:

Purpose:

Key Words:

See appendix 7 for key words in the New International Version and King James Version.

2 SAMUEL ‏שמואל ב‎
SHMU'EL BET

*T*he LORD is compassionate and gracious, slow to anger and abounding in lovingkindness. He will not always strive with us, nor will He keep His anger forever....As far as the east is from the west, so far has He removed our transgressions from us. Just as a father has compassion on his children, so the LORD has compassion on those who fear Him. For He Himself knows our frame; He is mindful that we are but dust" (Psalm 103:8-9,12-14).

These are the words of David. Were they written before or after he became king? Before or after he sinned with Bathsheba? We don't know for certain, but we do know David understood their meaning, as we will see in 2 Samuel.

THINGS TO DO

General Instructions

1. You should study 1 Samuel before you study 2 Samuel. In the Hebrew Scriptures they were written as one book and were not divided until later. Second Samuel records David's life from the time of Saul's death until the account of David's later years and death (which are recorded in 1 Kings). First Chronicles 10 through 29 covers the same period in David's life. As you observe this book, keep in mind what you have learned in 1 Samuel.

2. As you study 2 Samuel, you need to remember that you are studying a biographical account of a man whose frame is dust, but a man whom God would later say was a man after His own heart. Therefore, as you study chapter by chapter:

    a. Observe each chapter in the light of the "5 W's and an H." Ask questions such as: Who are the main characters in this chapter? What is taking place? Where is this happening? When is it occurring? Why did it happen? Why this response? What are the consequences? How was it handled? How did David (or whoever) respond? Record your insights in the margin.

    b. Mark all references to time with a ⏰ . Double-underline in green all geographical references and locate these on a map.

    c. In chapter 22 and throughout the Psalms, David wrote about the character of God. Watch for the references to God and note what you learn about God's character and His ways, even as David did.

    d. Watch and see what lessons you can learn for your life. Record these in the margin as you did in 1 Samuel under the heading "LFL" (Lessons for Life).

3. When you finish each chapter, record the theme or main event of the chapter on 2 SAMUEL AT A GLANCE and in your Bible.

Chapters 1–10: David Becomes King of Judah and Then Israel

1. As you read each chapter, in addition to following the "General Instructions," mark the following key words: *king, reigned, inquired, ephod, ark, covenant, before the Lord,* and *evil (iniquity).* Write these key words on an index card you can use as a bookmark. As you mark these words, observe what you learn and, in the margin, record any pertinent insights.

2. In chapter 5, refer to the chart "David's Family Tree" on page 75.

3. When you study chapter 7, give special attention to the Lord's promises to David. This is referred to as a covenant in 2 Chronicles 13:5; 21:7. Then observe what David does and how he responds to the Lord.

4. In 1 Samuel you marked every reference to *covenant*. In 1 Samuel 20 Jonathan and David make a covenant between their "houses" (families). When you study chapters 4 and 9 of 2 Samuel, keep in mind the covenant David and Jonathan made in regard to their houses and notice how David fulfills this covenant. Also when you study Mephibosheth, remember 2 Samuel 5:6-8. Mark *Mephibosheth* in a distinctive way.

Chapters 11–12: David's Sins

1. Make a new bookmark for this segment. Mark the following key words: *inquired, ark, evil (sinned, sin),* and every reference to fasting.

2. Carefully watch the progression of events in these two chapters. Note the progression of sin and the things which could have served as admonitions against sin had David heeded them. Also list the consequences of David's sin and how the consequences parallel his sin.

3. Remember to follow the "General Instructions." Don't forget the "Lessons for Life" (LFL).

4. Study Psalm 51. Note when the psalm was written.

Chapters 13–24: Consequences of David's Sins

1. Mark the following key words: *Absalom, Mephibosheth, inquired, ark, covenant (oath), before the Lord, evil (iniquity, sinned),* and *Spirit*. Make a new bookmark for this segment.

2. Follow the "General Instructions." Pay attention to who's who in these chapters— there are many key characters. Record their names in the margin. Note how they are described and observe the consequences of their actions.

3. Note who David's children are and how he deals with them. Watch Absalom carefully and keep a running record in the margin of what you learn about him. Record your "LFL" in the margin.

4. As you study these final chapters, give special attention to David's relationship to the Lord and to what David has to say about God even after God told him He would chasten him. Spend time meditating on chapter 22 and 23:1-7. When you come to *covenant*, review what you learned in chapter 7 and add any new insights.

5. Then complete 2 SAMUEL AT A GLANCE.

THINGS TO THINK ABOUT

1. What have you learned about sin and its consequences? Did you think that if God forgave you, you would never reap sin's harvest? What do you think now?

2. In light of all you have learned, why do you think God referred to David as a man after His own heart (1 Samuel 13:14; Acts 13:22)? Give this some serious thought. Then think about what such a statement about David, made after his death, would mean to you. If you wanted to be a man, a woman, a teen, a child after God's own heart, what do you think it would require on your part?

3. Review the "Lessons for Life" you marked in the margin. What did you see that you can make a matter of prayer? Did you learn anything about inquiring or sitting before the Lord? Did you learn anything from marking "before the Lord"?

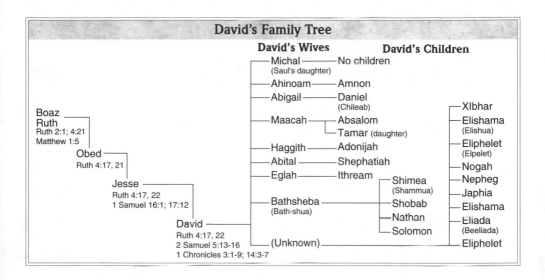

David's Family Tree

David's Wives — David's Children

Boaz
Ruth
Ruth 2:1; 4:21
Matthew 1:5

Obed
Ruth 4:17, 21

Jesse
Ruth 4:17, 22
1 Samuel 16:1; 17:12

David
Ruth 4:17, 22
2 Samuel 5:13-16
1 Chronicles 3:1-9; 14:3-7

David's Wives

- Michal — No children
  (Saul's daughter)
- Ahinoam — Amnon
- Abigail — Daniel
  (Chileab)
- Maacah — Absalom
  — Tamar (daughter)
- Haggith — Adonijah
- Abital — Shephatiah
- Eglah — Ithream
- Bathsheba
  (Bath-shua)
- (Unknown)

David's Children

- Shimea
  (Shammua)
- Shobab
- Nathan
- Solomon

- Xlbhar
- Elishama
  (Elishua)
- Eliphelet
  (Elpelet)
- Nogah
- Nepheg
- Japhia
- Elishama
- Eliada
  (Beeliada)
- Eliphelet

Theme of 2 Samuel:

SEGMENT
DIVISIONS

		CHAPTER THEMES	*Author:*
		1	
		2	*Date:*
		3	
		4	
		5	*Purpose:*
		6	
		7	*Key Words:*
		8	
		9	
		10	
		11	
		12	
		13	
		14	
		15	
		16	
		17	
		18	
		19	
		20	
		21	
		22	
		23	
		24	

See appendix 7 for key words in the New International Version and King James Version.

1 KINGS מְלָכִים א

MLAKHIM ALEPH

avid—the warrior, the great king, the man whom God both loved and chastised—was getting old. By the end of his life many people were vying for his throne. First Kings, which records the final events of David's life, marks the beginning of a new era for Israel, one that opens in resplendent glory and ends with apostasy.

The account of the kings who followed David is full of sobering lessons. It is an important chapter in the history of Israel and their God, who made them a people of His own possession.

We don't know who wrote 1 Kings. We only know that this is God's Word preserved "for our instruction, so that through perseverance and the encouragement of the Scriptures we might have hope" (Romans 15:4).

THINGS TO DO

General Instructions

Chapter 12 of 1 Kings records a dramatic, pivotal point in the history of Israel. Therefore, as we study 1 Kings, we will divide it into two segments with two sets of instructions.

Chapters 1–11

Read through this first segment of 1 Kings one chapter at a time.

1. Remember, you are studying the lives of real people. Observe the opportunities God gives them, His instructions to them, and how they respond. Watch when they succeed and when they fail; note why—and learn! Ask God to speak to your heart. In the margin of each chapter, if applicable, make a list of these two things: "Lessons for Life" (LFL) and "Insights about God" (△). Your insights on God will be most enlightening.

2. Mark in a distinctive way the following words and phrases: *word* (or any reference to *the word of the Lord), heart, pray (cry, cried), covenant, wisdom (wise), command (commandments), prophet, promise (promised), high places, house* (when it refers to God's house), and *sin (sinned)*. The first occurrence of the word *sin* is in chapter 8.

   a. List the key words on an index card and use it as a bookmark while you study. You might want to mark the beginning of a king's reign with a crown.

   b. When you read "*the Lord said,*" highlight or underline what the Lord said. Then underline anything you want to remember.

3. The main characters of these first chapters are David and Solomon.

   a. When you come to Solomon's reign, read Deuteronomy 7:2-6 and 17:14-20 to understand Solomon's actions as he took over the kingdom. Remember that sin was to be judged and murderers were to be put to death; otherwise the land would be polluted.

   b. Second Chronicles 1 through 9 is an excellent cross-reference on 1 Kings 1 through 11.

4. Mark every reference to time with a 🕐 and double-underline in green every geographical reference.

5. After you finish reading a chapter, record the theme or subject of that chapter in your Bible and on the appropriate place on 1 KINGS AT A GLANCE.

6. When you finish chapter 11, see if any of the first 11 chapters can be grouped under a common theme or as part of an event: e.g. the building of the temple. These are called segment divisions and can be recorded in the designated place on 1 KINGS AT A GLANCE.

Chapters 12–22

1. As you read chapter 12, study the chart ISRAEL'S DIVISION AND CAPTIVITY on the following page. Note the division of the kingdom, which occurred in 931 B.C. From this point on, whenever "Israel" is used, you will need to distinguish whether it is a reference to the ten tribes of the northern kingdom (which it will usually be) or to the nation of Israel as a whole.

2. Add *according to* to your key word list. When you come to this phrase, note what was "according to" what. You will gain some important insights. Also add *did evil, Elijah,* and *Elisha.* Mark your key words in this section.

3. Watch for insights the Lord gives you about Himself, His ways, and about life in general through the example of the kings and God's people. Record these in the margin under "Insights about God" or "Lessons for Life" just as you did in the first segment of 1 Kings.

4. When you read of a king or another key figure, consult THE HISTORICAL CHART OF THE KINGS AND PROPHETS OF ISRAEL AND JUDAH on pages 83 through 85. You might want to mark the beginning of each king's reign with a crown.

5. Each time you finish reading about a king, record your insights on the chart THE KINGS OF ISRAEL AND JUDAH on pages 86 and 87. Also fill in the information on Solomon.

   a. Make sure you note on the chart whether each king ruled over the northern kingdom (Israel) or southern kingdom (Judah) and whether they did good or evil.

   b. Mark every reference to time.

6. Compare 17:1 with Deuteronomy 28:1-2,12,15,23-24 and James 5:17-18. What could be the scriptural basis for Elijah's prayer and word to Ahab? Think about it.

7. Record the chapter themes and any segment divisions you see on 1 KINGS AT A GLANCE. Also fill in any other pertinent information. Choose a theme for 1 Kings that best describes what happens during this period in Israel's history.

8. Second Kings is a continuation of 1 Kings. You will want to study it next.

THINGS TO THINK ABOUT

1. Have you seen God's graciousness and long-suffering? God doesn't retaliate; rather, He seeks to bring us to repentance and obedience. What does this provoke in your heart? And how should you live if God is in control of your life?

2. Have you seen how a person can start well in his walk with the Lord and then turn away? What do you think causes this? What can you do to prevent this in your own life? Go back and review what you have listed in the margin regarding the kings and their relationship with the Lord. What lessons have you learned that you can apply to your life?

3. Did you notice the sovereignty of God—how He turns hearts, directs spirits, raises up and puts down kings and others in order to accomplish His purpose and will? Are you living in the light of this truth about God?

4. Have you been thinking that you had to be absolutely perfect before God could use you? Did you see how Elijah was a man "of like passions" just like you and yet God used him? What have you learned about this in 1 Kings? When David's life was over, didn't God call David a man after His own heart? Frailties and all, David was a man of God because he believed and obeyed God.

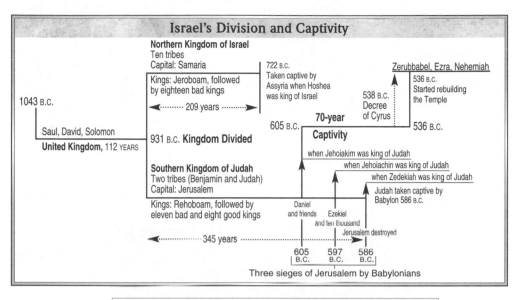

Israel's Division and Captivity

Northern Kingdom of Israel
Ten tribes
Capital: Samaria

Kings: Jeroboam, followed by eighteen bad kings

◄ ········· 209 years ········· ►

1043 B.C.

Saul, David, Solomon
United Kingdom, 112 YEARS

931 B.C. Kingdom Divided

Southern Kingdom of Judah
Two tribes (Benjamin and Judah)
Capital: Jerusalem

Kings: Rehoboam, followed by eleven bad and eight good kings

◄ ········· 345 years ········· ►

722 B.C.
Taken captive by Assyria when Hoshea was king of Israel

605 B.C.

70-year Captivity

538 B.C.
Decree of Cyrus

Zerubbabel, Ezra, Nehemiah
536 B.C.
Started rebuilding the Temple

536 B.C.

when Jehoiakim was king of Judah
when Jehoiachin was king of Judah
when Zedekiah was king of Judah

Judah taken captive by Babylon 586 B.C.

Daniel and friends

Ezekiel and ten thousand

Jerusalem destroyed

605 B.C.   597 B.C.   586 B.C.

Three sieges of Jerusalem by Babylonians

The Jewish Calendar

Babylonian names (B) for the months are still used today for the Jewish calendar. Canaanite names (C) were used prior to the Babylonian captivity in 586 B.C. Four are mentioned in the Old Testament. **Adar-Sheni** is an intercalary month used every two to three years or seven times in 19 years.

1st month	2nd month	3rd month	4th month
Nisan (B) Abib (C) March-April	Iyyar (B) Ziv (C) April-May	Sivan (B) May-June	Tammuz (B) June-July
7th month	*8th month*	*9th month*	*10th month*

5th month	6th month	7th month	8th month
Ab (B) July-August	Elul (B) August-September	Tishri (B) Ethanim (C) September-October	Marcheshvan (B) Bul (C) October-November
11th month	*12th month*	*1st month*	*2nd month*

9th month	10th month	11th month	12th month
Chislev (B) November-December	Tebeth (B) December-January	Shebat (B) January-February	Adar (B) February-March
3rd month	*4th month*	*5th month*	*6th month*

Sacred calendar appears in black • Civil calendar appears in gray

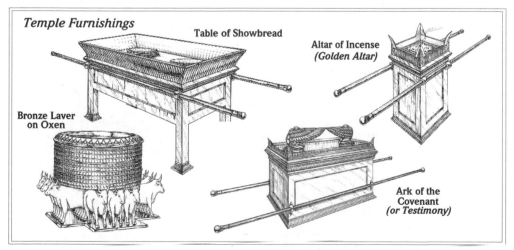

Temple Furnishings

Table of Showbread

Altar of Incense
(Golden Altar)

Bronze Laver on Oxen

Ark of the Covenant
(or Testimony)

Theme of 1 Kings:

SEGMENT DIVISIONS

PROPHETS	KINGS	CHAPTER THEMES
		1
		2
		3
		4
		5
		6
		7
		8
		9
		10
		11
		12
		13
		14
		15
		16
		17
		18
		19
		20
		21
		22

Author:

Date:

Purpose:

Key Words:

See appendix 7 for key words in the New International Version and King James Version.

2 KINGS מלכים ב
MLAKHIM BET

"*W*here is the LORD, the God of Elijah?" As you study 2 Kings, the continuation of 1 Kings, you will see God at work setting up and removing kings and kingdoms. And in the process you will be introduced to His spokesmen, the prophets, who faithfully speak forth His Word until Israel, and then Judah, are taken into captivity...because they did not listen.

THINGS TO DO

1. As you read through 2 Kings one chapter at a time:

   a. Mark the following key repeated words: *according to the Word of the Lord*, *Aram*, *Assyria*, *prophet*, *did evil*, *did right*, *heart*, *sin*, references to *mediums*, *spiritists*, and related terms, *high places*, *idols (gods)*, and *covenant*. Always watch for and mark words which are distinctive to a particular chapter, such as *customs* in chapter 17. Write these key words on an index card you can use as a bookmark while studying 2 Kings.

   b. Mark references to time with a clock ⊙ and double-underline in green all geographical locations.

   c. Observe what you learn about God: His requirements, His ways, His judgments, and His character. Record your insights in the margin of the text under a △. Also, be sure to note "Lessons for Life" (LFL).

   d. Watch for any reforms instituted by a king such as "he removed the high places". In the margin, note these reforms and the results. Mark the beginning of a king's reign with a crown. Record what you learn about each king on the chart THE KINGS OF ISRAEL AND JUDAH on pages 86 and 87.

   e. Record the theme or main event of each chapter on 2 KINGS AT A GLANCE and in your Bible.

2. Second Kings has some key or pivotal events:

   a. In 1:1 through 8:15 the prophetic ministries of Elijah and then Elisha are prominent. Mark *Elijah* and *Elisha* and then list in the margin the miracles accomplished through these men. Several miraculous things occur after 8:15; watch for them.

   b. Second Kings gives the account of the Assyrian invasion and subsequent captivity of the northern kingdom of Israel. Give special attention to the details of this invasion and why it came about, and mark in the margin when it happens.

   c. After the Assyrian captivity all that remains of the Hebrew nation is the southern kingdom—Judah. Watch how Judah conducts herself after seeing God's judgment on the northern kingdom. All this came to pass just as God's prophets said it would!

   d. Watch for the account of the Babylonian sieges of the southern kingdom (Judah) and the ensuing events. Record these in the margin as you did the Assyrian captivity.

3. Two charts identify the major characters and events of 2 Kings.

   a. The first chart, ISRAEL'S DIVISION AND CAPTIVITY, on page 79, gives a broad overview of the division of the kingdom through the three sieges of Jerusalem by the Babylonians.

   b. The second is a three-part chart: THE HISTORICAL CHART OF THE KINGS AND PROPHETS OF ISRAEL AND JUDAH, on pages 83 through 85. This chart shows the relationship of the kings and prophets to one another and to other foreign kings and their kingdoms. You might color these charts so that the kings of the northern and southern kingdoms and the prophets can be readily distinguished from one another.

   c. When you read of key figures or events in 2 Kings, consult these charts.

4. Complete the chart 2 KINGS AT A GLANCE. Considering the key events or personages featured in 2 Kings, see which chapters of 2 Kings can be grouped together under a common theme or topic. Record the theme of each segment under "Segment Divisions." Also, you might want to note on the chart the chapters that tell when the Assyrian and Babylonian invasions occur. Remember to record the theme of 2 Kings.

THINGS TO THINK ABOUT

1. As you consider the lives of Elijah and Elisha, what do you learn about faith and trusting God?

2. As you think about the captivity of Israel and Judah, and the reasons for their captivity, what do you learn about the necessity of living a righteous life? What practical applications can you make to your own life? Remember, walking your own way may be pleasurable for a while, but a just God must hold you accountable.

3. As you studied 1 and 2 Kings you saw that what God says will happen eventually comes to pass. Since His Word stands and none can alter it, can you see how critical it is that you believe God and hold to His Word no matter what others say or do?

Some of the Pagan Gods Worshiped by the Israelites		
The god:	**Ruled over / description:**	**Reference:**
Adrammelech	War, love	2 Kings 17:31
Anammelech	Demanded child sacrifice	2 Kings 17:31
Asherah	Wife of Baal	2 Kings 13:6
Ashima	God of Hittites	2 Kings 17:30
Ashtoreth (Astarte, Ishtar)	Sex, fertility, queen of heaven	2 Kings 23:13
Baal	Rain, wind, clouds, fertility of land	2 Kings 3:2
Baal-zebub	God of Ekron	2 Kings 1:2
Chemosh	Provider of land	2 Kings 23:13
Molech (Milcom)	National god of Moabites, worship involved human sacrifice	2 Kings 23:10
Nebo	Wisdom, literature, arts	1 Chronicles 5:8
Nergal	Underworld, death	2 Kings 17:30
Nibhaz	Worshiped by the Avvites (a people transplanted to Samaria from Assyria)	2 Kings 17:31
Nisroch	God worshiped in Nineveh	2 Kings 19:37
Rimmon	Thunder, lightning, rain	2 Kings 5:18
Succoth-Benoth	Mistress of Marduk, goddess of war	2 Kings 17:30
Tartak	Fertility (worshiped by Avvites)	2 Kings 17:31

THE HISTORICAL CHART OF THE KINGS AND PROPHETS OF ISRAEL AND JUDAH

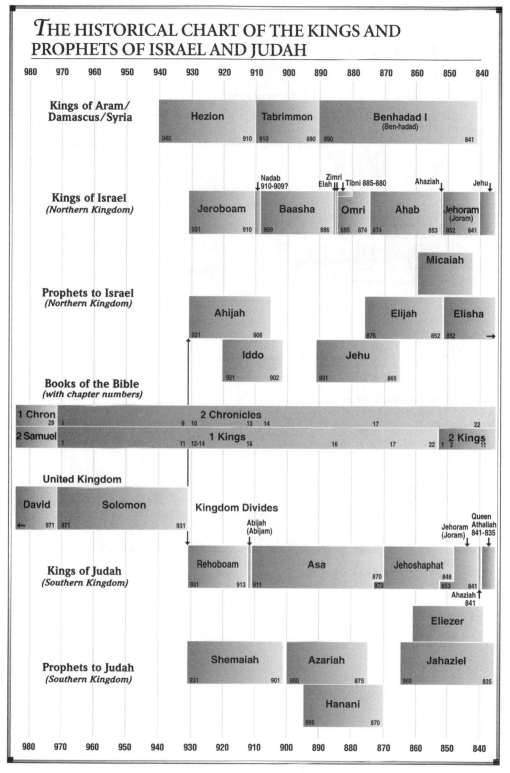

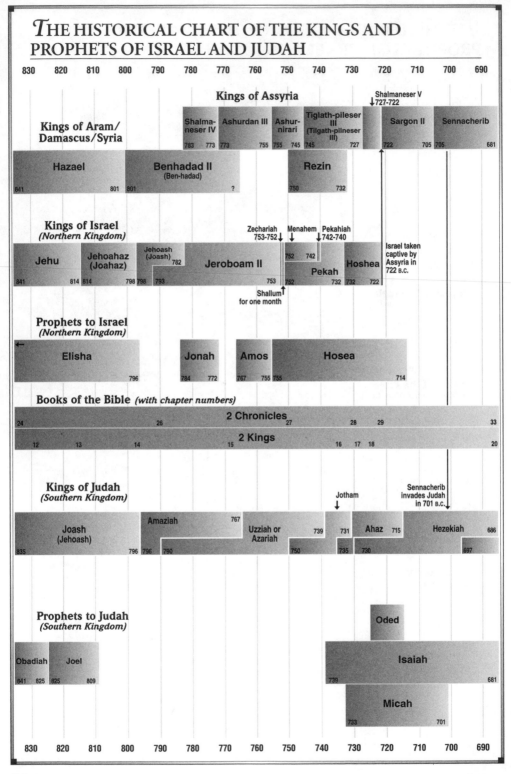

The Historical Chart of the Kings and Prophets of Israel and Judah

830 820 810 800 790 780 770 760 750 740 730 720 710 700 690

Kings of Assyria

Shalmaneser V ↓727-722

Kings of Aram/ Damascus/Syria

| Shalma-neser IV | Ashurdan III | Ashur-nirari | Tiglath-pileser III (Tilgath-pilneser III) | Sargon II | Sennacherib |

783 773 773 755 755 745 745 727 722 705 705 681

Hazael
841 801

Benhadad II (Ben-hadad)
801 ?

Rezin
750 732

Kings of Israel *(Northern Kingdom)*

Zechariah 753-752 ↓   Menahem ↓   Pekahiah ↓742-740

Israel taken captive by Assyria in 722 B.C.

Jehu — 841 814
Jehoahaz (Joahaz) — 814 798
Jehoash (Joash) 782 — 798 793
Jeroboam II — 793 753
752 742 — Pekah 752 732
Hoshea 732 722

Shallum↑ for one month

Prophets to Israel *(Northern Kingdom)*

Elisha — 796
Jonah — 784 772
Amos — 767 755
Hosea — 755 714

Books of the Bible *(with chapter numbers)*

2 Chronicles — 24 26 27 28 29 33

2 Kings — 12 13 14 15 16 17 18 20

Kings of Judah *(Southern Kingdom)*

Jotham ↓

Sennacherib invades Judah in 701 B.C.↓

Joash (Jehoash) — 835 796
Amaziah 767 — 796 790
Uzziah or Azariah 739 — 750
731 735 — Ahaz 715 730
Hezekiah 686 — 697

Prophets to Judah *(Southern Kingdom)*

Oded

Obadiah — 841 825
Joel — 825 809

Isaiah — 739 681

Micah — 733 701

830 820 810 800 790 780 770 760 750 740 730 720 710 700 690

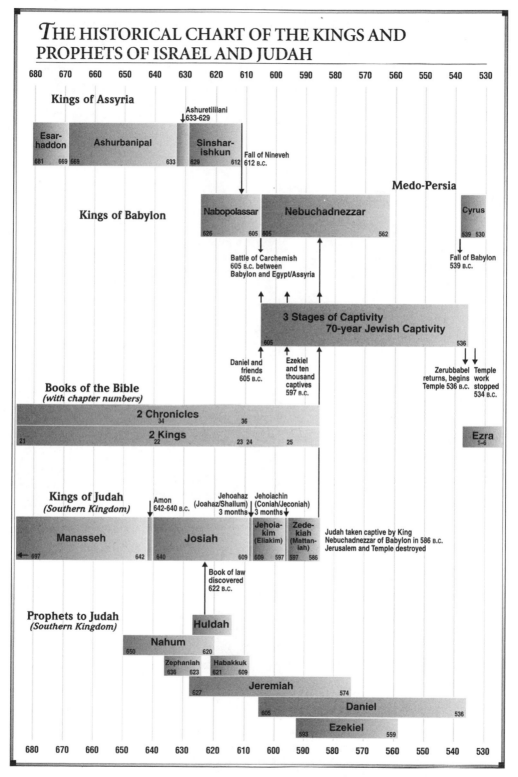

THE HISTORICAL CHART OF THE KINGS AND PROPHETS OF ISRAEL AND JUDAH

680 670 660 650 640 630 620 610 600 590 580 570 560 550 540 530

Kings of Assyria

Ashuretililani
↓633-629

Esar-haddon
681 669
Ashurbanipal
669 633
Sinshar-ishkun
629 612
Fall of Nineveh
612 B.C.

Medo-Persia

Kings of Babylon

Nabopolassar
626 605
Nebuchadnezzar
605 562

Cyrus
539 530

Battle of Carchemish
605 B.C. between
Babylon and Egypt/Assyria

Fall of Babylon
539 B.C.

3 Stages of Captivity
70-year Jewish Captivity
605 536

Daniel and
friends
605 B.C.

Ezekiel
and ten
thousand
captives
597 B.C.

Zerubbabel
returns, begins
Temple 536 B.C.
Temple
work
stopped
534 B.C.

Books of the Bible
(with chapter numbers)

2 Chronicles
34 36

2 Kings
21 22 23 24 25

Ezra
1–6

Kings of Judah
(Southern Kingdom)

Amon
↓642-640 B.C.

Jehoahaz
(Joahaz/Shallum)
3 months

Jehoiachin
(Coniah/Jeconiah)
3 months

Manasseh
←697 642
Josiah
640 609
Jehoia-kim
(Eliakim)
609 597
Zede-kiah
(Mattan-iah)
597 586

Judah taken captive by King
Nebuchadnezzar of Babylon in 586 B.C.
Jerusalem and Temple destroyed

Book of law
discovered
622 B.C.

Prophets to Judah
(Southern Kingdom)

Huldah

Nahum
650 620

Zephaniah
636 623

Habakkuk
621 609

Jeremiah
627 574

Daniel
605 536

Ezekiel
593 559

680 670 660 650 640 630 620 610 600 590 580 570 560 550 540 530

Dates	King	Kingdom Ruled over	Years Ruled	Insights on How King Lived and Died
971–931	**Solomon** son of:			
931–913	**Rehoboam** son of:			
931–910	**Jeroboam** son of:			
913–911	**Abijam** or **Abijah** son of:			
911–870	**Asa** son of:			
910–909	**Nadab** son of:			
909–886	**Baasha** son of:			
886–885	**Elah** son of:			
885	**Zimri** son of:			
885–874	**Omri** son of:			
873–848	**Jehoshaphat** son of:			
874–853	**Ahab** son of:			
853–852	**Ahaziah** son of Ahab			
852–841	**Jehoram** or **Joram** son of Ahab			
853–841	**Jehoram** or **Joram** son of Jehoshaphat			
841	**Ahaziah** son of Jehoram, grandson of Jehoshaphat			
841–835	**Queen Athaliah** mother of:			
841–814	**Jehu** son of:			
835–796	**Joash** or **Jehoash** son of:			
796–767	**Amaziah** son of:			

If a king ruled for any portion of a year, customarily that year was included as part of his reign.
An overlap in reigns indicates a co-regency, such as a son ruling alongside his father.

DATES	KING	KINGDOM RULED OVER	YEARS RULED	INSIGHTS ON HOW KING LIVED AND DIED
814–798	**Jehoahaz** or **Joahaz** son of:			
798–782	**Jehoash** or **Joash** son of:			
790–739	**Azariah** or **Uzziah** son of:			
793–753	**Jeroboam II** son of:			
753–752	**Zechariah** son of:			
752	**Shallum** son of:			
752–742	**Menahem** son of:			
742–740	**Pekahiah** son of:			
752–732	**Pekah** son of:			
750–731	**Jotham** son of:			
735–715	**Ahaz** son of:			
732–722	**Hoshea** son of:			
728–686	**Hezekiah** son of:			
697–642	**Manasseh** son of:			
642–640	**Amon** son of:			
640–609	**Josiah** son of:			
609	**Jehoahaz** or **Joahaz** or **Shallum** son of:			
609–597	**Jehoiakim** or **Eliakim** son of:			
597	**Jehoiachin** or **Coniah** or **Jeconiah** son of:			
597–586	**Zedekiah** or **Mattaniah** son of:			

If a king ruled for any portion of a year, customarily that year was included as part of his reign.
An overlap in reigns indicates a co-regency, such as a son ruling alongside his father.

Theme of 2 Kings:

SEGMENT DIVISIONS

PROPHETS	KINGS	CHAPTER THEMES	
		1	*Author:*
		2	
		3	*Date:*
		4	
		5	*Purpose:*
		6	
		7	*Key Words:*
		8	
		9	
		10	
		11	
		12	
		13	
		14	
		15	
		16	
		17	
		18	
		19	
		20	
		21	
		22	
		23	
		24	
		25	

See appendix 7 for key words in the New International Version and King James Version.

1 CHRONICLES א דברי הימים
DIVRE HAYYAMIM ALEPH

*J*udah had watched as Assyria captured the last Israel in 722 B.C. In 586 B.C., when the Babylonians besieged Jerusalem for the third and final time, Judah lost her temple and the city of David, bringing the reign of the sons of David to a halt. All seemed lost. Judah was held captive for 70 years. Then a Persian king, Cyrus, sent out a decree telling the exiles they could return and rebuild Jerusalem and their temple.

But if they did, could they be assured that the God of Abraham, Isaac, and Jacob would be with them? Had He abandoned His people and His promise to Abraham because of their sin? Would the northern and southern kingdoms ever be united again? Would God still send Messiah? Would David have a descendant who would sit on the throne of David forever?

And the temple? Between the time of Solomon and the Babylonian captivity, king after king had neglected it or desecrated it with idols. If they were to restore it, would it do any good?

What of the prophets? What was God's Word, the prophets' message, regarding Israel, Judah, and their future? Would the Word of God change? Would the words of the prophets be valid after Israel and Judah had so grievously sinned?

On returning from captivity, God's people had to be reminded "of the events or annals of the days, the years," and so Chronicles was written. We don't know for certain who wrote Chronicles; perhaps it was Ezra. However, we do know that it was part of God's plan, for God included it in the canon of Scripture.

THINGS TO DO

General Instructions

1. If possible, study 1 and 2 Samuel and then 1 and 2 Kings before you study 1 and 2 Chronicles. Chronicles is to these other historical books what John is to the synoptic Gospels (Matthew, Mark, and Luke). Both John and Chronicles are supplemental and yet bring unique insight and understanding. Study the HISTORICAL PARALLEL OF SAMUEL, KINGS, AND CHRONICLES on page 92.

2. First and 2 Chronicles have time gaps in them. Keep this in mind as you study. When you wonder about the timing of something, look at the HISTORICAL PARALLEL again.

3. Watch for and mark references to time with a clock ⏱. Double-underline in green all geographical references.

4. When you finish observing each chapter, record its theme on 1 CHRONICLES AT A GLANCE and in your Bible.

Chapters 1–9: The Genealogies of the Nation of Israel

1. This section may seem boring because it is primarily genealogies with a few historical sidelights. However, remember that this information has a purpose, and that is why God included it in His Word. Some genealogies, such as 4:1-23, are not included anywhere else.

   a. Don't skip this section; you will gain valuable insights which will help you in the study of the rest of the book.

   b. To discover the scope of the genealogies, read verses 1:1 and 9:1-2. Then write in the margin of 1:1 when the genealogies begin and end according to the historical events they represent. Keeping in mind what was said in the introduction to 1 Chronicles,

89

notice in 9:2 the words "the first who lived in their possessions in their cities."

2. In this segment the key words to mark or underline are the names of people who play vital roles in Israel's history.

   a. Mark the following key words in a distinctive way: *Adam*, *Noah*, and Noah's three sons: *Shem*, *Ham*, and *Japheth*. Then mark the phrases *the sons of Japheth*, *the sons of Ham*, and *the sons of Shem*.

   b. Mark *the sons of Abraham were Isaac and Ishmael*, and *Abraham became the father of Isaac*, and *the sons of Isaac were Esau and Israel* (remember that Israel was called Jacob until God changed his name to Israel).

   c. In chapter 2 mark *these are the sons of Israel*. Then count the sons. How many were there? They became the heads of the tribes of Israel. Record their names on an index card and look for any place where they are repeated in this segment. Use this card as a bookmark. Read Genesis 49:1-28, where Jacob (Israel) gives a prophetic blessing to each of these men.

   d. In 2:3-15 mark *the sons of Judah* and then look for *David*. In the margin, list David's genealogy from Judah through David's immediate father, Jesse. Remember that the author of Chronicles gives the genealogy of Judah before the other sons of Israel. Why? What would be important to the exiles who now repossessed their cities? Wouldn't it be God's promises to David? Keep this in mind as you study the second-to-last segment of 1 Chronicles.

   e. In 3:1, mark the names of the sons of David and list their names in the margin. Refer to "David's Family Tree" on page 75.

   f. First Chronicles 3:10-16 gives the line of kings that come from David through Solomon. List these names in the margin.

   g. First Chronicles 3:17-24 lists the genealogy through Jeconiah (Jehoiachin). He was the king who reigned three months and ten days before he was taken into exile in Babylon, put in prison, and then released. See 2 Kings 24:8-16 and 2 Chronicles 36:9-10.

3. When you read chapters 4 through 9, watch for any mention of the 12 sons of Israel and their genealogy. As you do:

   a. Notice that not all 12 are mentioned in chapters 4 through 9.

   b. Joseph's sons Manasseh and Ephraim are mentioned in Scripture as part of the 12 tribes of Israel. The reason for this is given in 1 Chronicles 5:1-2. Take special note of this.

      1) Write "Joseph's son" next to any mention of Manasseh and/or Ephraim.
      2) Manasseh is named twice. The tribe split when Canaan was divided. Half the tribe of Manasseh took land east of the Jordan and the other half went west of the Jordan; thus the reference to the "half-tribe of Manasseh."

4. Read the section on the sons of Levi carefully and either underline what they were to do or note it in the margin. Also observe and note what Aaron and his sons were to do. This will help when you come to the final chapters of 1 Chronicles.

5. Don't forget to record the chapter themes in the text and on 1 CHRONICLES AT A GLANCE.

Chapters 10–19: God Turns the Kingdom to David

1. As you read this segment, see how it fits with 1 and 2 Samuel. To do this consult the

chart HISTORICAL PARALLEL OF SAMUEL, KINGS, AND CHRONICLES.

  a. Read 1 Chronicles 10, mark any reference to *kingdom,* and list the events of that chapter.

  b. Also note where it says whose son David was. Keep in mind what you just studied in the first segment.

  c. Note in the margin why Saul died, who died with him, and what happened to Saul's body.

2. Read this segment chapter by chapter and do the following:

  a. Mark the following key words: *city of David, ark, covenant,* and *inquired of God.* Observe what you learn from these words and record your insights in your notebook.

  b. Ask the "5 W's and an H" as you read each chapter. Who are the key characters? What happens? When? (Mark references to time with a 🕐.) Where do events occur? Why do they occur? How do things happen? Record your insights in your notebook.

  c. Don't forget to record the chapter themes on 1 CHRONICLES AT A GLANCE and in the text next to the chapter number.

3. Watch for any prophecies (promises), speeches, songs, or psalms of praise. Who gives them? Why? What is said in each? Record your insights in your notebook. Also ask: How can I apply these truths in my life?

Chapters 20–29: David Builds an Altar and Prepares for God's House

1. Note where this portion of 1 Chronicles comes in respect to 2 Samuel.

  a. When you read chapter 20, compare the wording of verse 1 with 2 Samuel 11:1. Then as you look at the content of 2 Samuel 11–12, note what the author of Chronicles leaves out.

  b. Now compare 1 Chronicles 21 with 2 Samuel 24. Why was this event included in 1 Chronicles when David's other sin was omitted? Remember, the temple is very important to the returning exiles.

2. As you read each chapter, mark the following key words and note in the margin what you learn from each: *house (home, temple, sanctuary), ark, heart, Levi (Levites),* and *Aaron.*

  a. The word *house* has been used numerous times in 1 Chronicles; however, with one or two exceptions "house" referred to someone's family, such as the house of David. In this segment it is used primarily for the house of the Lord. As you mark it, note what you learn. Keep in mind that this is the book for the exiles who had returned to rebuild the temple and thus the emphasis is on the house of God and its importance. When difficulties arose, this historical account would affirm God's enduring purpose and promises.

  b. As you mark the references to the *Levites* and to *Aaron and his sons,* observe carefully the types of duties they were to perform and which Levite family was to perform each type of duty.

3. Read each chapter as you did in the last segment, asking the "5 W's and an H." Note in the margin what you observe. Also as you did in the last segment, watch for any speeches, prophecies, etc., and note the same things you looked for previously.

4. Complete 1 CHRONICLES AT A GLANCE. There are two lines for any additional segment divisions you might see and want to mark.

THINGS TO THINK ABOUT

1. Second Timothy 2:13 says, "If we are faithless, He remains faithful; for He cannot

deny Himself." What have you seen of the faithfulness of God in the book of 1 Chronicles? What assurance does this give you for your life?

2. You marked the word *heart* in this last segment. Go back over these references in chapter 29 and review what you observed about the heart. Also review what you observed as David blessed the Lord. Think about your own heart. What is your heart like in respect to the Lord? How can you turn what David did into a prayer to the Lord?

3. As you think about all you learned about the priests and their duties and you think of yourself and other Christians as a kingdom of priests unto God (Revelation 1 and 5), do you see any application you can make to your responsibilities as a priest unto God?

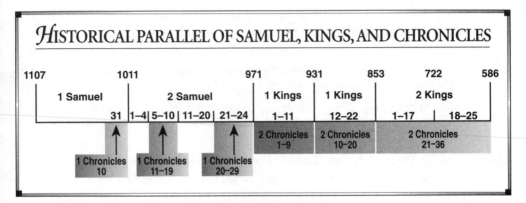

HISTORICAL PARALLEL OF SAMUEL, KINGS, AND CHRONICLES

1107	1011	971	931	853	722	586
1 Samuel	2 Samuel	1 Kings	1 Kings		2 Kings	
31	1–4 | 5–10 | 11–20 | 21–24	1–11	12–22	1–17	18–25	
		2 Chronicles 1–9	2 Chronicles 10–20	2 Chronicles 21–36		
1 Chronicles 10	1 Chronicles 11–19	1 Chronicles 20–29				

Theme of 1 Chronicles:

Segment Divisions

		Main Divisions	Chapter Themes	Author:
		The Genealogies of Israel	1	
			2	Date:
			3	
			4	
			5	Purpose:
			6	
			7	Key Words:
			8	
			9	
		God Turns Kingdom to David	10	
			11	
			12	
			13	
			14	
			15	
			16	
			17	
			18	
			19	
		David Builds Altar, Prepares for God's House	20	
			21	
			22	
			23	
			24	
			25	
			26	
			27	
			28	
			29	

See appendix 7 for key words in the New International Version and King James Version.

2 CHRONICLES רברי הימים ב

*K*ing David wanted to build a house for the Lord, but instead the Lord promised David that He would establish David's house forever and that David's son would build the temple. Second Chronicles records for us how this came to pass.

THINGS TO DO

If you haven't studied 1 Chronicles yet, you'll want to do so before you begin your study of 2 Chronicles.

Second Chronicles is filled with truths and lessons for life, which, if heeded, will help you in your pursuit of holiness. Second Chronicles focuses on the reigns of the kings of Judah and their relationship to God and His house from the time of Solomon until the Babylonian exile. Read all the instructions before you begin.

1. Examine every chapter in the light of the "5 W's and an H." Record your insights in the margin.

 a. Look for three *who's*: the king, the prophet, and the Lord. Of the three, the Lord and the king are most prominent. Ask: Who are the associates of the king? Who influences, opposes, or assists him?

 b. Look for *what* each king does, *what* God does in respect to that king, and *what* role the prophet plays, if any. In 2 Chronicles the "house" of God takes center stage; therefore, in each reign observe what the king's relationship is to the Lord and to His house.

 c. Also keep track of *when* events occur. Don't forget to note references to time with a clock ⏲.

 d. This is a historical book; watch *where* things occur and double-underline these references in green.

 e. Observing *why* events occur will bring insight into the character and sovereignty of God in the affairs of men and nations. Keep asking why. If the king does evil, ask why.

 f. Ask *how*. How did the king seek the Lord? How did the king do evil? How did God respond?

2. Record your insights on the kings mentioned in 2 Chronicles. Transfer these insights to the chart THE KINGS OF ISRAEL AND JUDAH located on pages 83 through 85.

3. On an index card make a list of the key repeated words printed on the 2 CHRONICLES AT A GLANCE chart. Use this list as a bookmark while you study 2 Chronicles.

 a. In your notebook, record all you learn from marking each of these key words. Note that after chapter 8, *ark,* one of the key words, is used once more—in chapter 35.

 b. You will also observe key words and phrases that will play a major role in only one or two chapters. Don't miss these. They will come to the surface as you prayerfully read and meditate on a chapter.

4. As you study each chapter, take notes in the margin of all you learn about God. You will gain rich and perhaps surprising insights. Also mark and record any lessons for life ("LFL").

5. Remember that 1 and 2 Chronicles were written as one book. Second Chronicles is a continuation of 1 Chronicles. Chronicles has a number of speeches, prophecies, and

prayers, some of which are not mentioned in Samuel or Kings. Watch for these and pay attention to what is said, by whom, and why. Highlight or note your insights in the margin.

6. When you finish reading each chapter, record its theme on 2 CHRONICLES AT A GLANCE and in your Bible. Also watch for the major historical events that occur in 2 Chronicles. Highlight these on the chart.

7. Complete 2 CHRONICLES AT A GLANCE. As you review the chapter themes you have recorded, see how this book could be segmented and record this under "Segment Divisions." Also, record the book's theme.

THINGS TO THINK ABOUT

1. Many lessons about prayer and seeking God can be learned from this book. Review what you have seen from marking the key words. Think about what you learned regarding sin, prayer, confession, and repentance in 2 Chronicles 6.

2. Second Chronicles is filled with illustrations of how people dealt with difficulties and testings. How did you relate to these people? What did you learn from their lives—men such as Asa, Jehoshaphat, Hezekiah, Uzziah? As you studied them, did God prick your heart? With what warnings or cautions?

3. What did you learn about the heart from this book? Do you serve the Lord wholeheartedly or halfheartedly? What did you learn about crying to the Lord? What happened to those who cried out to Him? Did they always deserve to be heard?

4. What did you learn about the sovereignty of God? How active or involved is God in the affairs of men? What were the different ways God afflicted those who disobeyed? Do you have a healthy fear of God?

Theme of 2 Chronicles:

Author:

Date:

Purpose:

Key Words:
house

ark

covenant

cry (cried)

seek (sought)

heart

pray
(prayer, prayed)

prophet(s)

sin

rebellion

glory of the
Lord (cloud)

the Spirit

humble

pride

did evil

did right

Segment Divisions			
		Kings	Chapter Themes
			1
			2
			3
			4
			5
			6
			7
			8
			9
			10
			11
			12
			13
			14
			15
			16
			17
			18
			19
			20
			21
			22
			23
			24
			25
			26
			27
			28
			29
			30
			31
			32
			33
			34
			35
			36

See appendix 7 for key words in the New International Version and King James Version.

EZRA עֶזְרָא

EZRA

$\mathcal{E}$ very seventh year the land was to lie fallow. This was God's ordinance to His people, part of His law by which they were to govern their lives.

However, for 490 years God's people had not paid attention to this statute, nor to others. The land had missed 70 Sabbaths. As prophesied by Jeremiah, God would exact 70 years for the land. Then the Spirit of God would move on behalf of His people. He would stir up the spirit of Cyrus, king of Persia, so that Cyrus would send out a written decree proclaiming, "The LORD, the God of heaven, has given me all the kingdoms of the earth, and He has appointed me to build Him a house in Jerusalem, which is in Judah. Whoever there is among you of all His people, may the LORD his God be with him, and let him go up!" (2 Chronicles 36:23).

And so a remnant returned from the land of exile to the land promised to Abraham, Isaac, and Jacob as an everlasting possession. Ezra tells us what happened.

THINGS TO DO

To better understand Ezra, look at Isaiah's prophecy in 44:28–45:7. This was written about 175 years before Cyrus was born.

Ezra falls into two main segments: chapters 1 through 6 and chapters 7 through 10. There is a lapse of approximately 58 to 60 years between these two segments.

Chapters 1–6

1. Read this segment chapter by chapter and do the following:

   a. In a distinctive way mark in the text the key words listed on the EZRA AT A GLANCE chart.

   b. Pay attention to any references to time. Mark these with a clock $\bigcirc$.

   c. When you come to a reference of a particular king, mark it and consult the historical chart THE TIMES OF EZRA, NEHEMIAH, AND ESTHER on page 101. This will help you appreciate the historical setting of the book of Ezra and see the relationship of Ezra to Esther and Nehemiah, who were contemporaries of Ezra.

   d. If specific people play a significant role, record their names in the margin and briefly describe what they did.

2. There are seven official documents or letters in the book of Ezra, all of which (except the first) were written in Aramaic, the international language of the times. The first document, written by Cyrus, the Persian king, is in Hebrew. These documents or letters are found in Ezra 1:2-4; 4:11-16; 4:17-22; 5:7-17; 6:2-5; and 6:6-12. The last one is in the second segment of the book, 7:12-26.

As you come to each document or letter in the text, underline who presented it. Then in the margin list the major points of the document or letter. This information will help you keep track of the opposition the Jews faced and how God moved on their behalf.

3. After you finish reading each chapter, identify the main subject, theme, or event and record it in your Bible next to the chapter number and on EZRA AT A GLANCE.

4. The book of Ezra records when the temple construction began and when it was completed. Write this information in the margin in bold print so you can easily find it.

5. For a better understanding of the Jewish feasts, consult the chart THE FEASTS OF ISRAEL on pages 48 and 49.

Chapters 7–10

1. This is the first time Ezra's name appears in this book. Note how he is described. Observe this man and the lessons you can learn from his life. List your insights in the margin under LFL, "Lessons for Life."

2. Mark key words as before, but add these to your list: every reference to *sin (iniquity, abomination, unfaithfulness,* etc.), *fast, covenant, guilt,* and *remnant.* Also, note your insights on the last official document in 7:12-26.

3. Watch for and mark references to time and to kings. Note these as you did before.

4. Record the theme of each chapter as you did in the first segment of Ezra.

5. How does the second segment of Ezra, chapters 7 through 10, differ from the first?

    a. Record the theme or subject of the first six chapters on EZRA AT A GLANCE under "Segment Divisions." Do the same for the last segment, chapters 7 through 10.

    b. On the second line for segment divisions write in the name(s) of the central character(s) of each segment.

    c. Consult the historical chart THE TIMES OF EZRA, NEHEMIAH, AND ESTHER on page 101 and then record on the chart the number of years covered in each segment.

6. What is the theme or teaching of Ezra? Record this and any other requested information in the appropriate place on EZRA AT A GLANCE.

THINGS TO THINK ABOUT

1. How did the people in Ezra's time deal with their sin? What showed you whether their sorrow led to repentance or simply regret? How do you deal with sin in your own life? How is it dealt with within your church congregation?

2. What did you learn about prayer and fasting? Are either of these integral parts of your walk with the Lord? Why?

3. As you review what you have learned in Ezra, what have you learned about God, His promises, and His ways? What difference can this knowledge make in your life?

Theme of Ezra:

	SEGMENT DIVISIONS				
Author:		YEARS COVERED	CENTRAL CHARACTERS		CHAPTER THEMES
Date:					1
					2
Purpose:					3
					4
Key Words:					5
house (or any reference to God's house)					6
decree					7
the law (of Moses, of the Lord, of your God)					8
					9
commandments					10

See appendix 7 for key words in the New International Version and King James Version.

NEHEMIAH נחמיה
NECHEMYA

Since the third millennium B.C., the cities of the Middle East had been surrounded by walls made of stones while guarded gates acted as sentinels. From the tops of these walls, watchmen could survey the landscape for great distances, seeing everyone who approached the city either as visitors or invaders.

The city fathers would gather at the city gates to carry out their business transactions and pass their judgments on civic affairs. The condition of the walls of the city was a matter of either pride or reproach.

Jerusalem's walls had been destroyed during the Babylonian invasion. The walls and their many gates stood in ruins, a rebuke to the newly returned exiles and a cause of mourning to Nehemiah, although he was over 600 miles away serving as cupbearer to Artaxerxes. Nehemiah had not forgotten his beloved city or her people.

While Ezra gives the account of the rebuilding of the temple under Zerubbabel, Nehemiah (Ezra's contemporary) gives the account of the rebuilding of Jerusalem's walls. His account begins in 445 B.C. in Susa, the Persian capital.

THINGS TO DO

1. Nehemiah is a continuation of Ezra. In fact, Ezra and Nehemiah were treated as one book in the earliest Hebrew manuscripts. Therefore, to put this book into context, study the historical chart THE TIMES OF EZRA, NEHEMIAH, AND ESTHER on page 101.

2. As you read Nehemiah chapter by chapter:

   a. Look for the theme of each chapter. Record this next to the chapter number on the NEHEMIAH AT A GLANCE chart and record it in your Bible next to the chapter number.

   b. Read each chapter again. This time make a list of the points you want to remember about the main topic or event within each chapter.

   1) For example, in chapter 1 the theme is Nehemiah's concern for Jerusalem. In the margin opposite the first three verses you could write "Remnant's Distress." Then underneath it write "walls broken down, gates burned."

   2) Then next to verses 4 through 11 you could write "Nehemiah's Prayer" and list the main parts or points of his prayer; for example, a) weeps, mourns, fasts, b) reminds God of who He is and His covenant, and c) confesses his and Israel's sins.

   3) As you summarize each chapter, list what you learn about God.

   c. While there are many key repeated words you could mark—such as *wall*, *gate*, *build*, *repairs*, etc.—you may want to observe them without marking them because of the nature of Nehemiah's writing. Some key words are used so many times within specific chapters that you may become overwhelmed by all the markings.

   1) Mark the key words listed on the NEHEMIAH AT A GLANCE chart.

   2) When you mark *command (commandments, ordinances, law)*, note in the margin what you learn.

   d. Note any references to time by drawing a clock ⊕ next to the verse.

   e. As you read through Nehemiah, note in the margin when the wall is started, when it is completed, and when it is dedicated.

3. There are valuable lessons to be learned from observing how Nehemiah handled situations. As you see how Nehemiah related to God in each situation, how he dealt with the people (including those who opposed him), and the example he set, you will see principles you can apply to your life. As you study, record your insights on the chart LESSONS FROM THE LIFE OF NEHEMIAH.

4. When you finish recording the theme of every chapter on NEHEMIAH AT A GLANCE, look for the main division of the book, where one emphasis ends and another begins. On the line under "Segment Divisions," record this division and the theme or subject of the two segments of the book. Also fill in the rest of the chart and record the theme of Nehemiah.

THINGS TO THINK ABOUT

1. Read Nehemiah chapter 9 again and think about the character of God and how He dealt with Israel. What can you learn about God and also about Israel's behavior that you can apply to your own life?

2. Have you thought about what could happen if the congregation of a church gathered together and publicly confessed their sins and then the sins of their nation?

3. What have you learned from Nehemiah's life? How are you going to apply it to your life in a practical way?

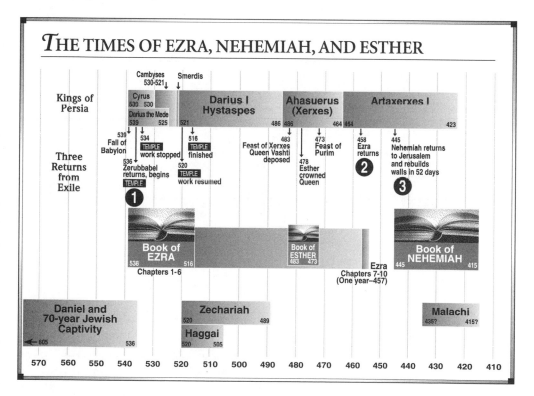

THE TIMES OF EZRA, NEHEMIAH, AND ESTHER

LESSONS FROM THE LIFE OF NEHEMIAH

THE SITUATION	HOW NEHEMIAH RELATED TO GOD	HOW NEHEMIAH RELATED TO PEOPLE	NEHEMIAH'S EXAMPLE

Theme of Nehemiah:

SEGMENT DIVISIONS

		CHAPTER THEMES	Author:
		1	Date:
		2	
		3	Purpose:
		4	
		5	Key Words:
		6	remember
		7	command (command-ments, ordi-nances, law)
		8	
		9	sin (iniquities)
		10	covenant
		11	fast
		12	prayer
		13	the book (book of the law, law of Moses)

See appendix 7 for key words in the New International Version and King James Version.

ESTHER אסתר
ESTER

*T*hroughout time people have attempted to destroy the nation of Israel, the "apple of God's eye." Why? Because from the Jews came the covenants, the promises, the law, and the Messiah—salvation for the world. The people of God are the enemy of Satan, the prince of this world, and the conflict is as old as Genesis 3:15.

While a remnant from Judah returned to the land promised to Abraham, Isaac, and Jacob, other Jews remained in the cities of their captivity. Some were welcomed as valued members of their communities, but others were despised and hated. Some were even targeted for extermination.

Esther tells the story. The book of Esther records a ten-year span during the 58- to 60-year interlude in the book of Ezra. Esther tells us of the inauguration of a feast that has endured over 2000 years because of one woman who, for the sake of her people, was willing to say, "If I perish, I perish."

THINGS TO DO

Esther is a story of intrigue—a divinely inspired one. It reveals the sovereignty of God, although God is never mentioned in this book. As you read:

1. Consult the historical chart THE TIMES OF EZRA, NEHEMIAH, AND ESTHER on page 105 in order to see the setting of Esther.

2. Observe the main events that occur in each chapter. Examine each chapter under the scrutiny of the "5 W's and an H": Who? What? When? Where? Why? and How? Ask: Who was involved? What happened? When did it occur? Where did it take place and why? How did it come about? etc.

   a. List in the margin the major points you want to remember about each event under the heading you give that event. For example, Esther 1:3-4 could be titled "King Ahasuerus's Banquet." Under the heading you could list these points: 1) attended by his princes, attendants, etc., 2) given to display riches, 3) lasted 180 days.

   b. While the main event of each chapter will not always be a banquet, banquets play an important role in Esther. So mark in a distinctive way each use of the words *banquet* or *feast*. Ask the "5 W's and an H" about each banquet and list your insights in the margin.

   c. Make sure you underline or mark in a distinctive way the main characters in each chapter. Study each person's character, as there is much to be learned.

3. Mark the key words on the AT A GLANCE chart. When you mark *Jew* or *Jews*, mark the pronouns and synonyms, such as *her people*, *my kindred*, or *people*. *Jews* was a term used to describe the people who came from Judah.

4. Mark every reference to time with a clock ⏰. This will help you quickly identify the timing of the events. Also consult the calendar on page 106 so you can keep track of the references to the various months.

5. When you finish studying each chapter, record the theme of that chapter in the appropriate place on the ESTHER AT A GLANCE chart. Also record this in your Bible.

6. In your notebook, list all you learn about Esther and then list all you learn about Mordecai.

7. When you finish reading Esther, complete ESTHER AT A GLANCE. See if any of the

chapters can be grouped according to events. If so, record these segment divisions on the AT A GLANCE chart.

THINGS TO THINK ABOUT

1. What can you learn from the lives of each of the main characters of this historical event? Review what you have listed about Esther and Mordecai. Have you ever realized that you too have come to the kingdom for such a time as this? What are the good works that God would have you do? Read John 15:16 and Ephesians 2:8-10.

2. Have you thought about why Mordecai was unwilling to bow before Haman? Have you "bowed" to someone or something and in so doing compromised your calling and position as a child of God? Read Galatians 1:10.

3. Esther and Mordecai relied heavily on fasting to turn the tide of events. What about you?

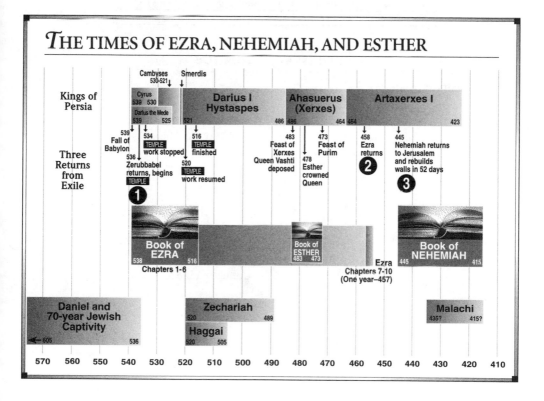

The Jewish Calendar

Babylonian names (B) for the months are still used today for the Jewish calendar. Canaanite names (C) were used prior to the Babylonian captivity in 586 B.C. Four are mentioned in the Old Testament. **Adar-Sheni** is an intercalary month used every two to three years or seven times in 19 years.

1st month	2nd month	3rd month	4th month
Nisan (B) Abib (C) March-April	Iyyar (B) Ziv (C) April-May	Sivan (B) May-June	Tammuz (B) June-July
7th month	*8th month*	*9th month*	*10th month*
5th month	**6th month**	**7th month**	**8th month**
Ab (B) July-August	Elul (B) August-September	Tishri (B) Ethanim (C) September-October	Marcheshvan (B) Bul (C) October-November
11th month	*12th month*	*1st month*	*2nd month*
9th month	**10th month**	**11th month**	**12th month**
Chislev (B) November-December	Tebeth (B) December-January	Shebat (B) January-February	Adar (B) February-March
3rd month	*4th month*	*5th month*	*6th month*

Sacred calendar appears in black • Civil calendar appears in gray

ESTHER AT A GLANCE

Theme of Esther:

SEGMENT DIVISIONS

Author:			CHAPTER THEMES
Date:			1
			2
Purpose:			3
Key Words:			4
anger (angry)			5
banquet, feast			6
Jew, Jews			
edict (decree)			7
fast			
destroy (destroyed, destruction)			8
			9
			10

See appendix 7 for key words in the New International Version and King James Version.

JOB אִיּוֹב
IYYOV

Job is a book born out of pain. Job's pain was so crushing he wanted to die, so unrelenting he wished he had never been born. His pain was compounded as his friends wrestled with the reason for his suffering. Job's affliction brought God's character and ways into question. Yet ultimately it brought deeper intimacy with God.

Job, the first and probably oldest of the poetical books of the Bible, is for those who need answers from God, for those who want to say with Job, "It is still my consolation, and I rejoice in unsparing pain, that I have not denied the words of the Holy One" (6:10).

THINGS TO DO

1. Chapters 1 and 2 provide the setting of Job's pain. Read through these two chapters. Mark every reference to Satan and to God. On the OBSERVATIONS CHART on page 109:

   a. List what you learn about Satan—his person and his relationship to God and to Job.

   b. List what you learn about God.

   c. List what you learn about Job: what God says about him; what Satan says; how he responds to God, to his pain, and to the counsel of his wife.

2. In order to understand Job and the ensuing discourses of his friends, read Job 1:8 and 2:3,11-13 and then Job 42:7-9. Do this before you proceed any further. Pay attention to what God says about Job and to what God says about what Job's three friends said.

3. In chapter 3 Job pours out his anguish, and then in chapters 4 through 42:6 there is a series of discourses given either by Job, his friends, or God Himself. Read through this section chapter by chapter and do the following:

   a. In your Bible, next to each chapter number, note who is speaking and to whom. Then record this under chapter themes on the JOB AT A GLANCE chart. You might want to color-code Job's and his friends' names so you can quickly distinguish who is speaking.

   b. Job 42:7 says that Job's friends did not speak what was right concerning God. Therefore, if one of these three men speaks, in the margin note how his reasoning is wrong in respect to God and to Job's suffering. Watch carefully to see where or how (if it tells) Job's friend came up with his conclusion. Then watch how Job answers each of his friends. Record pertinent notes in the margin.

4. As you read Job 4 through 42 observe what the text says about:

   a. Man and God

   b. What God expects from man and what He does not expect

   c. Nature

   d. Sin and righteousness

   e. Physical life and death

   f. How to deal with those in pain

   Record your insights on the OBSERVATIONS CHART as you read each chapter.

5. Mark key words or phrases that play a significant role in a particular chapter or which

recur throughout the book. These are listed on the AT A GLANCE chart. Note in the margin the insights you glean about God by marking *wisdom* and other key words. Also highlight or underline verses which speak to your heart.

6. Don't fail to compare Job's end with his beginning and to notice what came from Satan's challenge.

7. When you finish reading Job and you have filled in JOB AT A GLANCE, note how the book divides itself into a pattern of discourses. Record this under "Segment Divisions."

THINGS TO THINK ABOUT

1. Think about Job's end compared to his beginning and then ask yourself if Job's suffering was worth it. What about your suffering? What can it produce if you will respond in the proper way? What is the proper way? What did you learn from Job?

2. What have you learned about Satan and Satan's relationship to God from this book? How can those insights comfort you?

3. Read Job 31 again, and if you did not mark it the first time, mark in a distinctive way every *if* and every *if I have*. Think about how Job appealed to his own integrity in various matters of life. Examine those areas carefully. How does your own integrity measure up in those areas? What do you need to remember, do, hold onto, let go of, begin, or stop?

Job Observations Chart

INSIGHTS REGARDING SATAN

INSIGHTS REGARDING JOB

INSIGHTS REGARDING GOD

INSIGHTS REGARDING MAN

God's Power

Over Satan

Over Nature

INSIGHTS INTO LIFE AND DEATH

Over Man

Lessons I Learned About Dealing with Those in Pain

Theme of Job:

Segment Divisions

Author:		Main Speaker	Chapter Themes
			1
Date:			2
			3
Purpose:			4
			5
Key Words:			6
wisdom			7
sin (iniquity, transgression)			8
sons of God			9
righteous (right, righteousness)			10
			11
			12
			13
			14
			15
			16
			17
			18
			19
			20
			21

See appendix 7 for key words in the New International Version and King James Version.

Segment Divisions

	Main Speaker	Chapter Themes
		22
		23
		24
		25
		26
		27
		28
		29
		30
		31
		32
		33
		34
		35
		36
		37
		38
		39
		40
		41
		42

PSALMS תְהִילִים
THILLIM

*M*an needs to pour out his heart to God, to come before Him and honestly present what is on his heart—whether it be distress or joy, confusion or confidence.

Man, in right relationship to God, was made to sing, to lift his voice in worship, to speak to God and to others in psalms and hymns and spiritual songs, singing and making melody with his heart to the Lord (see Ephesians 5:19).

Thus many of the psalms—praises, prayers, and songs—are to be accompanied on stringed instruments. Therefore, David, himself the writer of many psalms, appointed Levites over the service of song in the house of the Lord. They ministered with song before the tabernacle of the tent of meeting until Solomon built the house of the Lord in Jerusalem (see 1 Chronicles 6:31-32).

Psalms is a book of prayer and praise, written by men but inspired by God. "For from Him and through Him and to Him are all things. To Him be the glory forever. Amen" (Romans 11:36).

THINGS TO DO

1. As you study Psalms, remember that the psalms are poetry whether they are prayers or songs. Hebrew poetry does not contain rhyme and meter. Rather, its distinctive feature is parallelism of some form, where one line relates to another in various ways. Usually the poetic lines are composed of two (or sometimes three) balanced segments in which the second is shorter than the first and repeats, contrasts, or completes the first segment.

The psalms vary in design. Nine are alphabetical, with each stanza beginning with the next letter from the Hebrew alphabet. The alphabetical psalms are 9; 10; 25; 34; 37; 111; 112; 119; and 145.

2. The majority of the psalms have a superscription at the beginning, which designates one or several things: the composer, the occasion of the psalm, who it is for, how it is to be accompanied, and what kind of psalm it is. If a psalm has a superscription, read it and consult the cross-references (if it is referenced). This will help put the psalm into context.

3. Watch for the theme of the psalm and how it is developed. Sometimes the theme will be stated at the very beginning of the psalm, while at other times the key thematic scheme will be found in the center of the psalm. Each will have a theme and will be developed in accordance with the author's design for the psalm.

   a. Some of the psalms give insights into the history of Israel, such as Psalm 78. Study these carefully. Note the events, God's intervention, and God's watchful care.

   b. If a psalm makes reference to a person or circumstance that is discussed in one of the historical books of the Bible, you might go back to that book and record the psalm that applies to that person or circumstance. For instance, in the margin of 2 Samuel 12, note "Psalm 51" as a cross-reference.

4. Key words bring out the theme of the psalm's song or prayer. Sometimes a key phrase will open and close the psalm. Watch for and mark these phrases. Also mark in a distinctive way the key words listed on the AT A GLANCE chart. Write these words on an index card and use it as a bookmark when you study and meditate on the psalms.

5. Don't miss the central focus of these psalms—God. There is so much to be learned about Him, and then He is to be worshiped and adored. Observe His names, His titles, His attributes, and how man is to respond to Him.

a. Don't forget to look for Jesus, who is God, one with the Father, for He said, "All things which are written about Me in the Law of Moses and the Prophets and the Psalms must be fulfilled" (Luke 24:44).

b. The psalms are for the heart and soul, but they also address the mind. In the margin record your insights about God (use a △ as a heading). As you do this, meditate on what you learn. Spend time in praise and prayer. Let the book of Psalms help you love the Lord your God with all your heart, mind, body, soul, and strength.

6. When you finish each psalm, record the theme of that psalm in your Bible next to the number of the psalm and on the PSALMS AT A GLANCE chart.

7. Psalms has five segments, which are marked on PSALMS AT A GLANCE.

a. Give each segment a title or record its theme.

b. Read Psalms 41:13; 72:18-19; 89:52; 106:48; and 150:6. Notice what is said and how each segment concludes.

c. Complete PSALMS AT A GLANCE.

THINGS TO THINK ABOUT

1. When you are distressed, confused, afraid, or hurt, or when you need to talk with Someone who will understand, turn to Psalms. With the psalmist, be still (cease striving) and know that He is God.

2. Think about the practical value of Psalms and let it serve as your primary counselor when you need wisdom and understanding. Remember, blessed is the man who does not walk in the counsel of the wicked, but whose delight is in the law of the Lord, and who meditates in that law day and night (see Psalm 1).

3. Have you thought about ending each day as the book of Psalms ends—with a psalm of praise? "Let the godly ones exult in glory; let them sing for joy on their beds. Let the high praises of God be in their mouth.... Let everything that has breath praise the LORD. Praise the LORD!" (Psalm 149:5-6; 150:6). Try it and see what God does.

Theme of Psalms:

SEGMENT DIVISIONS

		CHAPTER THEMES
		1
		2
		3
		4
		5
		6
		7
		8
		9
		10
		11
		12
		13
		14
		15
		16
		17
		18
		19
		20
		21
		22
		23
		24
		25

Author:

Date:

Geographical Location:

Purpose:

Key Words (and their synonyms):

affliction

take refuge

righteous

wicked (evil)

sin (iniquity)

prayer

praise (extol, glorify)

sing

fear

hope

save

cry

See appendix 7 for key words in the New International Version and King James Version.

Segment Divisions

		Chapter Themes
		26
		27
		28
		29
		30
		31
		32
		33
		34
		35
		36
		37
		38
		39
		40
		41
		42
		43
		44
		45
		46
		47
		48
		49
		50

SEGMENT DIVISIONS

			CHAPTER THEMES
		51	
		52	
		53	
		54	
		55	
		56	
		57	
		58	
		59	
		60	
		61	
		62	
		63	
		64	
		65	
		66	
		67	
		68	
		69	
		70	
		71	
		72	
		73	
		74	
		75	

SEGMENT DIVISIONS

		CHAPTER THEMES
		76
		77
		78
		79
		80
		81
		82
		83
		84
		85
		86
		87
		88
		89
		90
		91
		92
		93
		94
		95
		96
		97
		98
		99
		100

		Chapter Themes
		101
		102
		103
		104
		105
		106
		107
		108
		109
		110
		111
		112
		113
		114
		115
		116
		117
		118
		119
		120
		121
		122
		123
		124
		125

SEGMENT DIVISIONS

		CHAPTER THEMES
		126
		127
		128
		129
		130
		131
		132
		133
		134
		135
		136
		137
		138
		139
		140
		141
		142
		143
		144
		145
		146
		147
		148
		149
		150

PROVERBS מִשְׁלֵי
MISHLE

*W*hen God appeared to King Solomon in a dream, He said, "Ask what you wish me to give you." Solomon asked for an understanding heart so that he could lead the nation of Israel (see 1 Kings 3). In response to that prayer "God gave Solomon wisdom and very great discernment and breadth of mind, like the sand that is on the seashore. Solomon's wisdom surpassed the wisdom of all the sons of the east and all the wisdom of Egypt. For he was wiser than all men.... He also spoke 3,000 proverbs" (1 Kings 4:29-32).

Many of Solomon's wise sayings have been preserved for us in the book of Proverbs. A proverb is usually a short saying or maxim that gives insight on life and human behavior.

The book of Proverbs is a compilation of true sayings that give wisdom and instruction. However, these maxims should not be interpreted as prophecies, nor can they be held as absolute doctrines. For example, Proverbs says a man's enemies will be at peace with him when his ways please the Lord. We can accept this as a valid proverb which generally proves to be true, though not always. Our Lord's enemies were not at peace with Him even though He did only those things that pleased the Father.

The Proverbs are inspired by God; don't rush through them. Give yourself time for meditation and application. Although Proverbs was written between 971 and 686 B.C., these sayings are timeless. They can equip you for life in the home and the marketplace.

THINGS TO DO

1. Proverbs uses figurative language—similes and metaphors. Read the section called "Figures of Speech" on page 327 before you study Proverbs.

2. Read Proverbs 1:1-7 and note the author, purpose, and theme of the book in the margin of chapter 1. As you look for the purpose, watch the repeated use of *to*. The theme is also repeated in 9:10. Record these insights on the PROVERBS AT A GLANCE chart.

3. A wise person appreciates the wisdom of others. Look at PROVERBS AT A GLANCE and note the major segment divisions of this book. You will see that Solomon respected the wisdom of others. Look up the following verses and note whose words or proverbs follow: Proverbs 10:1; 22:17; 25:1; 30:1; 31:1.

4. Mark the key words listed on PROVERBS AT A GLANCE along with their synonyms. Keep a list of what you learn about wisdom, especially in the first nine chapters. Note how wisdom is personified. (An abstraction, such as wisdom, is personified when it takes on the characteristics of a person. Proverbs 1:20 is an example.)

5. Watch for and mark the phrase *my son (O son)*. Then listen as if it is God the Father speaking to you, His own dear child whom He wants to show the path of life.

6. Develop a code for marking the subjects covered throughout Proverbs: sexual morality, finances, discipline, the heart, the tongue, the company we keep, etc. As you read through Proverbs repeatedly you will learn more and more about mankind and will find yourself much wiser when it comes to living in the "fear of the Lord." You will have a collection of insights on the critical issues of life.

7. Record the theme or themes of each chapter on PROVERBS AT A GLANCE and in your Bible. You may find this difficult between chapters 10 and 29 because the proverbs are short and varied. However, simply listing the major topics of each chapter will help you find the major topics at a glance. Color-coding or marking each topic throughout the book will help you easily spot what Proverbs teaches about a particular subject. This will

be a great help as you share these truths with others or need wisdom on a specific topic.

THINGS TO THINK ABOUT

1. Are you walking in the fear of the Lord? To fear God is to have an awesome respect of who He is and a reverential trust in His Word and His character, and to live accordingly.

2. The wisdom of the world is different from the wisdom that comes from God. Which is of more value to you? How quick are you, beloved, to seek God's wisdom in the matters of everyday life?

3. What do you need to do or change in light of the insight and wisdom you have learned from these proverbs?

4. Since there are 31 chapters in Proverbs, some people read a chapter a day, month after month. This is good as long as you do not neglect other portions of the Word and as long as you give yourself adequate time to meditate on these proverbs.

   a. After chapter 9, many proverbs are only two to four lines long. You may want to choose one or two proverbs a day, evaluating your life and relationships in the light of them.

   b. Or you may want to select a theme you marked throughout Proverbs, list what you learned from the book as a whole, and then meditate on that theme. For example, you might meditate on what you learned about diligence versus laziness, or about the tongue.

Theme of Proverbs:

SEGMENT DIVISIONS

	MAIN DIVISIONS	CHAPTER THEMES	
			Author:
	THE CRY OF WISDOM, KNOWLEDGE, AND UNDERSTANDING	1	**Date:**
		2	
		3	
		4	**Purpose:**
		5	
		6	**Key Words:**
		7	
		8	my son (O son)
		9	
	THE PROVERBS OF SOLOMON AND WISDOM OF WISE MEN	10	wisdom (guidance, wise)
		11	
		12	knowledge
		13	understanding (insight, discernment)
		14	
		15	
		16	fear
		17	commandment(s)
		18	
		19	instruction (discipline, teaching)
		20	
		21	
		22	tongue
		23	fool (folly)
		24	
	SOLOMON'S PROVERBS TRANSCRIBED	25	righteous
		26	evil
		27	
		28	wicked
		29	
	COUNSEL OF OTHERS / WORDS &	30	
		31	

See appendix 7 for key words in the New International Version and King James Version.

ECCLESIASTES   קוהלת
QOHELET

*L*ife seems inconsistent, unpredictable, and unfair at times. Regardless of the generation, regardless of the time in history, the righteous and the wicked have the same experiences, face the same trials, grapple with the same problems—and all end up in the grave!

As people grow older they look back and see that life is but a breath, a vapor. It passes so quickly. What is its purpose? Have we sought after the right things? Have we lived as we should?

"What advantage does man have in all his work which he does under the sun?" (Ecclesiastes 1:3). And what is the conclusion of it all? Ecclesiastes not only asks questions, it also points toward the answers.

THINGS TO DO

General Instructions

1. A careful observation of Ecclesiastes gives insight into why this book is included in the Bible. So as you begin your study of this book, do the following:

   a. Remember that all you read must be considered in the context of the whole counsel of God.

   b. Read 1:1-3 and 12:13-14 to see how Ecclesiastes begins and ends. Keep these verses in mind as you study.

2. As you read Ecclesiastes, mark every reference to the author in a distinctive way:

   a. Who and/or what he is; how he describes himself; what he pursued, had, or experienced, and what gain it was to him. This is important. You may want to list your insights in your notebook as you go through Ecclesiastes.

   b. As you read the book, observe what the author has seen, come to know, commends, and concludes. Mark or note these insights in a special way, since these usually include important key repeated phrases.

   c. After chapter 4, mark or list in the margin the author's commands and warnings. For example, in 5:1 he tells us to guard our steps when we go into the house of God.

3. As you read each chapter, mark in a distinctive way the key words listed on the ECCLESIASTES AT A GLANCE chart. List these key words on an index card that you can use as a bookmark while observing this book.

4. When you finish observing each chapter:

   a. Look at every reference to God that you marked in the text. In your notebook, list all you learn about Him, what He does, and what we are to do in respect to Him.

   b. Mark the contrasting groups of people: the righteous and the wicked, the wise and the foolish. In your notebook, list what you learn about these persons from each chapter.

   c. Also make a list of what you learn about *riches (wealth)* and *labor.*

   d. When you have completed your study of the book, you may want to summarize in your notebook what you learned from compiling the above lists.

5. Record the theme of each chapter on ECCLESIASTES AT A GLANCE and in your Bible.

Chapters 1–8: Exploring Life's Inconsistencies

1. As you read, mark the key words listed on ECCLESIASTES AT A GLANCE. Also watch for and mark these words: *explore (explored)*, *discover (discovered)*, and *directed*.

2. The words *vanity, futile,* and *futility* are all from the Hebrew word *hebel,* which means "vapor" or "breath."

   a. *Hebel* appears more in Ecclesiastes than in any other book of the Bible; half of all its occurrences are in Ecclesiastes.

   b. Except for 11:8 and 12:8, all the occurrences of *vanity* and *futility* appear in this first segment of Ecclesiastes. Therefore after you finish marking in a distinctive way each occurrence of these words, you might want to record in your notebook everything you learn from the text about vanity and futility. Remember that although they are translated two different ways, they are the same Hebrew word.

Chapters 9–12: Explaining Life's Inconsistencies

1. Read 9:1 and mark the word *explain*. Do you see how this verse might be used as a pivotal point in the book? If so, watch for any explanations the author might give to life's inconsistencies.

2. When you finish observing chapter 10, review each reference to wisdom that you have marked and summarize everything you learned about wisdom from Ecclesiastes.

3. As you read 12:1-7, think of the human body and the effects of age on its members. See if you find any "pictorial descriptions" of the body and what happens as you get old (e.g., "the grinding ones which are few" might be a picture of losing some teeth).

4. Complete ECCLESIASTES AT A GLANCE.

THINGS TO THINK ABOUT

1. Where have you been searching for the meaning of life? Reflect on what you've been pursuing in order to find fulfillment or happiness. Has it worked?

2. According to God, where can the meaning of life be found? Where can't it be found?

3. The author of Ecclesiastes is Solomon, David's son, who was the richest and wisest of men. What can you learn from his experience that can help you?

4. Review all you have learned about God from this book. Since God is going to bring every act to judgment, even those of Christians (2 Corinthians 5:10; Romans 14:10), what are you doing that you should continue to do and what do you need to stop doing? Will you?

Theme of Ecclesiastes:

Author:

Date:

Purpose:

Key Words:
God

vanity
(futile, futility)

under the sun
(under heaven)

wisdom

righteous
(righteousness,
justice)

wicked
(wickedness)

wise

fool

evil

labor (labored,
toil)

riches (wealth)

SEGMENT DIVISIONS		CHAPTER THEMES
		1
		2
		3
		4
		5
		6
		7
		8
		9
		10
		11
		12

See appendix 7 for key words in the New International Version and King James Version.

SONG OF SOLOMON שיר השירים

Song of Solomon is a love story included in the canon of Scripture. On the eighth day of Passover the Jews would sing portions of the Song of Solomon, a book they compared to the most holy place in the temple.

Song of Solomon is a book never quoted by our Lord, but one from which many Christians sing, "I am my Beloved's, and He is mine" and "His banner over me is love."

Many waters cannot quench love,
>Nor will rivers overflow it;
If a man were to give all the riches of his house for love,
>It would be utterly despised (8:7).

THINGS TO DO

1. The Song of Solomon is a unified lyrical poem composed of a variety of songs. There is no other book like it in Scripture. Before you begin to analyze its content, sit down and read it through slowly without stopping. Remember, the phrases may seem different or unusual because of the culture of the Eastern people.

2. As you read Song of Solomon, notice who is speaking when. The reference notes of the NASB identify who speaks. If you prefer to identify the speaker yourself, do the following:

   a. Read the book again and mark every time the woman (bride) speaks and also when the man (bridegroom) speaks. Watch for the pronouns *he* and *she* and mark them in distinctive colors.

   b. As you read, you will notice there is a third party referred to in the text as "the daughters of Jerusalem" and in the reference notes in the margin as "Chorus." Note when "the daughters of Jerusalem" (the chorus) intervenes. When you see any other parties speaking, mark these as well. Note these under "Segment Divisions" on the SONG OF SOLOMON AT A GLANCE chart.

3. Now read through the Song of Solomon again. This time do the following:

   a. As you read, mark the key words listed on SONG OF SOLOMON AT A GLANCE.

   b. Watch for details about the bride and the bridegroom—their position, family, how they met, where they met, etc. A careful reading of the book as a whole can help you piece together these facts. You might want to write your observations on a piece of paper and then transfer them to the margin of the text.

   c. Watch for other segment divisions in the book. For instance, note when the courtship ends, when the wedding takes place, and what occurs in the marriage and why. (Watch for the word *wedding*.) Record these divisions on SONG OF SOLOMON AT A GLANCE.

   d. Record the theme of each chapter on SONG OF SOLOMON AT A GLANCE and then in your Bible. Complete the chart.

THINGS TO THINK ABOUT

1. There are many different interpretations in respect to the meaning of this book. Does Song of Solomon speak only about the emotional and physical relationship of love and marriage? Or does it symbolize something such as Israel's relationship to God, or the

church's relationship to Jesus, their heavenly bridegroom, or the individual's devotion to Christ? If it goes beyond the natural to the spiritual, what would you see that you might apply to your relationship with the Lord Jesus Christ?

2. If this book speaks merely of the physical and emotional bonds of marriage, what do you learn from it that you might apply to your relationship with your mate? Think about the way the bride and bridegroom communicated with each other, what they shared, what their physical relationship was like, what caused problems, and how they solved them.

3. What can you learn from Song of Solomon that would help you prepare for marriage? For instance, what can you learn from this book about understanding yourself, your future mate, and the importance of intimacy, purity, and physical oneness?

4. What do you think an adulterous relationship would do to the intimacy between the bride and the bridegroom? James 4:4 tells us that when we become friends with the world (the world system) we are committing spiritual adultery. What does this do to our intimacy with God? Read 2 Corinthians 11:2-3 and think about it.

SONG OF SOLOMON AT A GLANCE

Theme of Song of Solomon:

SEGMENT DIVISIONS

		CHAPTER THEMES	Author:
		1	Date:
		2	
		3	Purpose:
		4	Key Words:
		5	love
		6	beloved
		7	come (coming)
		8	beautiful

See appendix 7 for key words in the New International Version and King James Version.

*I*SAIAH   יְשַׁעְיָהוּ
YESHA'YAHU

*T*he messages of the Old Testament prophets addressed the people of Israel and Judah who lived between the years of 840 and 420 B.C. Isaiah is the first of the major prophets. Isaiah's name, *Yesha'yahu*, means "Jehovah Saves" or "Salvation of Jehovah." No other prophet offers more prophecies regarding the coming Messiah. Isaiah reveals the Messiah (Christ) as the Suffering Servant and the Conquering King. Under divine inspiration, Isaiah announces the things that will occur in the future so that God's people might know there is no God besides Him.

From Isaiah 37:37-38 we know Isaiah lived until at least 681 B.C., the year Esarhaddon, the son of Sennacherib, became king of Assyria after his father's death. Tradition says Isaiah died a martyr, sawn in two by Manasseh, the king of Judah who reigned after Hezekiah (2 Kings 21:16). If tradition is correct, Isaiah may be one of the heroes of faith referred to in Hebrews 11:37.

THINGS TO DO

The basic structure of Isaiah is easy to remember if it is compared to the Bible's structure. The Bible is comprised of 66 books, 39 in the Old Testament and 27 in the New Testament. Isaiah, which focuses on the Holy One of Israel, has 66 chapters, which fall into two main divisions: Isaiah 1 through 39 reveals God's character and judgment, and Isaiah 40 through 66 shows God's comfort and redemption. Because Isaiah is a long book filled with discourses and songs, it needs to be studied segment by segment so that you don't miss the wonder of its promises and prophecies. Ask God to help you understand the important message of this book.

General Instructions

1. As you read through Isaiah one chapter at a time, observe each chapter in the light of the "5 W's and an H." Ask general questions such as: Who does this chapter focus on? What happens or what is this about? When is this happening? Where will it happen? Why is this going to happen and how?

2. Mark any reference to God with a △ and observe any insights into His character, His power, His ways. Note these in the margin. If the verse mentions the sovereignty of God, note it in the margin with "△ Sovereignty." Also, watch for and mark any references to God as the Creator. Note these in the margin with "△ Creator."

3. Isaiah is a set of discourses, songs, or oracles rather than a historical chronology of events in the life of Israel. Periodically there are historical interludes, which are very important. In these interludes God often will tell Isaiah to do something that will act as a sign to the people. For instance, in Isaiah 8:3 Isaiah is to name his son *Maher-shalal-hash-baz*, which means "swift is the booty, speedy is the prey." His name pointed the people to the Assyrian invasion, which would come before Maher-shalal-hash-baz would learn to say Momma or Daddy. Observe these interludes carefully.

4. Isaiah recorded many prophecies regarding future events, including the captivity, the birth of Messiah, the reign of Messiah, and the last days. Watch for these prophecies and mark them in a significant way.

   a. As you read some of these prophecies, you will see that the first and second comings of Messiah (Christ) are prophesied without any indication that there is an interval of time between these comings. For instance, Isaiah 61:1-2a covers the first coming of Jesus Christ. In fact, Jesus read this passage in the synagogue in Nazareth and stopped at this point (Luke 4:18-19). Why? Because the next part of the verse, "And the day of vengeance of our God," skips to the day of the Lord, which encompasses Christ's judgment and His second coming.

    b. You will find it beneficial to read the section entitled "Guidelines for Interpreting Predictive Prophecy" on page 325.

    c. On page 132 is a chart called THE PROPHETIC POINTS OF HISTORY. This will help you distinguish the time periods to which Isaiah refers. Watch for and mark any references to the Lord's coming. Note which coming it is and the circumstances associated with it.

5. On the ISAIAH AT A GLANCE chart are key words to mark in a distinctive way. Put these on an index card now and use it as a bookmark. As you mark *in that day,* carefully observe what day it is referring to. Start a chart in your notebook on the day of the Lord (the day of wrath, the day of God) and use it throughout your study of the Bible. You might have four headings for this chart: the biblical reference, how the Bible describes the day, what happens in nature, and signs of the beginning or end of the day.

6. Babylon plays a significant prophetic role throughout Scripture, even in the day of the Lord. List what you learn about Babylon. Note the reference (book, chapter, and verse) from which you took your information. You will want this for future reference.

7. Note any references to time with a clock ⏲.

8. Finally, there's much you can learn about Isaiah himself. Mark in a distinctive color every reference to Isaiah that tells you something about him. You may want to record these insights at the end of Isaiah 66.

Isaiah 1–39: God's Character and Judgment

Chapters 1–12: Discourses Regarding Judah and Jerusalem

1. Read Isaiah 1 to get the spiritual and moral condition and the historical setting of this book.

    a. Read Isaiah 1 and color in a distinctive way every reference to God's people, Israel. Then on a separate piece of paper list what you learn about Israel just from this chapter.

    b. There is much to learn about Israel as a society around 700 B.C. Mark any reference that will give you insight into this nation's status or condition at this time.

    c. To put the book into its chronological setting, compare Isaiah 1:1 with the historical chart on page 132. Record your insights under "Author" and "Date" on the ISAIAH AT A GLANCE chart on pages 134 and 135.

2. As you read Isaiah 2–12 one chapter at a time:

    a. Add the following key words and mark them through Isaiah 39: *Samaria, Assyria, woe* (also 45:9-10), and *remnant* (also in 46:3).

    b. Mark references to time with a clock ⏲.

3. As you read each chapter observe the following:

    a. Note to whom God is speaking and what He says about their behavior.

    b. Observe the consequences of the behavior.

    c. See if there is an exhortation or plea followed by a promise of how God will cleanse them, bless them, or move on their behalf.

4. Isaiah 6 is a strategic chapter. It records Isaiah's call and commission from the Lord.

    a. To get the historical setting of this chapter, read 2 Kings 15. Uzziah is called Azariah in 2 Kings 15:1 (see 2 Chronicles 26:1). The reigns of Uzziah and Jotham overlapped because they served as co-regents for a time.

129

b. Observe the progression of events in this chapter and note them in the margin.

5. As you study each chapter, don't forget the "General Instructions." These are an important part of the process of carefully observing the text.

6. When you finish observing each chapter, record the theme of that chapter on ISAIAH AT A GLANCE and in your Bible.

Chapters 13–23: Oracles Against Various Nations

1. As you read this section chapter by chapter, watch for and mark in a distinctive way the key repeated phrase, *the oracle concerning* _____. Note who the oracle concerns and locate each of these on a map.

2. As you observe each chapter, note the following in the margin or mark it in the text:

   a. Observe if there is any judgment connected with those to whom the oracle is given and why.

   b. Watch where the judgment comes and if there is any effect on Israel.

   c. Watch for *when* something happens. Note this with the symbol of a clock.

   d. Notice how God's purposes are being worked out in history.

   e. Mark references to the day of the Lord.

3. Record the theme of each chapter in the same way you did previously. However, remember that this will not always be easy. The chapter divisions in the Bible are not part of the original Scriptures. Therefore, if you have a hard time summarizing the theme of each chapter, don't be discouraged. When it is not easy to settle on a chapter theme, pick a key verse that the truths of the chapter seem to pivot around, or simply choose some words from the first verse and record these on ISAIAH AT A GLANCE.

Chapters 24–27: Discourses Regarding "That Day"

1. As you read this segment, add *covenant* to your key words list.

2. As you read each chapter observe the following:

   a. What happens to the earth and its inhabitants (humans and animals)

   b. What the Lord of hosts will do and where He will be

   c. What the people's response will be

3. Record the theme of each chapter on ISAIAH AT A GLANCE and in the text.

Chapters 28–33: Six Woes

1. Mark the key words, and add *the* (or *My*) *Spirit* to your list. It is also used in Isaiah 11:2, so go back and mark it.

2. As you read each of these chapters, mark in the text the following:

   a. To whom the woe is given

   b. What was done to cause the woe

   c. What the Lord will do and what the result will be

3. Record the chapter themes on ISAIAH AT A GLANCE and in your Bible.

Chapters 34–35: God's Recompense and Ransom for Zion

1. As you read these two chapters, add the following key words and watch for them from this point onward: *sword, recompense, glory (the Lord's),* and *ransomed.*

2. Look for and record in your notebook on whom God's recompense will come, what it will be, and what will follow. Make sure you note what happens to the ransomed and the redeemed. Also note what this will mean to Zion.

3. Record the chapter themes on ISAIAH AT A GLANCE and in your Bible.

Chapters 36–39: Historical Account from the Threat of Assyria to the Threat of Babylon

1. Read these chapters and mark the following words: *Assyria, Sennacherib, Rabshakeh, Hezekiah, Isaiah, Babylon, remnant, Lord of hosts*, and *prayer (prayed)*.

2. Now read the chapters again, observing the words you marked. In your notebook, note what you learn about each of the characters and what they do, what happens as a result, and how God intervenes. List what you learn about God from these chapters. Don't miss what happens to Assyria and Babylon. This is a pivotal point in respect to these two powers and the nation of Israel.

3. For additional insight into Hezekiah, read 2 Kings 18–20 and 2 Chronicles 29–32.

4. Record the chapter themes on ISAIAH AT A GLANCE and in your Bible.

Isaiah 40–66: God's Comfort and Redemption

Chapters 40–48: Behold the Lord, Your Redeemer

1. Continue to mark any key words on your list. Also mark the following references to God in a distinctive way: *I am the Lord (God), no one besides Me (no other God)*, and *Redeemer*. Then list in your notebook all you see about God that you want to remember for future reference. Note God's character, what He does, and to what or whom He is compared.

2. As you do all this don't simply mark these and move on. Meditate on what you see. Think of what these insights can do for your relationship with God. Remember, He is not only Israel's Redeemer but yours also if you have repented and believed in the Lord Jesus Christ.

3. Also add and mark *servant*. As you read each chapter, check the context (the surrounding verses) in which *servant* is used. This is vital. Note whether *servant* refers to Israel (Jacob) or to the Lord Jesus Christ. Record your insights in your notebook. If it seems to be a prophetic reference to Jesus, check your Bible's reference notes and see if the New Testament verses show how this prophecy was fulfilled by Jesus. When you make your list in the margin put it under "Israel the Servant" or "Messiah the Servant."

4. Once again mark *remnant* (used only one time in this segment), *glory of the Lord, salvation, nation (nations)*, and *Babylon*. Record in your notebook what you learn about each.

5. Record your chapter themes as before. Fill in the second line of the segment division for these chapters: Discourses Regarding _____.

Chapters 49–57: Your Redeemer Will Save

1. Do everything you did under numbers 1 through 4 in the previous segment. Watch carefully all that the Lord can and will do; you might want to note it in your notebook. Observe the text carefully to see why this segment is titled "Your Redeemer Will Save." Watch for God's instructions and take them to heart.

2. Watch for prophetic verses that come in the midst of what Isaiah is saying. Give special attention to 50:6 and 52:13–53:12. After you observe Isaiah 53, read it through on your knees and substitute your name every time you see *we* or *us*. Mark every reference to *He* and *Him* from verse 2 onward. Then list all that the text tells you about Him.

3. Look for and record the theme of each chapter. If you think it will be helpful, summarize and list in the margin the subpoints covered in the chapter. Fill in the second line of the segment division for these chapters.

Chapters 58–66: Your Redeemer Will Come

1. Once again mark the key words on your bookmark. Also mark *redemption* and the

references to fasting. *Servant* becomes *servants* in this segment; don't miss it.

2. There is much in this segment about the events that surround or accompany the Lord's coming to reign and what will follow, even in regard to the new heaven and new earth. In your notebook list what you observe. Also watch for practical lessons and list what you learn. For instance, in Isaiah 58 you will gain insights on fasting.

3. Once again continue marking everything as you did under steps 1 through 4 (Isaiah 40–48).

4. Record your chapter themes and then complete ISAIAH AT A GLANCE. Fill in the second line of the segment division for these chapters. Write in any new segment divisions you have seen.

THINGS TO THINK ABOUT

1. God's character never changes; therefore what distressed Him in the days of Isaiah still distresses Him today. And what He had to judge then, He cannot overlook now. Is there anything in your life you must confess and forsake? And what if you are not willing to do so? Will God be able to overlook it? Think about what you learned about God and His ways.

2. God is sovereign. He ruled over the nations in the days of Israel. Does He do the same today? What, then, can you know? How might your nation fit into all this?

3. Amos says God doesn't do anything without first revealing it to His servants, the prophets (Amos 3:7). Therefore, from studying Isaiah, what do you know with an absolute certainty is going to come to pass? If the prophecies regarding the first coming of Jesus Christ literally came to pass (and they did), won't the prophecies regarding His second coming be literally fulfilled? How, then, are you to live?

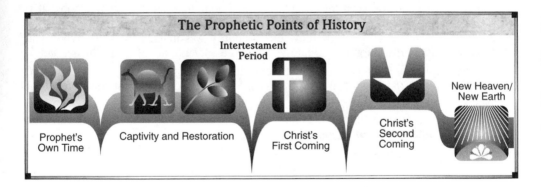

THE RULERS AND PROPHETS OF ISAIAH'S TIME

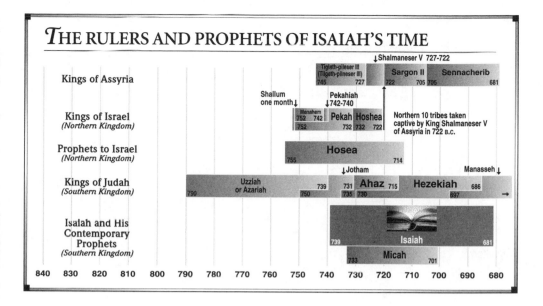

Kings of Assyria — ↓Shalmaneser V 727-722 / Tiglath-pileser III (Tilgath-pilneser III) 745-727 / Sargon II 722-705 / Sennacherib 705-681

Kings of Israel (Northern Kingdom) — Shallum one month↓ / Pekahiah ↓742-740 / Menahem 752-742 / Pekah 732 / Hoshea 732-722 / Northern 10 tribes taken captive by King Shalmaneser V of Assyria in 722 B.C.

Prophets to Israel (Northern Kingdom) — Hosea 755-714

Kings of Judah (Southern Kingdom) — Uzziah or Azariah 790-750 / 739 / ↓Jotham 735-731 / Ahaz 730-715 / Hezekiah 697-686 / Manasseh ↓

Isaiah and His Contemporary Prophets (Southern Kingdom) — Isaiah 739-681 / Micah 733-701

840 830 820 810 800 790 780 770 760 750 740 730 720 710 700 690 680

Theme of Isaiah:

Author:

Date:

Purpose:

Key Words:

in that day

Lord of hosts

Holy One of
Israel

earth

Babylon
(Babylonians,
Chaldeans)

nations (other
than Israel)

Israel (Jacob)

Judah

covenant

Zion
(Jerusalem)

sin (sinners,
evil, iniquity,
transgressions,
transgressed)

every reference
to the Lord's
coming

redeemed

woe

SEGMENT DIVISIONS

			CHAPTER THEMES
DISCOURSES REGARDING JERUSALEM	GOD'S CHARACTER AND JUDGMENT		1
			2
			3
			4
			5
			6
			7
			8
			9
			10
			11
			12
ORACLES			13
			14
			15
			16
			17
			18
			19
			20
			21
			22
			23
DISCOURSES REGARDING THAT DAY			24
			25
			26
			27
			28
WOES			29
			30
			31
			32
			33

See appendix 7 for key words in the New International Version and King James Version.

SEGMENT DIVISIONS

			CHAPTER THEMES
GOD'S RANSOM	GOD'S CHARACTER AND JUDGMENT	34	
		35	
HISTORICAL INTERLUDE		36	
		37	
		38	
		39	
DISCOURSES REGARDING:	GOD'S COMFORT AND REDEMPTION	40	
		41	
		42	
		43	
		44	
		45	
		46	
		47	
		48	
DISCOURSES REGARDING:		49	
		50	
		51	
		52	
		53	
		54	
		55	
		56	
		57	
DISCOURSES REGARDING:		58	
		59	
		60	
		61	
		62	
		63	
		64	
		65	
		66	

JEREMIAH ירמיהו
YIRMEYAHU

*I*saiah lived and prophesied one hundred years before the Babylonian captivity; Jeremiah prophesied just before and during Babylon's three sieges of Judah. Between these two great prophets there was about a 30-year period when God didn't speak. While the true prophets were silent, false prophets were very vocal, proclaiming peace rather than judgment—and the people loved it. This occurred during Manasseh's reign, a reign noted for its blasphemy and bloodshed.

Although Jeremiah was living at this time, his ministry as a prophet didn't begin until about 627 B.C., the same time that Nabopolassar began his rule of the Neo-Babylonian Empire. Josiah succeeded Manasseh as ruler over Judah, and when the Word of the Lord was found in the house of God, Josiah called the people to repentance, bringing about a revival.

Then, in 612 B.C., Nineveh, the capital of Assyria, fell to the Babylonians. In 609 B.C., as Egypt went to aid Assyria against Babylon at Carchemish, Josiah intercepted Neco, king of Egypt, on the plain of Megiddo. Although Neco had warned Josiah not to try to stop him, Josiah tried anyway, and as a result he was killed in battle (see 2 Chronicles 35:20-27).

The revival came to an end, and like her sister Israel, Judah played the harlot again. In 605 B.C., Egypt was defeated by Babylon at Carchemish, leaving Babylon the dominant world power, God's rod of judgment for His adulterous wife and the surrounding nations. And Jeremiah the prophet wept.

THINGS TO DO

Chapter 1: Understanding Jeremiah's Message

To understand Jeremiah's message you must understand Jeremiah's call and commission from the Lord. To do so, become thoroughly familiar with Jeremiah 1 before reading the instructions for Jeremiah 2 through 38.

1. Read the chapter, asking God for insight and understanding. Then read the chapter and mark any of the key words listed on JEREMIAH AT A GLANCE.

2. The first three verses give the historical setting of Jeremiah.

   a. The exile (1:3) refers to the final siege and destruction of Jerusalem by Nebuchadnezzar, king of Babylon, in 586 B.C. See "Israel's Division and Captivity" on page 79.

   b. Jeremiah contains many references to time, such as in Jeremiah 1:1-3. When you read one, try to determine who was reigning at the time and what his relationship was to the other kings. The book of Jeremiah is not chronological, so this will help you keep the timing of events in perspective. Mark every reference to time with a clock ⏱ and color it green for easy reference.

   c. Fill in "Author" and "Date" on the JEREMIAH AT A GLANCE chart.

3. Read Jeremiah 1 again. As you do, ask the "5 W's and an H." Ask questions such as: Who was Jeremiah? What was Jeremiah called to do or be? To whom was he appointed and by whom? When was he called and why? How did he respond? How will he be able to fulfill his appointment? What was he to say? How would the people respond? What was Jeremiah to do? What if the people didn't respond? What would God do?

   a. In your notebook, jot down your answers to these questions and any others you think of while observing the text. Don't read anything into the text; simply let it speak for itself.

b. In your notebook, you may want to list the main points about Jeremiah, his call, and the specifics of his commission. Record what you observed from examining the chapter in light of the "5 W's and an H." Be as specific as possible.

4. Mark references to God with a △, and note insights into His character, sovereignty, power, and ways. Draw a △ in the margin so you can note what the text tells you about Him.

5. Record the theme of this chapter on JEREMIAH AT A GLANCE and in your Bible.

6. The rest of Jeremiah revolves around Jeremiah's call and commission as a prophet to the nations. Everything Jeremiah says and does is rooted in chapter 1. Remember this as you study!

Jeremiah's critical and passionate message consists of discourses and narrative accounts of events in Jeremiah's life and in the history of Israel, Judah, and the nations.

Chapters 2–38: Judah's Sin and God's Warning to Return

Read all the instructions before you begin. Every now and then refresh your memory, since Jeremiah is a long book.

1. Study this segment chapter by chapter, doing the following:

a. When Jeremiah spoke he was to do two things—one negative and one positive. First, in respect to the nations, he was to pluck up, break down, destroy, and overthrow. Second, he was to build and plant. As you read, observe how Jeremiah does these in regard to Judah.

1) In your notebook, list their sins, their "wickedness" (1:16), which God has to deal with by plucking up, breaking down, destroying, and overthrowing.
2) Also note any promise of building and planting—restoration. Record what God will do on their behalf, when He will do it, and why.

b. Jeremiah had the assurance that God would perform His word (1:12). As you read, note what God says will happen to Judah in the way of judgment.

1) Watch for how God will bring about this judgment. In several places God has Jeremiah do some symbolic acts in order to get His point across to the people. Watch for these.
2) Watch for any verse that shows that God performed (accomplished or carried out) what He said He would do. Also note what God has to do because of the covenant (the law) He made with them.

2. Jeremiah was told to speak all God commanded him and that he would be opposed by kings, princes, priests, and people.

a. When you see Jeremiah encountering any opposition, write the word "opposition" in the margin. Observe Jeremiah's struggles and how he handles these. Also note how God delivers Jeremiah as He said He would in 1:8,18-19. (The height of Jeremiah's physical suffering is described in chapters 37–38.)

b. Also note what you learn about the leaders, the shepherds (spiritual), and the prophets.

3. As you noticed, Jeremiah prophesied during the reigns of the last five kings of Judah, starting with Josiah. Jeremiah 1–20 basically covers Jeremiah's ministry under Josiah's reign. Jeremiah 21–28 contains prophecies from the time of the other four kings. These are not in chronological order.

4. In chapter 20 the king of Babylon appears on the scene, for "out of the north the evil will break forth on all the inhabitants of the land" (1:14). From this point on, Babylon and Nebuchadnezzar are prominent. You might want to mark every reference to *Babylon (Chaldeans)* from this point onward and summarize your insights about them in the margin under the heading "Babylon."

5. Make a list of the key words on the AT A GLANCE chart, writing them on an index card. On the card, mark the words the same way as you will mark them in the text. Mark references to time with a clock ☾ and color them green for consistency and easy identification.

    a. As you mark every reference to *nation* or *nations* (except Babylon), observe which nation it is and record it.

    b. Watch for any words or synonyms that have to do with plucking up, uprooting, destroying, building, planting, or restoring. Mark these in a distinctive way or underline them in the text.

6. As you come to Jeremiah 31, you are going to find an exciting reference to the New Covenant. Record in your notebook what the New Covenant accomplished. Compare with Matthew 26:26-29 and Luke 22:17-20. See the insight on covenant on page 35.

7. As you finish observing each chapter, marking its key words and putting notes in the margin, record the theme of that chapter on JEREMIAH AT A GLANCE. Also record it in your Bible next to the chapter number.

Chapters 39–45: Jerusalem's Fall and Judah's Uprooting

1. Except for chapter 45, this section is narrative. Therefore, as you read each chapter:

    a. Note what happens, when it happens (mark references to time), where it happens, and why. Double-underline in green all the geographical references.

    b. Note who is involved. Mark in a distinctive way the main characters in each chapter. Then you might want to record who they are and anything significant you want to remember about them.

2. Record the theme of each chapter as you have done before.

Chapters 46–51: Jeremiah's Prophecy Concerning the Nations

1. As you read, note what the Lord says will happen and why. Also note the end result and if the Lord gives any hope for the future. Watch for and mark time phrases.

2. Pay attention to the references to the *north* and to the *Medes*. Also observe what you learn about Israel from these chapters.

3. These chapters contain critical information about Babylon that will help when you study prophecy and/or the book of Revelation. In your notebook, list what you learn about Babylon.

Chapter 52: Judah's Final Days of Exile

1. As you observe this chapter, mark the time phrases and note what was done to the kings, the city, the temple vessels, and who did it.

2. Record the theme of this chapter on JEREMIAH AT A GLANCE and then complete the chart. Record the segment divisions of Jeremiah.

THINGS TO THINK ABOUT

1. Judah played the harlot. How have you behaved as the bride of Christ? Do you relate to any of Judah's sins? In James 4:4 God calls those who are friends with the world adulteresses. What would He call you?

2. How faithful are you to proclaim God's Word to others? What can you learn from Jeremiah's life in this respect? Do you hesitate to share God's Word with others because of fear or because you think they wouldn't listen? Are you dismayed by their faces? What should you do? Think about all the times you marked *listened* and *hear* in Jeremiah. Judah didn't listen to God—only to those prophets who tickled her ears. How

carefully do you listen to God's Word?

3. Would God have relented of the calamity He was about to bring on Judah? Why? What do you learn from this?

4. God uses nations as His rod of judgment, and yet He holds them accountable for their actions. What does this tell you about God and about your accountability before Him?

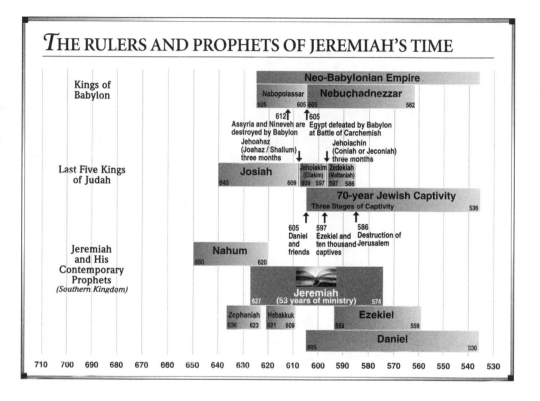

THE RULERS AND PROPHETS OF JEREMIAH'S TIME

Kings of Babylon

Neo-Babylonian Empire

Nabopolassar — 626 605
Nebuchadnezzar — 605 562

612↑ Assyria and Nineveh are destroyed by Babylon
↑605 Egypt defeated by Babylon at Battle of Carchemish

Last Five Kings of Judah

Jehoahaz (Joahaz / Shallum) three months
Jehoiachin (Coniah or Jeconiah) three months

Josiah — 640 609
Jehoiakim (Eliakim) 609 597
Zedekiah (Mattaniah) 597 586

70-year Jewish Captivity
Three Stages of Captivity — 536

605 Daniel and friends
597 Ezekiel and ten thousand captives
586 Destruction of Jerusalem

Jeremiah and His Contemporary Prophets (Southern Kingdom)

Nahum — 650 620

Jeremiah (53 years of ministry) — 627 574

Zephaniah — 636 623
Habakkuk — 621 609

Ezekiel — 593 559

Daniel — 605 536

710 700 690 680 670 660 650 640 630 620 610 600 590 580 570 560 550 540 530

Theme of Jeremiah:

Author:

SEGMENT DIVISIONS

CHAPTER THEMES

Date:

Purpose:

Key Words:

nations

word of the
Lord and
word(s) when
it refers to the
word of the
Lord

destroy (pluck,
uproot)

plant (build,
restore)

listen (hear)

return (repent,
turn)

wickedness
(sin, iniquity,
wicked)

heart

forsaken
(forsake)

heal (healing,
healed)

covenant

concerning

north

Babylon
(Chaldeans
from chapter
20 on)

calamity
(wrath)

woe

famine

		1
		2
		3
		4
		5
		6
		7
		8
		9
		10
		11
		12
		13
		14
		15
		16
		17
		18
		19
		20
		21
		22
		23
		24
		25
		26

See appendix 7 for key words in the New International Version and King James Version.

Segment Divisions

		Chapter Themes
		27
		28
		29
		30
		31
		32
		33
		34
		35
		36
		37
		38
		39
		40
		41
		42
		43
		44
		45
		46
		47
		48
		49
		50
		51
		52

LAMENTATIONS איכה
E K H A

*L*amentations is a book of wailings that are read annually by the Jews as a reminder of the fall of Jerusalem and destruction of the temple. They serve as a reminder of an avoidable tragedy caused by sin—and of a God who judges, but keeps His covenant forever.

These expressions of grief were written sometime between the destruction of Jerusalem and the return of the remnant after 70 years of captivity. Although Judah's plight is desperate, it is not hopeless when the people remember, "The LORD's lovingkindnesses indeed never cease, for His compassions never fail. They are new every morning; great is Your faithfulness" (3:22-23).

THINGS TO DO

1. There are five laments in this book; each begins a new chapter. Lamentations is written as poetry. Each chapter, except chapter 3, is 22 verses long—a verse for every letter of the Hebrew alphabet. As you read chapter by chapter, note how each lament begins and who or what the lament centers on.

2. Mark the key words (and their synonyms) listed on LAMENTATIONS AT A GLANCE.

3. Note the personification of Jerusalem and Judah. Jerusalem is personified as a woman. The personification is seen in the first lines of Lamentations: "How lonely sits the city… she has become like a widow." List what happened to Jerusalem and why; this is key. Note her emotions, the anguish because of her children, the thoughts and memories she has to deal with.

4. Carefully observe and list what you learn about God, His character, His judgments, and why He acts as He does. For example, 1:5 states that God caused Judah grief because of Judah's sin. God brought about Judah's captivity because of Judah's transgressions.

5. Lamentations gives a more definitive understanding of what took place during the Babylonian siege of Jerusalem. In the margin of the text, list what you learn. For example, 1:10 says the nations entered the sanctuary, the house of God, where only Jewish priests were to go. Verse 11 reveals there was a famine—people were seeking bread and giving away precious things in order to get it. (You saw this if you studied Jeremiah.)

6. Determine the theme of each chapter. Write the theme in your Bible next to each chapter number and on LAMENTATIONS AT A GLANCE.

7. Complete LAMENTATIONS AT A GLANCE.

THINGS TO THINK ABOUT

1. What would happen if we considered our future—if we weighed the consequences of our actions—before we acted?

2. God's judgment can take many forms. The sovereign God rules. None can stay His hand or say to Him, "What have You done?" for He does according to His will in the army of heaven and among the inhabitants of the earth (Daniel 4:34-35). Do you think you can sin and go unchastened by God? Judgment must begin at the house of God. Look at 1 Corinthians 11:31-32.

3. Why do you think God deals with sin as He does? How should you respond? Read chapter 3 on your knees so your "dancing" need not be turned into "mourning."

Theme of Lamentations:

Author:

SEGMENT DIVISIONS

CHAPTER THEMES

Date:

1

Purpose:

2

Key Words:

how

Zion (Jerusalem, the city)

3

anger (wrath)

transgressions (sin, iniquity, wickedness)

4

destroy (destroyed, destruction)

affliction (afflict)

desolate

5

little ones (children, infants)

eyes

See appendix 7 for key words in the New International Version and King James Version.

143

EZEKIEL יחזקאל
YEHEZQUEL

*I*n 622 B.C. the book of the law was found in the house of the Lord. When it was brought to King Josiah, he wept, for he saw the awfulness of Judah's sin and knew that God's wrath burned against them. Although Josiah was determined that Judah would walk after the Lord and keep His commandments, the prophetess Huldah told him that after his death God would have to bring judgment upon Judah, for they had forsaken God (see 2 Kings 22).

God's judgment on Judah began when King Josiah tried to stop Pharaoh Neco, king of Egypt, on his way to Carchemish on the Euphrates in 609 B.C. (see 2 Chronicles 35:20-27). Neco killed Josiah on the plain of Megiddo. Then four years later, in 605 B.C., Neco was defeated at Carchemish by Nebuchadnezzar, king of Babylon (see Jeremiah 46:2).

Ezekiel was 18 years old when a handful of the nobles and princes were captured by King Nebuchadnezzar and taken from Judah to Babylon. Among them were a 15-year-old boy named Daniel, and his three friends, Hananiah, Mishael, and Azariah. Ezekiel, however, was left behind. At age 30 he would be eligible for the priesthood and would spend his life in service to God in the temple at Jerusalem. Or so it seemed.

For almost ten years things were relatively quiet in Judah. The prophets were bringing good news, prophesying peace. The people loved it and continued in their sin. Only one lonely voice disturbed their peace—the voice of Jeremiah.

Then Jehoiakim, king of Judah, rebelled against Nebuchadnezzar (2 Kings 23:36–24:4). When Jehoiakim died, Jehoiachin became king, and in 597 B.C. Nebuchadnezzar once again besieged Jerusalem. This time 10,000 people were taken captive into Babylon, and Ezekiel, who would soon have been eligible for the priesthood, was among them. Never again would he see Jerusalem or the temple where he was to serve. Both would be destroyed by Nebuchadnezzar in 586 B.C.

But Ezekiel would see another temple and another Jerusalem—one which would be called *Jehovah-shammah,* the Lord is there! For at age 30, Ezekiel had a vision.

THINGS TO DO

In order to understand the depth and magnitude of the book of Ezekiel, you need to study it again and again. However, if you do the following, you will gain a good understanding of it.

General Instructions

1. Ezekiel has many references to time. These are important and need to be marked with a clock 🕐 and colored green for ease of identification. Ezekiel 1:1-2 establishes the historical setting of Ezekiel's ministry. The other references to time give you the historical timing of his visions and prophecies.

   a. Every time you mark references to time, look at the calendar on page 147 to see what month Ezekiel is referring to. (Follow the sacred calendar highlighted in black.)

   b. Ezekiel 1:2 is a parenthesis and serves as an explanation of the timing of verse 2. Read 2 Kings 24:8–25:21 for a good overview of the historical setting. This will help you understand the timing of Ezekiel's prophecies.

      1) As you read, look for Jehoiachin's name, mark it in a distinctive way, and watch when he goes into exile. Also note who is made king when Jehoiachin goes into exile.

      2) In the margins of 2 Kings 24–25, record the dates of Jerusalem's first, second,

and third sieges. (Jehoiachin was taken captive when Nebuchadnezzar besieged Jerusalem the second time.) The first siege is recorded in 2 Kings 24:1-7 and occurred in 605 B.C. The second siege is recorded in 2 Kings 24:10-16 and occurred in 597 B.C. (Ezekiel was taken captive during the second siege.) The third and final siege is recorded in 2 Kings 25:1-21. It began in 588 B.C., and by 586 B.C. the city was captured and destroyed.

3) Read Ezekiel 1:1-3 and record what you learn about Ezekiel under "Author" on the EZEKIEL AT A GLANCE chart.

4) Now read Numbers 4:3 and observe at what age a man began his priestly service. Then look at Ezekiel 1 and compare this with the way Ezekiel is described and the year he had his first visions from God. Verse 2 tells you what year it was in relationship to the second siege of Jerusalem, the year when Jehoiachin went into exile.

2. Now that you have the historical setting, as you read the dates of all the other visions or prophecies in Ezekiel, you can know that the dates are calculated from the time of Jehoiachin's and Ezekiel's exile in 597 B.C.

3. If you learn anything new about God, record your insight in the margin next to a △ (for God).

4. Key repeated words and phrases to mark throughout the book are listed on EZEKIEL AT A GLANCE. Write them on an index card, color code each in a distinctive way, and then use the card as a bookmark while you study Ezekiel. Double-underline in green all geographical locations. Record your insights on the DAY OF THE LORD chart we suggested in "Getting Started," page 25.

Chapters 1–3: Ezekiel's Call

1. Read chapters 1–3 and mark the key repeated words. Also, mark *listen,* and if it is negative, put a slash through it like this: \.

2. As you go through these chapters one at a time, interrogate the text with the "5 W's and an H." Ask questions such as: What does Ezekiel see? How are they described? Where are they? Where is Ezekiel? What is he told to do? Why is he told to do it? When is Ezekiel to speak?

3. You may want to summarize your observations in your notebook. Note what Ezekiel is called to do and how he is to do it. Also note to whom he is sent and why.

4. In summary form in your notebook, list everything you observe from the text about Ezekiel, the people to whom he was sent, and the glory of the Lord.

5. Record the theme of each chapter on EZEKIEL AT A GLANCE and in your Bible.

Chapters 4–24: Prophecies about Judah and Jerusalem

1. Read through this segment one chapter at a time. On the first reading of a chapter, mark every reference to the time of a vision. Also mark the key words that are on your bookmark.

a. Watch for and mark the phrase *know that I am the Lord*. This is a key phrase used throughout the remainder of Ezekiel, so add this to your bookmark. Every time you see this phrase, observe who is going to know and how they will know it.

b. When you mark *Spirit, heart,* and *the glory of God,* you may want to list what you learn about each from that chapter.

c. Add *covenant* to your list of key words. When it is used in a chapter, list what you learn about it in your notebook. Also watch for additional key repeated words.

2. Now read through each chapter again. Watch for every reference to the *son of man.* In your notebook, note God's instructions to Ezekiel, the son of man. Note to whom or

to what he was to speak and how. Note whether it was by symbolic acts, messages, visions, parables, or signs. Also note why he was to speak in that way and the significance of his action. Notice, too, when Ezekiel's mouth is shut and then later opened. This is important.

3. Record the theme of each chapter as you have done previously.

Chapters 25–32: Prophecies about the Nations

1. Read through this segment one chapter at a time. On the first reading mark the key words. Watch for the phrase *know that I am the Lord*, and again observe who is going to know and how they will know it.

2. On the second reading of the chapter, identify and record in the margin the nation to whom the prophecy is given and the ruler—if he is mentioned. Also observe and note what will happen to the nation and why.

3. Make sure you note or mark *when* the word of the Lord came to Ezekiel.

4. Record the theme of each chapter as you have done previously.

Chapters 33–39: Prophecies about Israel's Restoration

1. Read each chapter and once again:
    a. Mark the references to time, noting when the visions or prophecies were given to Ezekiel. As you look at these, you may want to consult the chart "The Prophetic Points of History" on page 132.
    b. Mark every key word. In your notebook list what you learn from marking *covenant* and then compare it with what you observed about covenant in Ezekiel 16–17.
    c. Continue noting the same observations from marking every occurrence of *know that I am the Lord*. Also list what you learn about the *Spirit, heart,* and *the glory of God*.

2. List God's instructions to Ezekiel ("the son of man"). Note to whom or to what he was to speak and what the message was to be. As you look at the prophecy, list what is going to happen, to whom or what it will happen, and when it will happen. Put a symbol next to any indication of timing. Also note any symbolic acts he was to perform and why.

3. List the theme of each chapter as before.

Chapters 40–48: Prophecies about the Temple

1. As you begin observing this final segment, read 40:1-5. In a distinctive way, mark when this final vision is given. Then in your notebook, record who gives it, how, where, and what Ezekiel is to do.

2. Read each chapter carefully and do the following:
    a. Mark key words as before; however, add to your list *temple (sanctuary, house), holy, offering,* and *gate (entrance)*. Watch for the reference to the Eastern Gate.
    b. Watch for and record the reason for the vision of the temple and its measurements. Also note what you learn about *the glory of the Lord,* the *Spirit,* and their relationship to the temple or sanctuary. Compare this with what you saw in Ezekiel 8–11.
    c. Warning: This last segment of Ezekiel may seem a little boring after the first 39 chapters. Don't get bogged down in all the temple measurements. Don't miss the last verse of Ezekiel, since it names "the city." It's *Jehovah-shammah!*
    d. In your notebook, list the main points, instructions, or events of each chapter.

3. See the chart "The Tribes, the Prince's Portion, the City, the Sanctuary" on page 148.

4. Record the theme of these chapters as you have done before. Then complete EZEKIEL AT A GLANCE. Go back to each vision Ezekiel had, note the year when it occurred, and from your calendar record the name of the month and the day. (Follow the sacred calendar highlighted in black.) Then transfer this information to the segment division portion of EZEKIEL AT A GLANCE.

THINGS TO THINK ABOUT

1. As you think about God's call on Ezekiel's life, what do you see about Ezekiel's responsibility as a watchman that you could apply to your own life? If the people wouldn't listen, was Ezekiel still to speak (Ezekiel 2–3; 33)? Remember that the things in the Old Testament were written for our example, encouragement, and perseverance (1 Corinthians 10:6,11; Romans 15:4).

2. Before Ezekiel ever shared God's message he was told to eat it, take it to heart, and listen closely to the Lord (Ezekiel 3). What lessons can you learn from his example? How would what you are doing in this inductive study Bible help you? What do you need to remember as you work your way through the Bible?

3. What have you learned about God and His ways from studying Ezekiel? God took Israel as His wife. Christians are espoused to Jesus Christ, their heavenly Bridegroom (2 Corinthians 11:2-3). Have you, like Israel, played the harlot spiritually and hurt God's heart (Ezekiel 6:9; James 4:4)? If so, what do you need to do? If not, what should you do so that you never do?

4. In Ezekiel 20:33 God tells Israel, "As I live...surely with a mighty hand and with an outstretched arm and with wrath poured out, I shall be king over you." Think about this verse in the light of the character and position of God and in the light of Philippians 2:5-11. Have you genuinely confessed Jesus Christ as your Lord, your King who has a right to rule over you?

5. What have you observed from marking the word *covenant*? What have you learned about the heart of stone and the Spirit dwelling within (Ezekiel 36)? Read 2 Corinthians 3 and see how this parallels what Ezekiel says. Do you have a heart of stone, or flesh? Where is the Spirit of God in relationship to you? Is He within? Read Ezekiel 36:26-27.

6. What have you learned about prophecy from Ezekiel that you could use in sharing God's Word with the Jews? What about the prophecies of Ezekiel 36–37 and the way they already are being fulfilled? And what do you learn about Israel's future in respect to Ezekiel 38–39? This is of great interest to Jews.

7. What have you learned about the holiness of God? What effect will it have on your life?

The Jewish Calendar

Babylonian names (B) for the months are still used today for the Jewish calendar. Canaanite names (C) were used prior to the Babylonian captivity in 586 B.C. Four are mentioned in the Old Testament. **Adar-Sheni** is an intercalary month used every two to three years or seven times in 19 years.

1st month	2nd month	3rd month	4th month
Nisan (B) Abib (C) March-April	Iyyar (B) Ziv (C) April-May	Sivan (B) May-June	Tammuz (B) June-July
7th month	*8th month*	*9th month*	*10th month*
5th month	**6th month**	**7th month**	**8th month**
Ab (B) July-August	Elul (B) August-September	Tishri (B) Ethanim (C) September-October	Marcheshvan (B) Bul (C) October-November
11th month	*12th month*	*1st month*	*2nd month*
9th month	**10th month**	**11th month**	**12th month**
Chislev (B) November-December	Tebeth (B) December-January	Shebat (B) January-February	Adar (B) February-March
3rd month	*4th month*	*5th month*	*6th month*

Sacred calendar appears in black • Civil calendar appears in gray

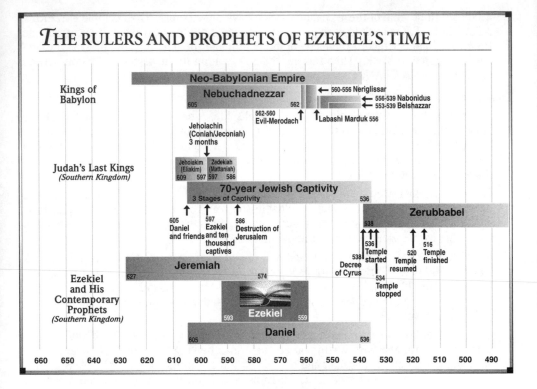

THE RULERS AND PROPHETS OF EZEKIEL'S TIME

Kings of Babylon

Neo-Babylonian Empire

Nebuchadnezzar
605 — 562

560-556 Neriglissar
556-539 Nabonidus
553-539 Belshazzar

562-560 Evil-Merodach

Labashi Marduk 556

Judah's Last Kings
(Southern Kingdom)

Jehoiachin (Coniah/Jeconiah) 3 months

Jehoiakim (Eliakim) 609 — 597

Zedekiah (Mattaniah) 597 — 586

70-year Jewish Captivity
3 Stages of Captivity — 536

605 Daniel and friends
597 Ezekiel and ten thousand captives
586 Destruction of Jerusalem

Zerubbabel
538

538 Decree of Cyrus
536 Temple started
534 Temple stopped
520 Temple resumed
516 Temple finished

Ezekiel and His Contemporary Prophets
(Southern Kingdom)

Jeremiah
627 — 574

Ezekiel
593 — 559

Daniel
605 — 536

660 650 640 630 620 610 600 590 580 570 560 550 540 530 520 510 500 490

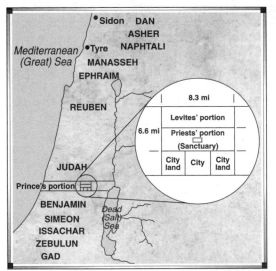

*The Tribes,
the Prince's
Portion,
the City,
the Sanctuary*

Sidon   DAN
ASHER
Mediterranean (Great) Sea   Tyre   NAPHTALI
MANASSEH
EPHRAIM
REUBEN
JUDAH
Prince's portion
BENJAMIN
SIMEON   Dead (Salt) Sea
ISSACHAR
ZEBULUN
GAD

8.3 mi
Levites' portion
6.6 mi   Priests' portion (Sanctuary)
City land | City | City land

Theme of Ezekiel:

Author:

Date:

Purpose:

Key Words:

the word of the Lord

prophesy

son of man

covenant

vision(s)

the glory of God (the Lord)

Spirit (spirit)

know that I am the Lord

iniquity (sin, abominations)

rebelled (rebellious)

sword

wrath (anger, fury)

mountain(s)

heart

harlot (harlotries, adultery)

blood

sanctuary (temple)

the day of the Lord

woe

		CHAPTER THEMES
		1
		2
		3
		4
		5
		6
		7
		8
		9
		10
		11
		12
		13
		14
		15
		16
		17
		18
		19
		20
		21
		22
		23
		24

See appendix 7 for key words in the New International Version and King James Version.

SEGMENT DIVISIONS

		CHAPTER THEMES
		25
		26
		27
		28
		29
		30
		31
		32
		33
		34
		35
		36
		37
		38
		39
		40
		41
		42
		43
		44
		45
		46
		47
		48

DANIEL דָּנִיֵּאל
DANIYYEL

*D*aniel's prophetic ministry began and ended in Babylon. When Nebuchadnezzar first besieged Jerusalem in 605 B.C., Daniel, who was about 15 years old, was among the captives taken to Babylon.

As Moses predicted, Israel lost her place of supremacy among the nations because she did not obey God. Instead of being the head, Israel became the tail to be wagged by the Gentiles (Deuteronomy 28). Yet, because the gifts and calling of God are irrevocable, when the fulness of the Gentiles is complete, all Israel will be saved, for the Deliverer will come out of Zion and take away Israel's sin (see Romans 11:25-30). All this becomes evident as the prophecies of Daniel unfold.

THINGS TO DO

What the skeleton is to the body, Daniel is to prophecy. All the other prophecies in the Old and New Testaments add flesh to Daniel's bones. If you carefully and thoroughly observe Daniel and discover exactly what the text says, you will find that Daniel's prophecies become increasingly clear and more exciting with every new observation.

General Instructions

Read through Daniel one chapter at a time. Don't hurry. Simply do the following assignment on each chapter. Record all your notes in the margin of the chapter. As you read, answer the following questions and record the answers in the margin of the text:

1. When do the events of this chapter occur? Mark every reference to time with a clock ⏰, using a distinctive color so you can see it immediately.

2. What king/kingdom is ruling at the time? Record this in the margin along with a notation of the "when" of the chapter. For instance, in the margin of chapter 1 you would put the following:

> Third year of Jehoiakim, king of Judah
> Nebuchadnezzar was king of Babylon

3. Who are the main characters in the chapter?

4. What, in general, is the chapter about?

5. Record the theme or event of the chapter on the DANIEL AT A GLANCE chart and in your Bible. Then in the margin list the key points or happenings connected with the main event of the chapter.

6. If a vision or dream is recorded, note in the margin who had the vision or dream and what the vision or dream was about. Also, if you sketch or draw the vision or dream, you will better remember and understand it.

Chapters 1–6

1. Read Daniel 1 through 6 again chapter by chapter. This time do the following:

   a. Color code every reference to God. Watch for the repeated reference to God as the "Most High" and color this also. When you gain a new insight into God's character, power, ways, or sovereignty, put a △ in the margin and record what you learned. Then meditate on how you can apply each truth to your own life.

   b. In your notebook, list everything you learn about Daniel: his character, his relationship to God and to others, and how he handles and responds to various situations.

c. Mark in a distinctive way the following key repeated words: *kingdom (dominion)*, *rules (ruler)*, *dream*, *mystery (mysteries)*, and *Nebuchadnezzar* (including pronouns). Put these on an index card and use it as a bookmark. Also watch for and mark key repeated words that appear in individual chapters. If there is room, you may want to summarize in your notebook what you learn about Nebuchadnezzar.

2. Study the historical chart on page 156. In the light of what you have observed in the text and on the chart, see if the first six chapters of Daniel come in chronological order.

Chapters 7–12

1. As you prepare to go through these final chapters of Daniel, review what you have observed in chapters 7 through 12 and what you recorded on DANIEL AT A GLANCE. Do you see any difference between the first six chapters of Daniel and the last six?

a. Are the last six chapters chronological?

b. Who had the dreams/visions in each of these major segments?

c. Record your insights to these two questions on DANIEL AT A GLANCE under "Segment Divisions." Show the chronology or lack of it on one line, and then on the other write the main theme or emphasis of these two major divisions of Daniel.

2. Read Daniel 7 through 12 again chapter by chapter. Do the following:

a. As you read each chapter mark the following key words: *vision, kingdom (empire, authority, power, dominion), horn(s), saints, man of high esteem, end (end time, appointed time, time of the end), covenant, Michael, Gabriel,* and *God*. Mark every reference to the fourth beast in Daniel 9.

b. List everything you learn about Daniel from observing the text.

Understanding the Visions and Dreams in Daniel

1. When you come to a vision, observe the details of the vision carefully. Watch the references to numbers. See if the text interprets the vision. In chapter 7, list in the margin or your notebook all that you learn about the little horn.

2. After you observe chapter 7, compare it with chapter 2.

a. If you didn't do a sketch of the vision in chapter 2, stop and do it. Then do a sketch of the vision in chapter 7. What parallels do you see? Which chapter gives more details of the events encompassed in the vision? Pay attention to those details when you sketch out the vision.

b. Mark any references to time with a clock. In biblical reckoning "time, times, and half a time" is the equivalent of 3 1/2 years. Note what precedes a period of time and what brings it to an end.

3. When you observe chapter 8, list everything you learn about the ram and the goat. In a distinctive way mark every pronoun which refers to the small horn of 8:9. Then list everything you observe from the text about this horn. Ask the "5 W's and an H": Where did it come from? What does it do and where? When does it happen? How long does it last?

4. When you observe Daniel 9:24-27, follow those verses chronologically.

a. Number from 1 to 6 in the text the six things in Daniel 9:24 that will be accomplished in 70 weeks (sevens).

b. Observe who the 70 weeks pertain to. Then in your notebook draw a line and put in the sequence of events. For example:

|Seven weeks|_____(you complete the drawing).
Decree

Note when the prophecy begins (what starts it) and what happens at each interval of time. Note what happens after the seven weeks and 62 weeks and what happens during the last week (the seventieth week) mentioned in 9:27.

c. Observe who destroys the city and the sanctuary, and their relationship to the prince who is to come in 9:27. A historical fact that might help is that Jerusalem was destroyed in A.D. 70 by Titus, a Roman general.

5. Read chapters 10–12 as one unit and then concentrate on the message and vision of chapters 11–12.

a. Mark every reference to time, including the word *then,* which shows the sequence of events.

b. Chapter 11 is not an easy chapter to understand apart from a grasp of history. It was written years before the fact, but many people are not familiar with this period of time. When you read about the kings of the south and the north, keep in mind that they are so named because of their geographical relationship to Israel, the Beautiful Land.

c. As you read through the chapter, consult the chart HISTORY OF ISRAEL'S RELATIONSHIP TO THE KINGS OF DANIEL 11 on page 155. In 11:1-35 there are approximately 135 prophetic statements, which have all been fulfilled. The accuracy of Daniel's prophecies regarding the Gentile nations and their relationship to Israel has staggered the minds of some theologians. Many even say that because of its historical accuracy, Daniel had to be written sometime after the Maccabean period in the second century B.C. However, the book of Daniel clearly refers to Daniel as the author, and so does our Lord Jesus Christ (see Matthew 24:15).

d. If you have not done so, make a list of everything you learned about the despicable person in Daniel 11:22-35. Many scholars link this description to Antiochus IV Epiphanes. To date, no person in history has yet fulfilled the description given in 11:36-45.

e. Reading *Josephus, the Essential Writings* (Kregel, 1988) will help you understand the intertestament period, the 400 silent years from Malachi to Matthew. It also gives insight into Rome's role in Israel's history and tells more about the various kings mentioned in Daniel 11:1-35, especially Antiochus IV Epiphanes.

f. Observe the transition from 11:45 to 12:1 chronologically. Mark all references to time and the events connected with them. Observe this chapter very carefully.

6. When you study the dreams and visions in Daniel, remember that Nebuchadnezzar's dream in chapter 2 gives a broad overview and that every vision that follows begins to fill in the details. Now that you have finished observing Daniel, you might want to study the chart PROPHETIC OVERVIEW OF DANIEL on page 156 and see how it compares with the text and your understanding of it.

7. Finally, determine how the book of Daniel can be segmented. Note these under "Segment Divisions" on DANIEL AT A GLANCE. Then complete the chart.

THINGS TO THINK ABOUT

1. Keeping in mind the meaning of Daniel's name, "God is my judge," think about how Daniel lived. Review what you observed of his life and character and determine to be a Daniel. You have His promise, "The people who know their God will display strength

153

and take action" (Daniel 11:32b). If you are God's child, you also have God's Spirit and His grace (John 14:17; 1 Corinthians 15:10).

2. What did Daniel know about God that would help him accept what happened to him? How does this understanding of God help you deal with the situations and circumstances of your life?

3. How does your understanding of future events help you understand and deal with what is happening in history? Have you thought about using Daniel as a tool in sharing the gospel with others? Many times prophecy will open the door when nothing else will.

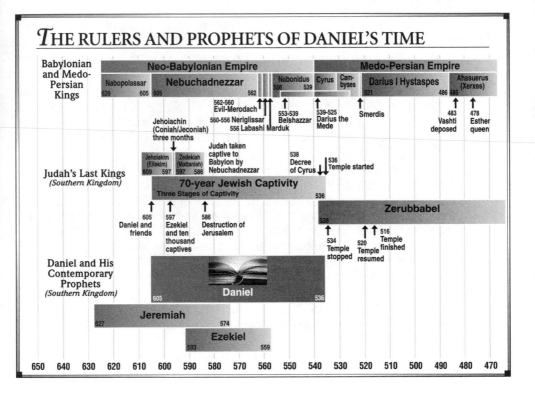

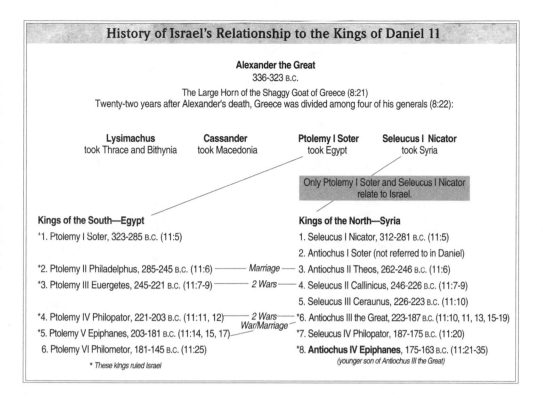

History of Israel's Relationship to the Kings of Daniel 11

Alexander the Great
336-323 B.C.

The Large Horn of the Shaggy Goat of Greece (8:21)
Twenty-two years after Alexander's death, Greece was divided among four of his generals (8:22):

Lysimachus	**Cassander**	**Ptolemy I Soter**	**Seleucus I Nicator**
took Thrace and Bithynia	took Macedonia	took Egypt	took Syria

Only Ptolemy I Soter and Seleucus I Nicator relate to Israel.

Kings of the South—Egypt

*1. Ptolemy I Soter, 323-285 B.C. (11:5)

*2. Ptolemy II Philadelphus, 285-245 B.C. (11:6) ——— Marriage ———

*3. Ptolemy III Euergetes, 245-221 B.C. (11:7-9) ——— 2 Wars ———

*4. Ptolemy IV Philopator, 221-203 B.C. (11:11, 12) — 2 Wars —
War/Marriage

*5. Ptolemy V Epiphanes, 203-181 B.C. (11:14, 15, 17)

6. Ptolemy VI Philometor, 181-145 B.C. (11:25)

* These kings ruled Israel

Kings of the North—Syria

1. Seleucus I Nicator, 312-281 B.C. (11:5)

2. Antiochus I Soter (not referred to in Daniel)

3. Antiochus II Theos, 262-246 B.C. (11:6)

4. Seleucus II Callinicus, 246-226 B.C. (11:7-9)

5. Seleucus III Ceraunus, 226-223 B.C. (11:10)

*6. Antiochus III the Great, 223-187 B.C. (11:10, 11, 13, 15-19)

*7. Seleucus IV Philopator, 187-175 B.C. (11:20)

*8. **Antiochus IV Epiphanes**, 175-163 B.C. (11:21-35)
(younger son of Antiochus III the Great)

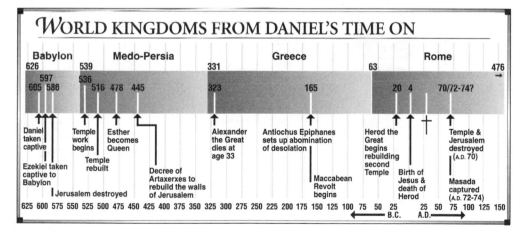

WORLD KINGDOMS FROM DANIEL'S TIME ON

Babylon 626 · 597 · 605 586 — **Medo-Persia** 539 · 536 · 516 478 445 — **Greece** 331 · 323 · 165 — **Rome** 63 · 20 4 · 70/72-74? · 476 →

Daniel taken captive

Ezekiel taken captive to Babylon

Jerusalem destroyed

Temple work begins

Temple rebuilt

Esther becomes Queen

Decree of Artaxerxes to rebuild the walls of Jerusalem

Alexander the Great dies at age 33

Antiochus Epiphanes sets up abomination of desolation

Maccabean Revolt begins

Herod the Great begins rebuilding second Temple

Birth of Jesus & death of Herod

Temple & Jerusalem destroyed (A.D. 70)

Masada captured (A.D. 72-74)

625 600 575 550 525 500 475 450 425 400 375 350 325 300 275 250 225 200 175 150 125 100 75 50 25 · 25 50 75 100 125 150
← B.C. A.D. →

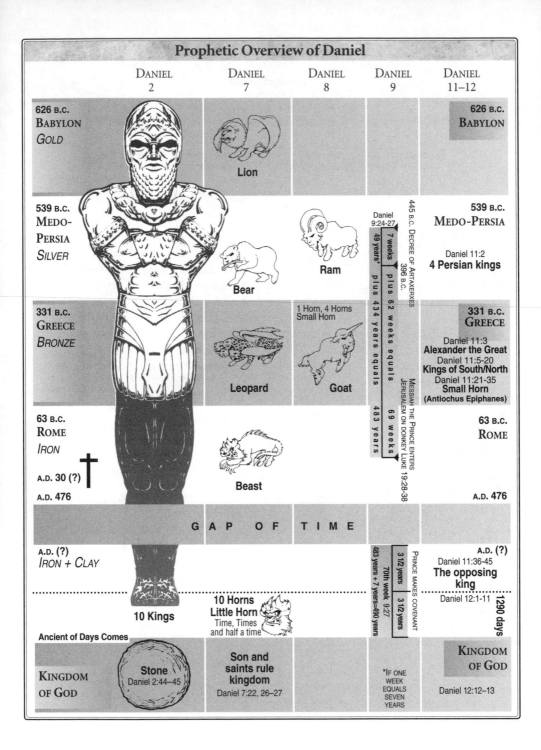

Prophetic Overview of Daniel

	DANIEL 2	DANIEL 7	DANIEL 8	DANIEL 9	DANIEL 11–12
626 B.C. BABYLON GOLD		Lion			626 B.C. BABYLON
539 B.C. MEDO-PERSIA SILVER		Bear	Ram	Daniel 9:24-27	539 B.C. MEDO-PERSIA Daniel 11:2 4 Persian kings
331 B.C. GREECE BRONZE		Leopard	1 Horn, 4 Horns Small Horn Goat		331 B.C. GREECE Daniel 11:3 Alexander the Great Daniel 11:5-20 Kings of South/North Daniel 11:21-35 Small Horn (Antiochus Epiphanes)
63 B.C. ROME IRON A.D. 30 (?) † A.D. 476		Beast			63 B.C. ROME A.D. 476
	G A P O F T I M E				
A.D. (?) IRON + CLAY		10 Kings			A.D. (?) Daniel 11:36-45 The opposing king Daniel 12:1-11
KINGDOM OF GOD	Ancient of Days Comes Stone Daniel 2:44–45	10 Horns Little Horn Time, Times and half a time Son and saints rule kingdom Daniel 7:22, 26–27		*IF ONE WEEK EQUALS SEVEN YEARS	KINGDOM OF GOD Daniel 12:12–13

445 B.C. DECREE OF ARTAXERXES

Daniel 9:24-27
49 years* — 7 weeks — 396 B.C.
plus 434 years equals — plus 62 weeks — 483 years — 69 weeks

MESSIAH THE PRINCE ENTERS JERUSALEM ON DONKEY LUKE 19:28-38

483 years + 7 years=490 years

70th week 9:27
3 1/2 years — 3 1/2 years

PRINCE MAKES COVENANT

1290 days

156

Theme of Daniel:

Author:		SEGMENT DIVISIONS			
			KINGS/ KINGDOM		CHAPTER THEMES
Date:					1
					2
Purpose:					3
					4
Key Words:					5
					6
					7
					8
					9
					10
					11
					12

See appendix 7 for key words in the New International Version and King James Version.

HOSEA ‏הושע‎
HOSHEA

Ｇod had entered into a covenant with Israel. Yet from the time of Jeroboam son of Nebat's reign through that of Jeroboam (II), son of Joash, the northern kingdom of Israel continued to play the harlot. God begged her to return to Him, but she would not listen. God's heart was grieved. If only Israel could understand; if only she could see what she was doing to the One who had betrothed her to Himself. If only she could see what her infidelity was doing to her children! Then the word of the Lord came to Hosea with a surprising message: "Go, take to yourself a wife of harlotry and have children."

THINGS TO DO

Chapters 1–3

1. The first three chapters of Hosea provide the setting for Hosea's prophetic message to the northern kingdom of Israel. Read these three chapters as you would a story; just remember it is a true story.

2. Read through Hosea 1 again. As you read:

   a. Mark every occurrence of the word *harlotry*.

   b. In your notebook, draw a simple family tree that shows whom Hosea married and the names of their children. Under each family member write a brief description of what the person was like or what his or her name meant. If your Bible has reference notes in the margin, consult them if you have problems discerning the meanings of the children's names.

   c. Observe what this chapter teaches about the sons of Israel and the sons of Judah.

3. Now go back and read the introduction, which precedes "Things to Do." Then:

   a. Read 1 Kings 11:26-40, where God tells Jeroboam what He will do after King Solomon's death. Notice why God does what He does.

   b. Read 1 Kings 12, which tells of the fulfillment of God's word to Jeroboam. This chapter describes how the kingdom of Israel was divided into the northern kingdom, consisting of ten tribes, and the southern kingdom, consisting of two tribes. Pay attention to what Jeroboam does, since the northern kingdom no longer has access to Jerusalem and the temple, where they were to worship God three times a year.

   c. Read Hosea 1:2 again and then Hosea 3:1. Watch the word *as* in 3:1.

   d. In the margin of chapter 1 write why Hosea was told by God to marry Gomer. This will help you see why chapters 1 through 3 provide the setting for Hosea's message to the northern kingdom of Israel.

4. Keeping in mind what you have seen thus far, read Hosea 2 and do the following:

   a. Mark every occurrence of the word *harlotry* and the phrase *in that day*.

   b. Check your Bible's reference notes for 2:1 and either write in the text what *Ammi* and *Ruhamah* mean or highlight the reference note.

   c. Carefully observe what the children are to say to their mother and why.

   d. Read chapters 1 and 2 and underline every occurrence of *the Lord said* or *declares the Lord*. Then highlight or mark in a distinctive way every occurrence of *I will*. Then decide who is speaking throughout chapter 2 and who the *her* and *she* refer to.

   e. Finally, read each *I will* in chapter 2. Watch the sequence of events and summarize the type of action taken in these "I wills." Also watch what happens to *her*. Record your insights in your notebook.

    f. When you come to 2:23, read your Bible's reference notes on this verse and compare this with 1:6,9; 2:1.

5. In the light of all you have seen in chapters 1 and 2, read chapter 3 and do the following:

    a. In a distinctive way mark the word *love.*

    b. Summarize in your notebook what God tells Hosea to do and why.

    c. Read 3:5 and mark *in the last days,* but before you choose how to mark it, see if you notice any parallel to *in that day* in chapter 2. If you think any of these references pertain to the day of the Lord, record your insights.

6. Write the themes of each of the first three chapters on the HOSEA AT A GLANCE chart. Then record the chapter theme in your Bible.

Chapters 4–14

1. Keeping in mind the setting of Hosea 1–3, read through Hosea 4–14 chapter by chapter. As you do:

    a. Mark in a distinctive way the following key words (with their synonyms or pronouns): *harlot (harlotry), knowledge, covenant, return, woe, iniquity (guilt, wickedness, sin).* Also mark the phrases *I will, from Me,* and *against Me (the Lord).* Write these words on an index card and use it as a bookmark.

    b. Also mark *Judah, Israel,* and *Ephraim,* each in its own distinctive way. As you do, remember that Ephraim was one of the ten tribes that comprised the northern kingdom of Israel. After Pekah took the throne in Israel, Tiglath-pileser, king of Assyria, came against him and took all of the kingdom captive in 733 B.C. except Ephraim and western Manasseh. Ten years later the remainder of the northern kingdom was completely destroyed by the Assyrians in 722 B.C. Thus Ephraim refers to what remained of Israel in those last ten years. Remember this as you read.

2. After you read a chapter and mark key words and the references to *Judah, Israel,* and *Ephraim,* compile your insights on a chart.

3. As you read through the remainder of Hosea, remember that this is a passionate discourse because of God's relationship to Israel, the relationship of a husband to his wife (Ezekiel 16; Jeremiah 3:6-8), and of a father to his children (Hosea 11:1-3; Jeremiah 31:20). Remember also that because it is passionate, there is quite a bit of repetition, but not without purpose.

4. As you finish reading each chapter, summarize the theme of each one and record it on HOSEA AT A GLANCE and in your Bible. Also, when you finish the book, decide on its theme and record it on the chart. Then fill in the remainder of the chart.

THINGS TO THINK ABOUT

In 2 Corinthians 11:2 Paul wrote, "I am jealous for you with a godly jealousy; for I betrothed you to one husband, so that to Christ I might present you as a pure virgin."

1. Are there any similarities between your relationship to Jesus Christ and Israel's relationship to God? How are you pleasing your heavenly Bridegroom? Are you breaking God's heart in any way?

2. What do you need to do?

3. How do you think God will respond, and why?

Theme of Hosea:

Segment Divisions

Author:			Chapter Themes
Date:			1
			2
Purpose:			3
			4
Key Words:			5
			6
			7
			8
			9
			10
			11
			12
			13
			14

See appendix 7 for key words in the New International Version and King James Version.

THE RULERS AND PROPHETS OF HOSEA'S TIME

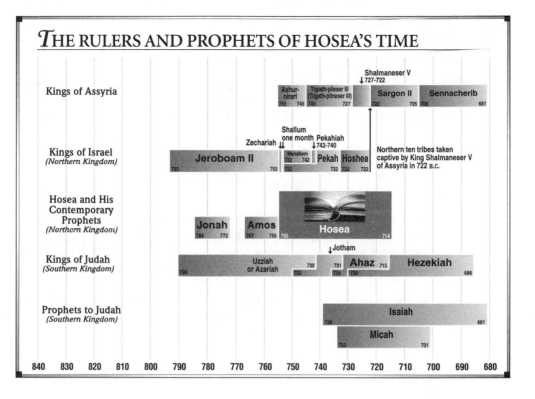

| | 840 | 830 | 820 | 810 | 800 | 790 | 780 | 770 | 760 | 750 | 740 | 730 | 720 | 710 | 700 | 690 | 680 |

JOEL 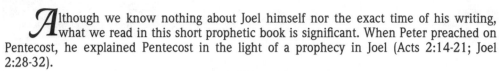 יוֹאֵל

YO'EL

*A*lthough we know nothing about Joel himself nor the exact time of his writing, what we read in this short prophetic book is significant. When Peter preached on Pentecost, he explained Pentecost in the light of a prophecy in Joel (Acts 2:14-21; Joel 2:28-32).

Joel uses a present-day plague to call God's people to repentance. As he does this, Joel, like the other prophets, warns them of the coming day of the Lord—a day that is as sure as the promises of God.

THINGS TO DO

1. Read through Joel and mark the key words listed on the JOEL AT A GLANCE chart.

2. To correctly interpret Joel, you must pay attention to the time when certain events occur. Joel switches from the present to the future. To pick this up, watch for and mark the words *then* and *now*. Mark any references to time with a clock 🕐. Also, observe the sequence of events.

3. As you read through Joel, note the following and record what you learn in the appropriate section on the JOEL OBSERVATIONS CHART on page 164.

    a. What is going to happen to the people, the land, the nations, and the animals and who or what is going to do it.

    b. What the people are to do and why.

    c. How God will respond and the effect it will have on the people.

    d. When applicable, note when any of the above will happen.

4. Although we don't know when Joel prophesied, many believe it was during the days of Joash. See the chart THE RULERS AND PROPHETS OF JOEL'S TIME on page 163.

5. Record the theme of each chapter on JOEL AT A GLANCE as well as in your Bible. Then fill in the rest of the chart. Be sure to record the theme or message of Joel.

6. The day of the Lord is an important day prophetically. Record your insights. As you do, note the reference (book, chapter, and verse) that you took your information from so you can find it later.

THINGS TO THINK ABOUT

1. What do you see happening in the world, in your nation? Could it be the judgment of the Lord? What could you and others learn from Joel's exhortations? What could you do?

2. Have you failed God in any way? According to what you have seen in Joel, is there a chance to return to Him? What could you do? How can you apply the message of Joel to your life? What do you think would happen if your church collectively repented and returned to the Lord in this manner? Think about it and ask God what to do.

Theme of Joel:

Author:

Date:

Purpose:

Key Words:

locust

Zion

day of the Lord

return

I will

never again

then

now

nations

sackcloth

Spirit

land (God's)

Segment Divisions		Chapter Themes
		1
		2
		3

See appendix 7 for key words in the New International Version and King James Version.

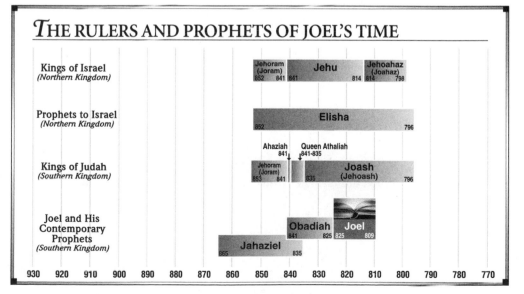

THE RULERS AND PROPHETS OF JOEL'S TIME

Kings of Israel *(Northern Kingdom)*	Jehoram (Joram) 852 · 841 | Jehu 841–814 | Jehoahaz (Joahaz) 814–798
Prophets to Israel *(Northern Kingdom)*	Elisha 852–796
Kings of Judah *(Southern Kingdom)*	Ahaziah 841 · Queen Athaliah 841–835 · Jehoram (Joram) 853–841 | Joash (Jehoash) 835–796
Joel and His Contemporary Prophets *(Southern Kingdom)*	Jahaziel 865–835 · Obadiah 841–825 · Joel 825–809

930 920 910 900 890 880 870 860 850 840 830 820 810 800 790 780 770

What Happens to the People   What the People Are to Do   What Is the Effect on People

What Happens to the Land Before and During Judgment   What Happens to the Land After Judgment

What Happens to the Animals   What God Will Do—"I will"

What Happens to the Nations and Why

The Day of the Lord

ᴬMOS עָמוֹס
AMOS

While the cows of Bashan (the best of breeds raised in Canaan) grazed and were pampered in the northern Transjordan region, the Israelites of the northern kingdom went up to worship at Bethel, burning incense and presenting their sacrifices at the altar.

Bethel was one of two places where Jeroboam son of Nebat, the first king of Israel (the northern kingdom), had set up the golden calves (see 1 Kings 12–13). He felt he had to. When the 12 tribes divided into two kingdoms, those of the northern kingdom were cut off from Jerusalem. Jerusalem now belonged to the two tribes of the southern kingdom, Judah and Benjamin. If Jeroboam's people went to celebrate the feasts in Jerusalem at the temple as God commanded, they might defect to the southern kingdom.

So Jeroboam commissioned his own priests and instituted his own feast. The people would worship as they pleased, where they pleased. Those who did not go to Bethel could go to Gilgal, another principal place of worship. In Gilgal they could present their thank offerings with leaven, proclaim their freewill offerings, and even worship other gods.

Israel became prosperous and politically secure. It was a golden era. Surely God was pleased with Israel—or that is what they supposed until a shepherd from the small city of Tekoa, just ten miles south of Jerusalem, appeared on the scene.

Then the Word of the Lord came.

THINGS TO DO

General Instructions

1. In order to understand the historical setting of Amos, do the following:
   a. Read Amos 1:1 and then record what you learn about Amos on the AMOS AT A GLANCE chart under "Author." Then under "Date" record the information that gives you a clue as to the time of these visions (see Zechariah 14:5). Under "Purpose" fill in Amos's reason for writing (see Amos 1:1).
   b. Study the historical chart on page 161, which shows Amos's relationship to the kings of Israel and Judah. Remember, Amos is a prophet to the northern kingdom.
   c. Read 2 Chronicles 26:1-23; 2 Kings 14:23–5:7. When you come across Azariah, remember that this is another name for King Uzziah, who ruled over the southern kingdom.

2. Record the key words on AMOS AT A GLANCE on an index card and use this as a bookmark. Other key words will be added in the upcoming segments. As you mark the key words, compile a list of the information you glean by examining the key word in the light of how it might answer the "5 W's and an H."

3. Observe references to God carefully. Note the extent of His sovereignty. Draw a △ in the margin of every verse that reveals God's authority and power and what He is sovereign over.

As you read through Amos, you will find three key phrases that divide the book into three segments. Therefore, your instructions will be divided accordingly.

Chapters 1–2

1. Read Amos 1 and 2 and mark each occurrence of the phrase *Thus says the Lord, for three transgressions of* _____ *and for four*. Note whose transgressions God is going to deal with in each incident.

165

2. Read what follows each of the statements you have marked. Look for another key repeated phrase and mark or color it in a distinctive way.

3. Then observe why God will not revoke their punishment and what the punishment will be. Note their punishment by marking each occurrence of *I will*.

4. In 2:4,6 God deals with the southern kingdom, Judah, and with the northern kingdom, Israel. To understand why God speaks to them separately, look at Amos 1:1 and notice to whom Amos was sent as a prophet (see the chart on page 161). Keep this in mind as you study Amos.

5. Record the theme of the first two chapters on AMOS AT A GLANCE and in your Bible.

Chapters 3–6

1. The second key repeated phrase is *hear this word.* Read Amos 3–6 and distinctively mark each occurrence of this phrase.

2. Read Amos 3–6 a second time. As you read these messages from the Lord, ask the "5 W's and an H." Ask questions such as: Who is speaking? To whom? What is being said? What is going to happen? When will it happen? Where will it take place? Why will it happen? How will it happen? (Remember, you won't always find answers to every question.)

3. Mark key repeated words or phrases. Marking every *I will* as it refers to God and asking the "5 W's and an H" will help you see what God is going to do. Watch for *yet* and *returned* in chapter 4 and *seek* in chapter 5. Mark every reference to *the day of the Lord* and record your insights on the chart "The Day of the Lord" we suggested in "Getting Started" on page 25.

4. In your notebook, list important insights about God, Israel, what the people are doing wrong, and what they don't like.

5. Record the chapter themes as you have done previously.

Chapters 7–9

1. The key repeated phrase that sets off the last segment of Amos is *thus the Lord God showed me.* Read these last three chapters and mark each occurrence of this phrase.

2. As you read through this final segment of Amos, watch what Amos was shown and how he responds. Also observe the response to Amos's prophecy and how Amos deals with this.

3. In chapter 8 you see one final *hear this.* Pay careful attention to what God is going to do. Compare 8:8 with 1:1.

4. Although the phrase *thus the Lord God showed me* is not used in 9:1, can you see that *I saw the Lord...and He said* could be Amos's fifth vision, which parallels those you marked in chapters 7 and 8? If so, mark it as you did the others.

5. Mark the *I will's* of God and any other key words or phrases.

6. Record the chapter themes along with the theme of Amos.

7. Record your insights from Amos on the day of the Lord.

8. Finally, watch how the book of Amos closes. What is God's promise? Recall any reference to the land. Has this promise regarding the land of Israel been fulfilled? Think of Israel's history.

THINGS TO THINK ABOUT

1. Has wealth, the ease of life, the possession of things, the pursuit of happiness led to complacency in your worship? Are you worshiping God His way or your way?

2. Review the list of Israel's sins. Are you guilty of any of these? According to what you read in Amos, could Israel or the other nations sin and not reap the consequences? Can you?

3. What is the purpose of God's judgments? When God decides to judge, what can we do? What can we expect?

THE RULERS AND PROPHETS OF AMOS'S TIME

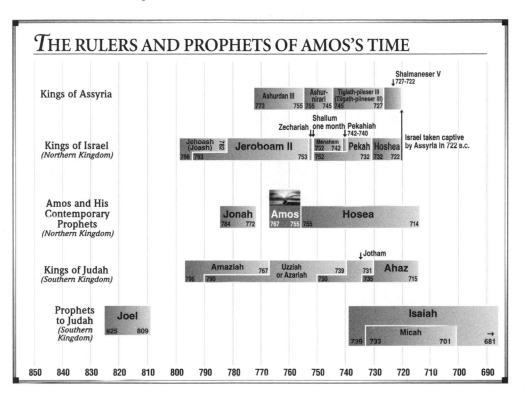

Theme of Amos:

Segment Divisions

		Chapter Themes
		1
		2
		3
		4
		5
		6
		7
		8
		9

Author:

Date:

Purpose:

Key Words:

Amos

Israel

land

nations (other than Israel)

Edom

covenant

any reference to the name of the Lord

any reference to famine

See appendix 7 for key words in the New International Version and King James Version.

OBADIAH עֹבַדְיָה
O V A D Y A

*G*od said that whoever touched Israel touched the apple (pupil) of His eye. According to Obadiah 1:10-14, Edom had touched God's eye.

Scholars are divided about whether the incident referred to in these verses occurred during the reign of Jehoram (853–841 B.C.), when the Philistines and the Arabs invaded Jerusalem, or during Babylon's sieges of Jerusalem (between 605 and 586 B.C.). However, the exact date is not critical to the message of the book. What we do know is that in both instances Edom did not respond as God wanted, and thus came this report through "the Lord's servant," which is the meaning of Obadiah's name.

THINGS TO DO

1. Read this book once without stopping in order to get an overview of Obadiah's message.

2. Read through Obadiah again, and in a distinctive way mark the key words (along with their synonyms and pronouns) listed on the OBADIAH AT A GLANCE chart.

3. Remember that Jacob and Esau were brothers, born to Rebekah and Isaac. If you want to refresh your memory, read Genesis 27:1–28:9; 32:1–33:20; Romans 9:10-13; and Numbers 20:14-21. Genesis 36 gives the genealogy of Esau and says, "Esau is Edom." It also names Esau as the father of the Edomites.

Although the people of Edom (descendants of Esau) and Israel (descendants of Jacob) are related (Amos 1:11-12), biblical history records many conflicts between them. Look at a map and notice the proximity of Edom to Israel. Edom was a constant threat to Israel, repeatedly thwarting the nation and blocking Judah's access to the Gulf of Elat (Aqaba).

4. Now read through Obadiah again, asking the "5 W's and an H." Ask questions such as: Who is speaking? To whom? Why? What is the message? What is going to happen? To whom? How? Summarize your observations in the margin of the text.

5. Look at a map and find the Negev and the other places mentioned at the end of Obadiah. These are real lands and real people, and what God says will happen to them *will* happen.

6. Since Obadiah is just one chapter, record the theme (subject) of each paragraph on OBADIAH AT A GLANCE and then fill in the rest of the chart, including the theme of Obadiah.

7. The day of the Lord is an important day prophetically. Record your insights on the day of the Lord on the DAY OF THE LORD chart we suggested in "Getting Started," page 25.

THINGS TO THINK ABOUT

1. Sometimes when tragic and unjust things happen, we wonder where God is. If He is righteous, just, and omnipotent, why doesn't He intervene? What do you learn from Obadiah that helps answer these questions? What can you learn from this for your own life?

2. How should we respond to the tragedies of others, the dark hours of our enemies? What does God think when we use their tragedy to our advantage?

Theme of Obadiah:

SEGMENT DIVISIONS

		PARAGRAPH THEMES
		VERSES 1-9
		VERSES 10-14
		VERSES 15-21

Author:

Date:

Purpose:

Key Words:

the day

day of the Lord

Edom (Esau)

Jacob (Judah)

the nations

Mount Zion (My holy mountain)

declares the Lord (or any phrase having to do with the Lord speaking or reporting)

See appendix 7 for key words in the New International Version and King James Version.

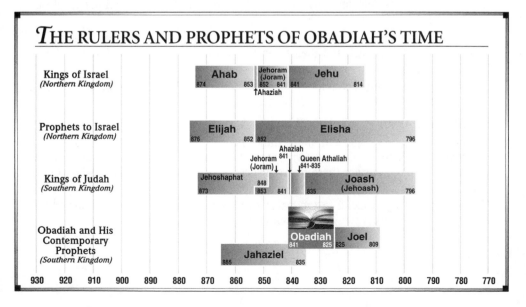

THE RULERS AND PROPHETS OF OBADIAH'S TIME

Kings of Israel (Northern Kingdom)
Ahab 874 — 853 | Jehoram (Joram) 852 841 | Jehu 841 — 814
↑Ahaziah

Prophets to Israel (Northern Kingdom)
Elijah 876 — 852 | Elisha 852 — 796

Kings of Judah (Southern Kingdom)
Jehoshaphat 873 — 853 | Jehoram (Joram) 848 841 | Ahaziah 841 | Queen Athaliah 841-835 | Joash (Jehoash) 835 — 796

Obadiah and His Contemporary Prophets (Southern Kingdom)
Jahaziel 865 — 835 | Obadiah 841 825 | Joel 825 809

930 920 910 900 890 880 870 860 850 840 830 820 810 800 790 780 770

*J*ONAH יוֹנָה
YONA

*J*ust before God commissioned Amos and Hosea as prophets to the northern kingdom to warn Israel of the impending invasion by the Assyrians, He appointed the prophet Jonah to go to Nineveh, the capital of Assyria. Yet 50 years later, in 722 B.C., Assyria would take the last portion of the northern kingdom into captivity.

God knew what Assyria would do. Why, then, did He bother to send Jonah to the wicked city of Nineveh? Because of who God is. The focus of Jonah is not a man trapped in the belly of a great fish; the focus is people engraved on the heart of God.

THINGS TO DO

1. Before you read through Jonah, look up 2 Kings 14:23-27, which mentions Jonah and his ministry during the reign of Jeroboam II son of Joash, king of Israel. At that time Shalmaneser IV was king of Assyria.

2. In a distinctive way mark the key words listed on the JONAH AT A GLANCE chart. Double-underline in green every geographical reference. Mark all references to time with a clock ⏲.

3. What you learn about God in this book is awesome. As you mark the references to Him, you might want to put a triangle in the margin of the text noting what God does.

4. Record the theme of each chapter on JONAH AT A GLANCE and in your Bible next to the chapter number. Then fill in the rest of the chart.

THINGS TO THINK ABOUT

1. What or who evokes compassion in your heart? Contrast Jonah's heart with God's heart. How does your heart compare with God's? Does it long for the same things? Why?

2. Is there something that you know God wants you to do that you haven't done? What can you learn from Jonah's life?

3. How did Jesus view the story of Jonah? Read Matthew 12:39-41; 16:4. Will you accept as truth what Jesus accepted as fact—or did Jesus compare His resurrection to a mythological tale?

Theme of Jonah:

Author:

Date:

Purpose:

Key Words:

Jonah

compassion
(compassionate,
concerned)

relent(s)

turn (turned)

pray (any refer-
ence to prayer
or calling out
to God)

perish *(die)*

Lord (God)

appointed

anger (angry)

calamity
(and synonyms)

Segment Divisions		Chapter Themes
		1
		2
		3
		4

See appendix 7 for key words in the New International Version and King James Version.

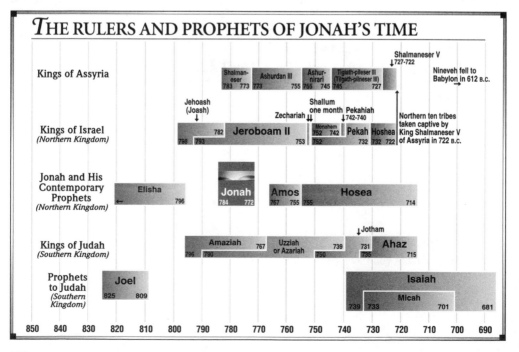

THE RULERS AND PROPHETS OF JONAH'S TIME

Kings of Assyria
Shalman-eser 783 773 | Ashurdan III 773 755 | Ashur-nirari 755 745 | Tiglath-pileser III (Tilgath-pilneser III) 745 727 | Shalmaneser V 727-722 | Nineveh fell to Babylon in 612 B.C.

Kings of Israel *(Northern Kingdom)*
Jehoash (Joash) | 798 793 782 Jeroboam II 753 | Zechariah | Shallum one month | Menahem 752 742 | Pekahiah 742-740 | Pekah 752 732 | Hoshea 732 722 | Northern ten tribes taken captive by King Shalmaneser V of Assyria in 722 B.C.

Jonah and His Contemporary Prophets *(Northern Kingdom)*
Elisha 796 | Jonah 784 772 | Amos 767 755 | Hosea 755 714

Kings of Judah *(Southern Kingdom)*
Amaziah 796 790 767 | Uzziah or Azariah 750 739 | Jotham 731 735 | Ahaz 715

Prophets to Judah *(Southern Kingdom)*
Joel 825 809 | Isaiah 681 | Micah 739 733 701

850 840 830 820 810 800 790 780 770 760 750 740 730 720 710 700 690

MICAH מִיכָה
MIKHA

*M*icah knew his calling and was ready to fulfill it, for Micah knew his God. What a contrast he is to the prophet Jonah! Micah, whose name means "who is like Jehovah," reminds a rebellious people that "the LORD is coming forth from *His* place."

THINGS TO DO

1. Micah 1:1 gives the historical setting of Micah. Read it carefully and answer as many of the "5 W's and an H" as you can concerning the who, when, where, why, what, and how of this book.

The reigns of Jotham, Ahaz, and Hezekiah, three kings of Judah, cover the years 750–686 B.C. Remember that Assyria conquered the northern kingdom in 722 B.C. and Babylon destroyed the southern kingdom in 586 B.C.

2. For the historical background of the kings of Judah mentioned in Micah 1:1, read 2 Kings 15:32–20:21 and 2 Chronicles 27:1–33:20.

3. Read through Micah to get an overview of the book. It divides into three messages, each of which starts with "hear" or "hear now." Mark Micah 1:2; 3:2; 6:1. Study the book accordingly.

4. Read one chapter of Micah at a time or, if you prefer, one message at a time. As you observe the text of each chapter:

   a. Mark the key words listed (with their synonyms and pronouns) on the MICAH AT A GLANCE chart. You will find it helpful to record these on an index card that you can use as a bookmark while you study Micah.

   b. Mark references to time with a clock ⏱, such as *when, then, in that day, in the last days*.

   c. Since Micah's prophecy concerns Samaria (representing the northern kingdom of Israel) and Jerusalem (representing the southern kingdom of Judah), next to the word *Samaria* in Micah 1:1 write "NK" for northern kingdom. Next to the word *Jerusalem* write "SK" for southern kingdom.

   As you observe the text, watch which kingdom Micah is referring to. Observe what is said regarding their sins, the consequences of their sin, their future, and the remnant. If it will help, list your insights in your notebook.

   d. Watch what God is going to do and to whom. Always note to whom Micah is referring.

   e. List everything you learn about Micah and what he is to do.

   f. Record the theme or subject of each chapter in your Bible and on MICAH AT A GLANCE. When you finish the last chapter of Micah, complete the chart.

5. Record your insights from Micah on the last days if you think these pertain to the day of the Lord.

THINGS TO THINK ABOUT

1. Review what you have learned about God the Father and the Son in this book. Meditate on these truths. Tell God you want to know Him more intimately and ask Him to open the eyes of your understanding. Ask Him to show you how to live in light of who He is.

2. Micah 4:12 says the nations do not know the thoughts of the Lord, nor do they understand His purpose. Yet the child of God can know these things through studying His Word. Amos said, "Surely the Lord GOD does nothing unless He reveals His secret

counsel to His servants the prophets" (3:7). God's secret counsel and His plan for the future is in the Word of God. Are you ordering your life in such a way that you take time to study His Word?

3. What have you learned about the unchanging love and compassion of God in pardoning your sins? Are you living accordingly?

4. Although you may not be able to trust in others, can you trust in God? Are you trusting Him? Can He trust you? In Micah 6:6-8 God tells you how to approach Him and what He requires. Will you live accordingly?

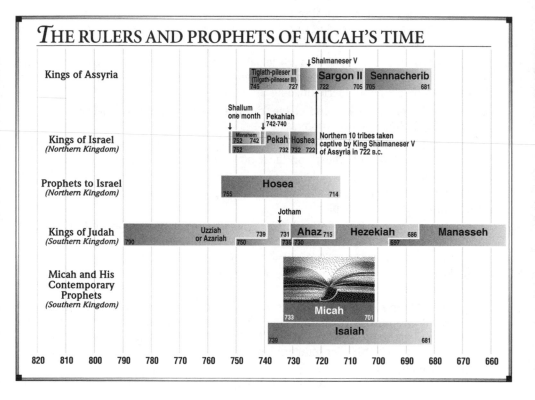

THE RULERS AND PROPHETS OF MICAH'S TIME

Theme of Micah:

SEGMENT DIVISIONS

Author:

CHAPTER THEMES

Date:

		1
		2
		3
		4
		5
		6
		7

Purpose:

Key Words:
- Samaria
- Jerusalem
- Jacob
- Israel
- Judah
- Zion
- destroy(ed) (destruction)
- remnant
- in that day (in the last days)
- My (Your, His) people
- woe
- sin (iniquity, evil, rebellious acts)

See appendix 7 for key words in the New International Version and King James Version.

NAHUM נחום
NACHUM

One hundred years had passed since Jonah went to Nineveh to proclaim its destruction. Now another prophet, Nahum, proclaims his vision from God regarding Nineveh, the capital of Assyria. What a sharp contrast between Nahum's prophetic message and the meaning of his name—comforter!

Assyria sat smugly on her throne. Assyria had conquered Israel in 722 B.C. In 701 B.C., under Sennacherib's rule, the Assyrians had invaded Judah. Rabshakeh, Sennacherib's general, had boasted to Judah that none of the gods of the nations they had conquered had been able to deliver their people. To Hezekiah, king of Judah, he proclaimed, "Do not let your God in whom you trust deceive you saying, 'Jerusalem will not be given into the hand of the king of Assyria.' Behold, you have heard what the kings of Assyria have done to all the lands, destroying them completely. So will you be spared?" (2 Kings 19:10-11).

But God did spare Judah. Sennacherib, king of Assyria, returned to Nineveh and died there.

Yet that wasn't the end of the story. God had a message for Nineveh, the capital of Assyria, who at the time of Nahum's prophecy sat at the pinnacle of wealth and power, secure behind her impregnable walls. Or so she thought.

THINGS TO DO

1. If you have time, read Jonah to see what God said to the people of Nineveh 100 years earlier and how they responded.

2. Begin your study by reading through Nahum and marking every reference to *Nineveh* (pronouns and synonyms such as "wicked one", or "bloody city") in a distinctive color or way. Sometimes you will find it difficult to discern who the "you" refers to—Nineveh or someone else such as Jacob in 2:1. Do not mark the text until you are sure.

3. Study the historical chart on the next page to see the context of the book.

4. Read Nahum chapter by chapter and do the following:

   a. Mark each in its own distinctive way the following two phrases: "I am against you" and "I will."

   b. Many believe chapter 2:3-12 is a prophetic discription of Nineveh's destruction by the Babylonians under Nabopolassar in 612 BC. The description of the warriors fits historically with the military attire of the Babylonians.

   c. Nahum tells us much about God. Carefully observe the text and then in the margin summarize what you learn about God. For instance, 1:4 tells us that God rules over nature. Write that in your list in the margin under the title "God" or the symbol △.

   d. Look at every place you marked *Nineveh.* List in your notebook what you learn from marking these references.

5. Record the theme or subject of each chapter on NAHUM AT A GLANCE and in your Bible. Also, record the theme of the book and complete any other information requested on the chart.

THINGS TO THINK ABOUT

1. What do you learn about the justice of God and the certainty of His Word from this book? Is this the kind of God you can trust? Why?

2. Is there anything that can stop God from doing what He says or plans?

3. Can compassionate people deliver this kind of message? What if you were impressed by God to bring this kind of warning to others? Would you? What would motivate you or hinder you? By the way, remember the meaning of Nahum's name.

NAHUM AT A GLANCE

Theme of Nahum:

SEGMENT DIVISIONS

		CHAPTER THEMES	Author:
		1	Date:
		2	Purpose:
		3	Key Words: I am against you I will Nineveh (and all references to it)

See appendix 7 for key words in the New International Version and King James Version.

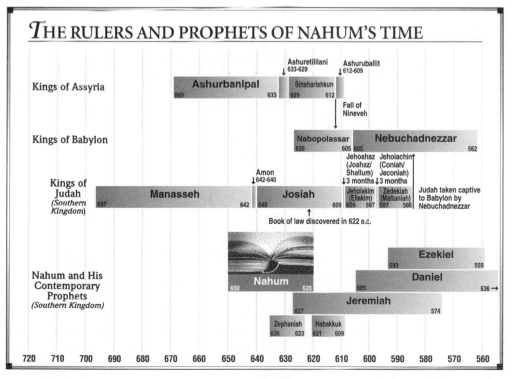

THE RULERS AND PROPHETS OF NAHUM'S TIME

HABAKKUK חֲבַקּוּק
CHAVAQQUQ

"The righteous will live by his faith." This verse, which pierced Martin Luther's heart and as a result brought about a reformation, comes from Habakkuk 2:4. Paul echoed it in Romans and Galatians, but its roots are in the Old Testament, where God affirms that salvation has always been by faith and faith alone.

And what is the setting of the verse that unshackled Luther and brought him into a vital relationship with the living God? You will discover this as you study Habakkuk, a book that ends with a crescendo of faith even in anticipation of Judah's darkest of hours.

THINGS TO DO

General Instructions

As you read Habakkuk it is critical for you to know whether God is speaking or Habakkuk. Since the book is only three chapters long, read through Habakkuk and note in the margin when God speaks or when Habakkuk speaks. Try it on your own and then look at the HABAKKUK AT A GLANCE chart for the segment divisions, which show who is speaking when.

Chapter 1

1. An "oracle" can be translated "a burden." What is Habakkuk's burden; what is bothering him? Mark the key repeated word *why* and you'll discover the answer.

2. Read through Habakkuk 1 and mark every reference to *Habakkuk* in one color and every reference to the *Lord* (including personal pronouns) in another color. Then observe (and list, if you want) everything you learn about the Lord as a personality and what He is going to do.

3. The Chaldeans, another name for the Babylonians, invaded the southern kingdom of Judah three times. In 605 B.C., Daniel and many nobles were taken captive. Then in 597 B.C., Ezekiel and 10,000 others were taken captive. The final siege occurred from 588 to 586 B.C., when Jerusalem and the temple were destroyed. Mark every reference to the *Chaldeans*—and observe what they will do and what will happen to them. Also, from this point onward, mark *nations.*

4. Study the historical chart on the next page and notice the relationship between the time of Habakkuk's writing and the Babylonian invasion.

Chapter 2

1. Mark every reference, including pronouns, to the *proud* or *haughty man.* Then in your notebook, list what he is like and with whom he is contrasted.

2. Mark each use of *woe* and observe to whom the woe is going to come, why it will come, and what will happen when it comes. If you want to, summarize this in your notebook.

3. Mark every reference to the *Lord* and record in the margin any new insights about Him.

Chapter 3

1. Habakkuk's prayer is an intensely emotional poem. A statement is made and is followed by a similar statement that heightens the meaning or repeats the truth in another way. Read the prayer again, keeping its form in mind.

178

2. As you read, ask the "5 W's and an H": Who is doing what? To whom or what? When will it be done? Why will it be done? What specifically is going to happen? How? Observe everything you learn about the Lord from this chapter.

3. What does this chapter say about Habakkuk and his relationship to God? Record this in your notebook. Then compare what you write with 2:4. How is Habakkuk going to live? Have his circumstances changed?

4. Fill in the appropriate sections of HABAKKUK AT A GLANCE, recording the theme of each paragraph, each chapter, and the book itself. Fill in any other information asked for on the chart. Also record the theme of each chapter in your Bible.

THINGS TO THINK ABOUT

1. What do you learn about God—His ways, His Word, His character? If He is the same yesterday, today, and forever, how would such insight into God influence your relationship to Him and to His Word? How would this affect your response to your circumstances?

2. What have you learned about the haughty or proud? God says in James 4 that He resists the proud. Can you understand why? Can you see any element of pride or haughtiness in your life that you need to deal with?

3. Review what you learned about the woes pronounced by God. Ask God to search your heart. Would these woes be applicable to you because of your lifestyle? Do you need to confess anything to God and receive His forgiveness and cleansing (see 1 John 1:9)?

4. As you look at how Habakkuk begins and ends, think about what effected the difference in Habakkuk and then apply it to your own life. Are you questioning or doubting God and His ways, and is it causing despair? What do you need to do?

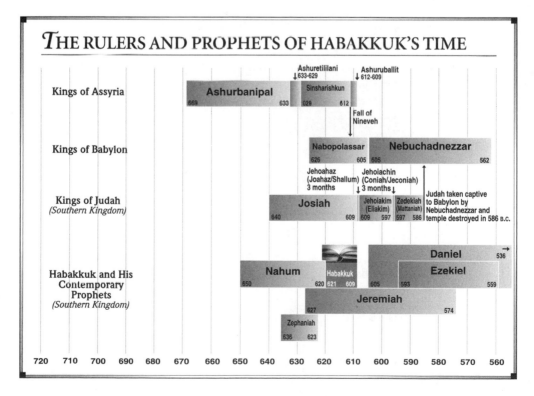

THE RULERS AND PROPHETS OF HABAKKUK'S TIME

Theme of Habakkuk:

SEGMENT DIVISIONS

	WHO IS SPEAKING	PARAGRAPH THEMES	CHAPTER THEMES	
	HABAKKUK SPEAKS	1:1-4	1	*Author:*
	GOD SPEAKS	1:5-11		*Date:*
	HABAKKUK SPEAKS	1:12-17		*Purpose:*
		2:1-3	2	*Key Words:*
	GOD SPEAKS	2:4-5		
		2:6-8		
		2:9-11		
		2:12-14		
		2:15-17		
		2:18-20		
	HABAKKUK PRAYS	3:1-2	3	
		3:3-7		
		3:8-15		
		3:16-19		

See appendix 7 for key words in the New International Version and King James Version.

ZEPHANIAH צְפַנְיָה
TZFANYA

*D*uring the latter years of King Josiah's reign, Israel was a spiritual oasis surrounded by apostasy—the abandonment of faith.

We do not know exactly when Zephaniah's prophecy came, although it was during Josiah's reign (640–609 B.C.). However, some argument can be made from the text that Zephaniah's prophecy motivated Josiah's reforms. In 2 Chronicles 34:3 we read "in the eighth year of his (Josiah's) reign (about 632 B.C.) while he was still a youth, he began to seek the God of his father David; and in the twelfth year he began to purge Judah and Jerusalem…" In 622 B.C., the book of the Law was found in the house of God. Whenever Zephaniah's prophecy came, it came full gale, a stormy blast calling God's people to humility and righteousness in the face of the day of the Lord's anger.

THINGS TO DO

1. Zephaniah 1:1 gives the genealogy of Zephaniah and also the historical setting of the book. Record your insights about the author on the ZEPHANIAH AT A GLANCE chart. If you want a more thorough picture of the historical setting of Zephaniah, read 2 Kings 22:1–23:30 and 2 Chronicles 34:1–35:27.

2. Consult the historical chart on the next page to see the relationship of his prophecy to the Babylonian captivity and the destruction of Nineveh.

3. Read Zephaniah paragraph by paragraph, watching carefully for the references to the different peoples and places. Double-underline in green every reference to the various peoples and cities (Moab, Ammon, etc.). Note what is said about each one.

   a. Be careful to note when there is a change of subject. Watch carefully what happens in 3:1. Although Jerusalem is not mentioned by name at the beginning of chapter 3, the prophecy changes from Nineveh (the Assyrian capital) to Jerusalem.

   b. Decide on the theme or subject covered in each paragraph and record this under "Paragraph Themes" on ZEPHANIAH AT A GLANCE.

4. Now read Zephaniah chapter by chapter and mark the key words listed on ZEPHANIAH AT A GLANCE.

   a. Watch for any other key words as you read chapter by chapter and mark these.

   b. As you mark *the day*, *in* or *on that day*, and *the day of the Lord* notice what will happen in that day and how it relates, if at all, to the day of the Lord. (Remember, prophecy can have a near and a distant fulfillment. If you are not familiar with interpreting prophecy, you can read "Guidelines for Interpreting Predictive Prophecy" on page 325.)

   c. Note what God will do, to whom, and why. Also note what effect it will have on Israel.

5. Record what you learn about the day of the Lord on the chart we suggested in "Getting Started," page 25.

6. Fill in ZEPHANIAH AT A GLANCE. Record the theme of each chapter and of the book in the designated spaces. Then record the chapter theme in your Bible.

THINGS TO THINK ABOUT

1. The day of the Lord is also mentioned in the New Testament. One such reference is

181

in 1 Thessalonians 5:1-11. If the day of the Lord is yet future, what should you be doing to prepare for the time of its approaching?

2. What do you learn about the nation of Israel and its future? Are you using these truths in sharing the good news of Jesus Christ with God's people, the Jews?

3. Think about what you have learned about God from Zephaniah and how such knowledge should affect the way you live.

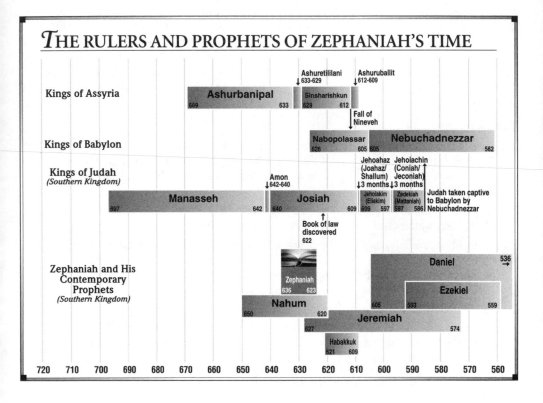

THE RULERS AND PROPHETS OF ZEPHANIAH'S TIME

Kings of Assyria
Ashurbanipal 669–633
Sinsharishkun 629–612
Ashuretililani ↓633-629
Ashuruballit ↓612-609
Fall of Nineveh

Kings of Babylon
Nabopolassar 626–605
Nebuchadnezzar 605–562

Kings of Judah *(Southern Kingdom)*
Manasseh 697–642
Amon ↓642-640
Josiah 640–609
Book of law discovered 622
Jehoahaz (Joahaz/ Shallum) ↓3 months
Jehoiachin (Coniah/ Jeconiah) ↓3 months
Jehoiakim (Eliakim) 609–597
Zedekiah (Mattaniah) 597–586
Judah taken captive to Babylon by Nebuchadnezzar

Zephaniah and His Contemporary Prophets *(Southern Kingdom)*
Zephaniah 636–623
Nahum 650–620
Jeremiah 627–574
Habakkuk 621–609
Daniel 605–536
Ezekiel 593–559

720 710 700 690 680 670 660 650 640 630 620 610 600 590 580 570 560

Theme of Zephaniah:

SEGMENT
DIVISIONS

	PARAGRAPH THEMES	CHAPTER THEMES
	1:1-6	1
	1:7-13	
	1:14-18	
	2:1-3	2
	2:4-7	
	2:8-11	
	2:12-15	
	3:1-7	3
	3:8-13	
	3:14-20	

Author:

Date:

Purpose:

Key Words:

I will (the Lord will, He will)

the day of the Lord (the day, in or on that day)

remnant (remainder)

every reference to God's people, nation (daughters of Zion)

nations (kingdoms, peoples)

desolation, destruction

in your midst

woe

seek

anger

all the earth (face of the earth)

Assyria (and Nineveh)

See appendix 7 for key words in the New International Version and King James Version.

183

HAGGAI חַגַּי

Discouragement reigned. Only a remnant returned to Jerusalem after the 70 years of exile—a small remnant in comparison to the number of people taken captive. Many Jews were reluctant to leave Babylon to return to Jerusalem. The land of their captors had become home. The Babylonians had allowed them to establish businesses and build houses. Their children, while born in captivity, were secure. Why should they leave?

It was a small remnant that returned to rebuild the temple, which soon became a discouraging task. Their zeal dwindled. What was begun enthusiastically was forgotten before God's house was completed. For about 16 years the temple stood unfinished and ignored.

Then about 520 B.C., the word of the Lord came to Haggai.

THINGS TO DO

1. Read through the book of Haggai once, and then read it again and mark in a distinctive color every occurrence of the word *people* (the people in general), including the appropriate pronouns. Also, mark every reference to *the house of the Lord,* also called *the temple*.

2. Having done that, did you notice a pattern to the book of Haggai? Read through the text again and mark with the symbol of a clock Ⓛ every reference to specific dates as seen in 1:1,15 and 2:1,10,20. The sacred portion of the Jewish calendar on page 185 can help you see the "when" of the message.

3. Now read Haggai again and, in a distinctive way, mark every occurrence of the phrases *the word of the Lord came by the prophet Haggai, the word of the Lord came by Haggai the prophet,* and *Haggai, the messenger of the Lord spoke by commission of the Lord.* When you finish, you will see that Haggai is a series of messages.

4. Now read Haggai, one message at a time.

   a. As you do, mark the key words listed on the HAGGAI AT A GLANCE chart, along with their synonyms and pronouns.

   b. After you have read each message and marked key words, observe the content of each message by asking the "5 W's and an H." Ask: What is the specific message, and to whom was it given? What has happened? To whom? Why? What is going to happen? What are they to believe or do? Summarize and record what you learn about each message in the section for "Paragraph Themes" on HAGGAI AT A GLANCE.

   c. Observe what you learn from marking *Lord of hosts,* with the appropriate pronouns, *people, temple, consider,* and *shake.* It would be good to make a list of what you observe about each.

5. To get the historical setting of Haggai, read Ezra 4:24–6:22. Then study the two charts on the next page. The first gives the historical setting of Haggai. Note who Darius is, and note that Darius is mentioned in Haggai. Also note when the temple work started and stopped under Ezra and when it resumed under Haggai.

6. Complete HAGGAI AT A GLANCE. Record the theme of each chapter in the appropriate places. Then record the chapter theme in your Bible next to the chapter number. Finally, write out the theme of the book and fill in any other information needed.

THINGS TO THINK ABOUT

1. Have you given too much attention and time to your personal affairs and needs but neglected the things of God that are important for the spreading of the gospel or the furtherance of His work?

2. What might God be trying to say when cataclysmic events take place? Do you take advantage of these things to turn people's attention and thoughts to God?

3. When discouraged in your service to God, do you quit, or do you courageously persevere, determined to be faithful and to leave the outcome to God?

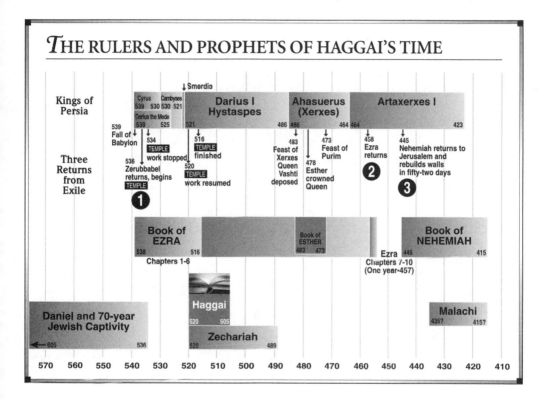

THE RULERS AND PROPHETS OF HAGGAI'S TIME

The Jewish Calendar

Babylonian names (B) for the months are still used today for the Jewish calendar. Canaanite names (C) were used prior to the Babylonian captivity in 586 B.C. Four are mentioned in the Old Testament.
Adar-Sheni is an intercalary month used every two to three years or seven times in 19 years.

1st month	2nd month	3rd month	4th month
Nisan (B) Abib (C) March-April	Iyyar (B) Ziv (C) April-May	Sivan (B) May-June	Tammuz (B) June-July
7th month	*8th month*	*9th month*	*10th month*
5th month	**6th month**	**7th month**	**8th month**
Ab (B) July-August	Elul (B) August-September	Tishri (B) Ethanim (C) September-October	Marcheshvan (B) Bul (C) October-November
11th month	*12th month*	*1st month*	*2nd month*
9th month	**10th month**	**11th month**	**12th month**
Chislev (B) November-December	Tebeth (B) December-January	Shebat (B) January-February	Adar (B) February-March
3rd month	*4th month*	*5th month*	*6th month*
Sacred calendar appears in black • Civil calendar appears in gray			

185

Theme of Haggai:

SEGMENT
DIVISIONS

	PARAGRAPH THEMES	CHAPTER THEMES	
	1:1-11	1	*Author:*
	1:12-15		*Date:*
	2:1-9	2	*Purpose:*
	2:10-19		*Key Words:*
	2:20-23		

Author:

Date:

Purpose:

Key Words:

people

the house of the Lord (the temple)

Lord of hosts

consider

shake

See appendix 7 for key words in the New International Version and King James Version.

ZECHARIAH זְכַרְיָה
ZEKHARYA

*T*he earth was peaceful and quiet. All the nations were at rest...except for Israel. From Israel's perspective, it looked as if God had abandoned His people and forgotten His holy city, Jerusalem. Jerusalem's walls were torn down, Solomon's temple had been destroyed, and now a partially rebuilt temple stood on its site. Even if this temple were to be completed, it would not begin to equal Solomon's.

The majority of God's people had settled in their land of exile and were reluctant to return to Jerusalem. Only a remnant had come back, and they were a discouraged lot who soon abandoned the rebuilding of the house of God. But then the word of the Lord came—first through Haggai and then Zechariah.

Born in Babylon, Zechariah was among the remnant who returned to Jerusalem under the leadership of Zerubbabel and Joshua. Although he belonged to the priestly line, Zechariah, like Haggai his predecessor, was to be God's prophet to the discouraged remnant.

And so, about 520 to 519 B.C., the word of the Lord came to Zechariah—a needed word, an encouraging word...a word for the future, a word of hope.

THINGS TO DO

General Instructions

If you are going to have a good understanding of Zechariah, it will help to put the book into its historical context. Although this will take extra study, it will be worthwhile.

Ezra gives the historical setting of Zechariah; therefore, if you have not studied Ezra, read it before you start Zechariah. Ezra, like Zechariah, is a post-exilic book, which simply means it was written after the Jews were in exile under the Babylonians (Chaldeans). Ezra records the return of a remnant to Jerusalem under the reign and decree of Cyrus, a Persian king who ruled from 539 to 530 B.C. The Babylonians conquered Judah, and then the Medes and Persians conquered the Babylonians.

1. As you read Ezra, observe what is said regarding rebuilding the temple, since the temple plays a key role in Ezra and Zechariah. Also, watch for any reference to Zerubbabel and to Jeshua, who is called Joshua in Zechariah. Joshua is also called Jeshua in Nehemiah, another post-exilic book that focuses on the rebuilding of the walls of Jerusalem.

2. If you have not studied Haggai, study it next since Haggai and Zechariah are contemporaries.

Chapters 1–8

1. The book of Zechariah divides into two segments: chapters 1 through 8 and chapters 9 through 14. As you read the first segment, mark every occurrence of the phrase *the word of the Lord came*. There will be slight variations to the wording (e.g., *the word of the Lord of hosts came*). However, mark each occurrence the same way. Then in the margin, note the main point of the Lord's message. Also, if the text tells you when the word came, draw a clock ⊕ in the text. Consult the historical chart on page 189 for the chronological setting of these messages.

2. As you read, also watch for the phrases *what do you see?, the Lord showed me, I saw*, and *I lifted up my eyes*. In the margin write "Vision," and then note briefly what the vision was. As you do this, you will see many correlations between *the word of the Lord* and the vision.

3. Watch for and mark in a distinctive way the following key words or phrases, along with their synonyms or pronouns: *listen (stopped their ears from hearing), return, again,*

temple (house of the Lord), nations, Judah, Jerusalem, I will dwell in your midst (I will be the glory in her midst or any reference to the Lord's coming), remnant, and seventy years.

Record these key words and phrases on an index card and use it as a bookmark as you study Zechariah. You will find it helpful to color or mark these phrases in the same way you mark them in the text.

4. Zechariah contains many prophecies regarding the Messiah's first and final comings, the nation of Israel and Jerusalem, and the future of the nations. Therefore, as you read Zechariah chapter by chapter, watch for these prophecies and note them under the appropriate columns on the chart ZECHARIAH'S PROPHETIC REVELATIONS on page 190.

5. God's name, Jehovah-sabaoth, Lord of hosts, is used repeatedly. Mark these occurrences. Then as you study Zechariah, in your notebook keep a list of all you learn about God.

6. After you study each chapter, record its theme (subject) on the ZECHARIAH AT A GLANCE chart under the appropriate chapter number and then in your Bible next to the chapter number.

Chapters 9–14

1. As you read through this segment, watch for the same key words and/or phrases you marked in chapters 1 through 8, but add to your list covenant, in that day, and any reference to the Lord as King.

2. Also mark the phrase the burden of the word of the Lord. The occurrences of this phrase divide these final chapters of Zechariah into segments.

3. After you mark the key words and phrases in this segment, list in the margin or on the chart ZECHARIAH'S PROPHETIC REVELATIONS what you learn about each. If you believe that day refers to the day of the Lord, also record your insights on the "Day of the Lord" chart we referred to in "Getting Started," page 25.

4. When you read chapter 13, watch what will happen to the two parts and the third. Watch the pronouns they and them. Mark the third part as remnant. You may want to record in your notebook all you learn about the third—the remnant that survives.

5. In chapter 14 you will see a reference to the Feast of Booths. On pages 48 and 49, you will find a chart called THE FEASTS OF ISRAEL. As you look at the chart, note the significance of the Feast of Booths (or Tabernacles, as it is sometimes called).

6. Record the theme of each chapter as you did previously. When you finish, write the theme of Zechariah on ZECHARIAH AT A GLANCE. Record the main theme of the two major segment divisions and fill in the other information requested on the chart.

7. Since Haggai and Zechariah were contemporaries, it would be interesting to note how the messages given by the Lord to these two prophets correlate in time. After you have studied both books, look at the "time symbols" in both books and note when the messages came in relationship to each other. List the messages in the order of their occurrence.

THINGS TO THINK ABOUT

1. As you studied Zechariah, were you touched by the awesomeness of God's sovereignty? What does it mean to you personally to realize that God reigns supreme over the nations? That He has declared things before they have come to pass, and that as He has purposed, so it shall be? If He can handle nations, can He handle your life?

2. Do you take time to listen—really listen—to what God says in His Word? If you have not listened, God's invitation to return to Him is still there in Zechariah for you. Believe Him...and return.

3. How can you apply the truth of Zechariah 4:6-7 to your own life? Remember, the things that were written in the Old Testament were written for our encouragement and perseverance. They are not simply historical records; they are the bread of life by which we live.

4. God said, "The Lord is coming; He will dwell in our midst." Revelation 22:12 tells us that when He comes, He will reward us according to our deeds. Are you prepared? According to 1 John 3:2-3 the coming of the Lord is a purifying hope. What do you need to do in order not to be ashamed at His coming?

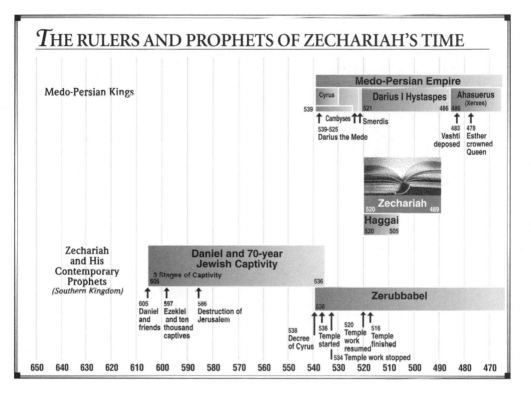

CONCERNING MESSIAH, JUDAH, AND JERUSALEM	CONCERNING THE NATIONS	CONCERNING MESSIAH, THE SAVIOR AND KING

Theme of Zechariah:

Author:

Date:

Purpose:

Key Words:

SEGMENT DIVISIONS

		CHAPTER THEMES
		1
		2
		3
		4
		5
		6
		7
		8
		9
		10
		11
		12
		13
		14

See appendix 7 for key words in the New International Version and King James Version.

MALACHI מַלְאָכִי
MAL'AKHI

*B*ecause they had not obeyed the word of the Lord, in 586 B.C. the children of Israel were taken into captivity. The nation that was once the head became the tail, just as God had spoken through His prophet Moses. And just as God had decreed through Jeremiah the prophet, the children of Israel's captivity lasted for 70 years.

In 538 B.C. Cyrus, the king of Persia, issued a decree allowing the children of Israel to return to Jerusalem and rebuild their temple. It was just as God had said when Isaiah prophesied 150 years earlier. Zerubbabel finished the temple, just as God promised. In 445 B.C. the Persian King Artaxerxes permitted Nehemiah to return to Jerusalem and rebuild its walls, just as Daniel had prophesied.

Over and over, the children of Israel saw that God stood by His word. Just as Solomon wrote in Proverbs, the hearts of kings were in God's hands, and He could turn them wherever He wanted. Why, then, did the remnant of Israel think that they could live and worship any way they wanted once they returned from their 70 years of exile and settled again in Israel? Had they grown tired of waiting for the fulfillment of the prophecies that promised that the Messiah would reign as King over all the earth? Had God abandoned them as He had Esau's descendants? Did they think He would allow the heathen nations who had come against them to go unpunished? Or were they entertaining thoughts that God really did not love them, that He would not keep His covenant promises?

Whatever it was, once again the remnant became apathetic in their relationship with God. So He spoke one more time through Malachi, whose name means "my messenger." It was sometime around 433 B.C. And then came a famine for hearing the word of the Lord (Amos 8:11).

THINGS TO DO

1. Since Malachi is a short book, read it without interruption so you can get a perspective of the book as a whole before you observe it chapter by chapter. As you read, catch the atmosphere of this book. Remember, this was written to people who had been sent into exile because of disobedience and then had returned to their land, just as God had promised.

2. Now read through Malachi one chapter at a time, doing the following:

   a. In a distinctive way or color mark the key words listed on the MALACHI AT A GLANCE chart. Write these key words on an index card you can use as a bookmark while you study Malachi.

   b. As you mark every reference to *you say* or *said,* watch what the priests and/or the people say and how God answers.

   c. You may want to note in the margin with whom God is upset, why He is upset, and what He tells them to do or what He is going to do as a result.

   d. Observe what will happen to those who fear His name and to those who do not.

   e. Note God's call to return to Him, how they are to return, and what will happen if they do.

3. When you finish each chapter, decide what the main subject or theme of that chapter is and record it on MALACHI AT A GLANCE and in your Bible.

4. As you read the final chapter of Malachi, read Deuteronomy 28–30, which speaks of the blessings or curses upon those who obey or disobey the law given by Moses.

5. God was silent for 400 years after He spoke through His prophet Malachi. His silence was broken when an angel appeared to Zacharias with the news that he and Elizabeth would give birth to a son. Read Luke 1:5-17 and Matthew 11:2-15, and see how these passages relate to God's final promise in Malachi. Record the essence of that promise in the margin of Malachi 4, and write next to it the cross-references in Luke and Matthew.

6. Record what you learn about the day of the Lord on the chart we suggested in "Getting Started," page 25.

THINGS TO THINK ABOUT

1. What do you learn from God's word to the priests that you can apply to your own life? Read through the list you compiled on "the priests" and remember that if you belong to the Lord Jesus Christ, you are part of a kingdom of priests to God. What kind of a priest are you? In principle, do you think God expects anything less of you as a Christian? For instance, what do you offer the Lord of your time and talents, your tithe and offering? Do you give others instructions according to the Word of the Lord or according to the current philosophy of the world? What about your covenant relationship with your mate?

2. Are you tired of serving God? Or do you fear Him? If so, what is God's promise to you?

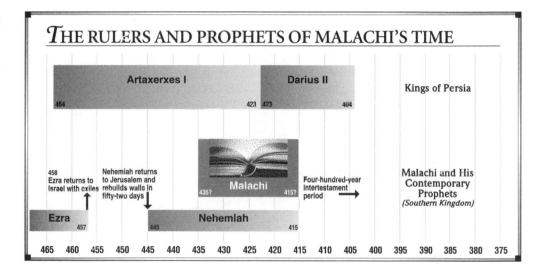

THE RULERS AND PROPHETS OF MALACHI'S TIME

| Artaxerxes I | | Darius II | Kings of Persia |

464 — 423 — 423 — 404

458 Ezra returns to Israel with exiles — Nehemiah returns to Jerusalem and rebuilds walls in fifty-two days — Malachi 435? 415? — Four-hundred-year Intertestament period — Malachi and His Contemporary Prophets *(Southern Kingdom)*

Ezra 457 — Nehemiah 445 — 415

465 460 455 450 445 440 435 430 425 420 415 410 405 400 395 390 385 380 375

Theme of Malachi:

	Chapter Themes	Author:
1		Date:
2		Purpose:
3		Key Words: Lord of hosts you say (said) profane (profaned) My name (or Your name) priest(s) offering (sacrifices) curse covenant treacherously fear (reverence) divorce
4		

See appendix 7 for key words in the New International Version and King James Version.

MATTHEW

God promised Abraham that all the nations of the earth would be blessed through his seed (Genesis 12:3; 15:1-6). Where was this son of Abraham?

God promised Isaiah that a child would be born, a son would be given, and the government would rest on His shoulders. His name would be Wonderful Counselor, Mighty God, Eternal Father, Prince of Peace. There would be no end to the increase of His government or of peace. He would occupy the throne of David (Isaiah 9:6-7). Where was this son of David?

No one knew until a baby's cry went up from Bethlehem Ephrathah. Magi from the East arrived in Jerusalem saying, "Where is He who has been born King of the Jews?" The One who was to be ruler in Israel (Micah 5:2), the son of David, the son of Abraham, had been born. Matthew writes about this King of the Jews.

THINGS TO DO

1. From the first verse, Matthew's purpose is clear: to show that Jesus was the long-awaited King, the son of David, the Messiah whose coming was prophesied throughout the Old Testament.

There is a pattern to Matthew that repeats itself and divides the Gospel into six segments. Matthew presents certain facts concerning the person and work of Jesus, which he then follows with an account of Jesus' teaching. Each teaching account is brought to a conclusion with one of the following three phrases: "When Jesus had finished these words," "finished giving instructions," or "finished these parables."

Therefore before you read through Matthew chapter by chapter, mark in a distinctive way each occurrence of a dividing phrase in 7:28; 11:1; 13:53; 19:1; and 26:1. Remember, these phrases conclude that particular teaching. Then the cycle begins again.

2. Now read Matthew chapter by chapter, keeping in mind these six segments. As you read:

   a. In a distinctive way mark in the text the key words listed on MATTHEW AT A GLANCE. Mark every reference to time with a green clock ⏰. Double-underline in green all geographical locations and locate them on a map.

      1) List on page 212 what you learn about *king* or *kingdom.*

      2) In addition to these key words, watch for other key repeated words or phrases.

   b. Using the same color each time, underline or highlight each reference to or quotation from an Old Testament prophecy that shows Jesus as the promised King. Then in the margin, write the word "prophecy." (In the NASB, you can easily spot the Old Testament quotes because they are printed in small capital letters.)

   c. Watch for the events, works, or facts that demonstrate who Jesus Christ is.

   d. When you read Jesus' teaching on a particular subject, in your notebook make a list of the main points covered in His teaching. If it is a prophetic teaching, pay attention to time phrases or indicators, including *then* and *when.* Watch for the progression of events.

   e. Record the main theme or event of each chapter in your Bible next to the chapter number and on MATTHEW AT A GLANCE.

3. Chapters 26 through 28 give an account of the final events in the life of Jesus. Record the progression of events on the chart THE ARREST, TRIAL, AND CRUCIFIXION OF JESUS

CHRIST on page 211. Make a similar chart in your notebook called THE ACCOUNT OF JESUS' RESURRECTION. Note the chapter and verse of each insight for future reference.

4. When you record the circumstances surrounding the resurrection of Jesus Christ, also note any postresurrection appearances that are recorded in Matthew. After you do this for all four Gospels you will have comprehensive notes on all that took place. Remember, Luke gives the consecutive order of events and therefore becomes a chronological plumb line for the other Gospel records.

5. List and consolidate everything you learn from Matthew about the kingdom of God in your notebook. Be sure to note the chapter and verse for future reference.

6. Complete MATTHEW AT A GLANCE. Under "Segment Divisions," record the theme of each segment of Matthew. There is also a blank line for any other segment divisions you might see.

THINGS TO THINK ABOUT

1. Have you bowed your knee to Jesus as King in your life? Read Matthew 7:21-27 and think about the difference between *merely hearing* something and *hearing and living accordingly.* Which best describes you?

2. Can you explain from Scripture why Jesus is the King of the promised kingdom?

3. Do you realize that Jesus' final words to His disciples in Matthew 28:19-20 are your responsibility also? What are you doing in order to fulfill His Great Commission? As you go, are you making disciples? Are you teaching them to observe all that He has commanded?

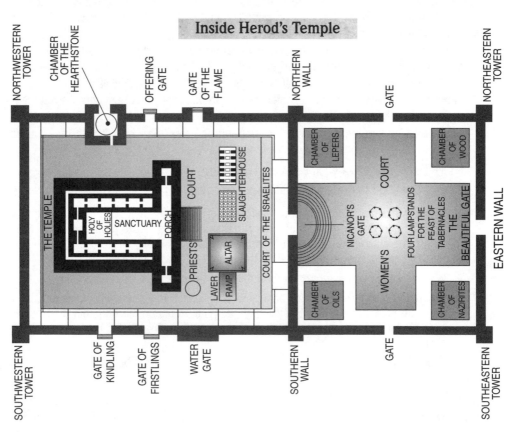

Inside Herod's Temple

Theme of Matthew:

SEGMENT DIVISIONS

		CHAPTER THEMES
Author:		

		1
Date:		2
		3
		4
Purpose:		5
		6
Key Words:		7
king (kingdom, kingdom of heaven, kingdom of God)		8
		9
fulfilled		10
mark every reference to the devil or demons		11
		12
		13
covenant		14
Spirit (Holy Spirit)		15
believe (faith)		16
disciples (disciple)		17
sign (signs)		18
Christ (Messiah)		19
sin(s)		20
heart		21
		22
		23
		24
		25
		26
		27
		28

See appendix 7 for key words in the New International Version and King James Version.

MARK

*J*esus was clearly born to be King of the Jews, as Matthew points out. However, the gospel was not just for the Jews; it was for the whole world. Before Jesus would reign as King of kings, He would be servant of all by dying for mankind. Mark writes of the works and authority of the One who came not to be served but to serve, and to give His life a ransom for many.

THINGS TO DO

Mark is a fast-paced Gospel which emphasizes Jesus' works rather than His teachings. Although Jesus is referred to as a teacher a number of times, Mark shows Jesus' power and authority through the works He does as He goes about His Father's business.

In reading this Gospel you will notice the repeated use of the word *immediately* as Mark takes his reader from one event in the life of Jesus to another. These events and the works of Jesus show the reader Jesus' power and authority as the servant of God and man.

Chapters 1–13

Read through all of the instructions below before you begin working on chapters 1–13.

1. Although the emphasis in the Gospel of Mark is on the works of Jesus that show His divine power, Mark opens his Gospel by declaring the deity of Jesus Christ. He also gives an account of the events that took place prior to and in preparation for Jesus' ministry. Read Mark 1:1-13 and list in your notebook the following:

    a. The facts that declare the deity of Jesus Christ.

    b. The events that took place in Jesus' life prior to His public ministry.

2. Now read Mark chapter by chapter, and in a distinctive way mark in the text the key words listed on the MARK AT A GLANCE chart.

    a. Record these key words on an index card and use it as a bookmark while you study this Gospel. Mark references to time with a green clock ⏰ so they're distinctive.

    b. Double-underline in green each geographical location, whether it is a city, a region, or a place, such as the temple or the synagogue. Noting these will help in your overall understanding of the events in Jesus' life.

3. Chapters 1–3 cover events (including healings and miracles) that demonstrate Jesus' authority.

    a. As you look at each event, observe how it demonstrates Jesus' authority, how the people respond, and what Jesus has authority over.

    b. Record your insights in your notebook by listing the event and then under that event noting how the people, religious leaders, disciples, and others responded. For example:

Healing on Sabbath
Pharisees counsel to destroy Him

    c. After you have recorded these demonstrations and responses, be sure to record the scope of Jesus' authority. For example, next to the illustration above, you might write, "Authority over Sabbath." Look at His works. Watch for Jesus' power over nature, demons, disease, and so on. Ask God to show you how this demonstration of Jesus' power declares His deity. Also, notice how these events portray Jesus as a Servant.

d. Throughout these chapters, Jesus faces the accusations and rejection of the Jewish religious leaders of His day. Each time the scribes, Pharisees, or Sadducees accuse Jesus, He reasons with them. Mark that conflict in the margin with a star.

4. Record in your notebook the main points of Jesus' teachings, whether the teaching comes as a result of healing, casting out demons, working a miracle, or responding to a question from either the disciples or the multitude. Also note the response of those who hear the teaching.

5. Look at every reference to the kingdom of God you marked and do the following:

a. Note when Jesus increases His emphasis on the kingdom of God.

b. Underline every prediction of Jesus' death and resurrection and note how it coincides with Jesus' emphasis on the kingdom of God.

c. Observe that in the first part of Mark, Jesus defines the kingdom of God, and then at chapter 9 the emphasis shifts to how to enter the kingdom.

d. Compile the *main* teachings from Mark about the kingdom of God on page 212. Note the chapter and verse as you do this.

6. After you finish reading and marking each chapter, record the theme of that chapter on MARK AT A GLANCE. Also record it in your Bible.

Chapters 14–16

1. When you read Mark's account, record the progression of events during the trial, death, burial, and resurrection of Christ on the charts on page 211 and in your notebook. Note the chapter and verse beside each insight.

a. When you record the circumstances surrounding the resurrection of Jesus Christ, also note any postresurrection appearances recorded in Mark. After you do this for all four Gospels you will have comprehensive notes on everything that took place at this time in our Lord's life.

b. As you do this, remember that because Luke gives the consecutive order of events, it is a plumb line for the other Gospel records.

2. Complete MARK AT A GLANCE. Fill in any segment divisions you have seen from studying the book.

THINGS TO THINK ABOUT

1. People often say that Mark shows the servant aspect of Jesus' ministry. Although the word *servant* is used only four times, Mark 10:45 says that Jesus "did not come to be served, but to serve, and to give His life a ransom for many." How like your Lord are you in that respect? Would others regard you as a servant? Or do they see you as having to be "number one"? What is it to be "number one" in God's eyes?

2. Jesus talks about discipleship in this Gospel. According to Jesus, what is required of disciples? Can you consider yourself a true disciple of Jesus Christ? Why? Think about Mark 8:34-36 and 10:28-31.

3. Can you say with Peter, "You are the Christ, the Son of the living God"? (Matthew 16:16). And will you listen to Jesus as the Father commands?

Theme of Mark:

SEGMENT DIVISIONS

		CHAPTER THEMES
		1
		2
		3
		4
		5
		6
		7
		8
		9
		10
		11
		12
		13
		14
		15
		16

Author:

Date:

Purpose:

Key Words:

immediately

authority (power)

kingdom of God

mark every reference to Satan or demons

covenant

Spirit

Christ (Messiah)

disciple(s)

See appendix 7 for key words in the New International Version and King James Version.

*L*UKE

*I*n Matthew we see Jesus as King of the Jews. In Mark we see Him as the Servant who came to give His life a ransom for many. Then Luke, writing with the carefulness of a historian, takes us "in consecutive order" through the days of the Son of Man. In this Gospel we see the fulfillment of the things written about Him in the law of Moses, the Prophets, and the Psalms, things that no other Gospel records.

THINGS TO DO

1. Luke's purpose in writing is stated in Luke 1:1-4; record this.

2. As you read chapter by chapter, be sure to do the following:

   a. Mark in the text the key words listed on LUKE AT A GLANCE.

   b. Mark references to time with a green clock ⏰. The references will come in many different forms, from the mention of actual days or years to the naming of a Jewish feast, a chief priest, or a king. The chart on Herod's family tree on page 209 will help. This part of your study will keep before you the timing and sequence of the events in Jesus' life. These are critical to Luke's purpose.

   c. It is also important to note where each event takes place. Double-underline in green every reference to places, cities, or regions. Locate these on a map.

   d. Observe the main events and teachings covered in each chapter. (Note: Much of the material in Luke 1–3; 10–18 is unique to Luke.)

   1) As you list each event in the margin of the text, color code or mark it in a distinctive way so it can be recognized as an event. This will help you see at a glance the chronology of events in Luke. Consult the chart THE LIFE OF CHRIST on page 210.

   2) Pay attention to the setting and the response of those who are listening or participating in what is happening. Observe where Jesus is, His relationships to people, what social events He is involved in, and what He expects from people.

   e. *Disciple(s)* is a key word. You may want to make a list of everything you learn from marking it.

   f. If Jesus tells a parable or tells of an incident such as the rich man and Lazarus dying (Luke 16), note what provokes Jesus to do so.

   g. Record the theme of each chapter in your Bible and on LUKE AT A GLANCE. Do the same for the theme of the book as you complete the chart.

3. Record the facts concerning Jesus' betrayal, arrest, trial, crucifixion on page 211. In your notebook, record the facts concerning the resurrection, postresurrection appearances, and ascension. Note the chapter and verse for each insight. After you do this for all four Gospels you will have comprehensive notes on what took place at this time in our Lord's life.

4. Record on page 213 the information you glean from marking every reference to the *kingdom of God* in Luke.

THINGS TO THINK ABOUT

1. Have you been slow of heart to believe all that Moses and the prophets wrote about Jesus Christ? Do you see Jesus as the Son of Man, the fulfillment of prophecy, the Christ, the Son of God? Have you bowed to Him as Lord of your life? Are you a true disciple?

201

2. Jesus reached out to the hurting, the sinners, and the outcasts. He visited in their homes. He was available and accessible. What about you? Do you have compassion on these people? Are you wasting your life on self or are you investing in others? What did you learn from watching Christ's response to others that you can apply to your life?

3. If Jesus needed to withdraw often to a lonely place to pray, what about you? Is prayer a high priority in your life? Do you understand and incorporate the principles of prayer that Jesus taught in the Gospel of Luke?

Theme of Luke:

SEGMENT DIVISIONS

Author:

Date:

Purpose:

Key Words:

kingdom (king-
dom of God)

Son of Man

mark every
reference to
the devil or
demons

covenant

pray (prayer, etc.)

disciple(s)

sins (sinner)

every reference to
Jesus' second
coming

Christ (Messiah)

		CHAPTER THEMES
		1
		2
		3
		4
		5
		6
		7
		8
		9
		10
		11
		12
		13
		14
		15
		16
		17
		18
		19
		20
		21
		22
		23
		24

JOHN

God in the flesh! What would He be like? What would He do? How would He live in relationship to the Father once He came to earth? And how would people know He was God? Would He force people to believe in Him? What about those who refused to believe He was God? And what of those who believed, who followed Him? What would God in the flesh expect from them?

God in the flesh. The incarnation would be hard for some to believe, but their belief or unbelief would be a matter of life or death.

Three other Gospels had been written, and years had passed. One more Gospel was needed, one which would answer these questions and more, one which would illumine the shadows of doubt. So the apostle John answered God's call to write a fourth and final Gospel to explain the One who came to reveal the Father. It was about A.D. 85.

THINGS TO DO

1. Although the author of John is not identified by name, tradition holds that it was the apostle John. Read John 21:20-25 and note how the author identifies himself. You might want to put this reference or information under "Author" on the JOHN AT A GLANCE chart.

2. To understand the purpose of John read John 20:30-31. Record this on JOHN AT A GLANCE. Keep John's purpose in mind as you study this Gospel.

Chapters 1–12

1. Carefully read this segment chapter by chapter, observing what the author includes to accomplish his purpose.

   a. Mark the following key words and their synonyms: *believe, life, sign, judge (judgment), witness, love, sin, true (truth), Spirit,* and *king (kingdom)*.

   b. Write the key words on an index card and mark them in the same way you mark them in your Bible. Use this as a bookmark.

   c. Also mark any other repeated key words that are pertinent to the message of the chapter.

2. As you read each of the first 12 chapters, ask the "5 W's and an H": Who? What? Where? When? Why? and How? Observe the events and the people.

   a. *Events:* What is happening? For example, "Nicodemus came to Jesus by night."

   b. *Geographic locations:* Where is this event taking place? For example, John was baptizing at Bethany beyond the Jordan. Double-underline in green all geographical locations.

   c. *Timing of events:* When is this event taking place? For example, "on the third day," or "before the Feast of the Passover." Mark time phrases with a green clock ⏲. When Jesus attends a feast, put a clock in the margin and write the name of the feast.

   d. *Portrayals of Jesus Christ:* How is Jesus pictured or described? For example: "the Word," "the Lamb of God," etc. You may want to note this in the margin.

   e. *Signs and Miracles:* The signs John recorded were for the purpose of leading people to believe that Jesus is the Christ, the Son of God. Look for these signs or miracles and note them with a special symbol in the margin. For example, Jesus turned water into wine. The text says this was the beginning of His signs.

204

f. *References that show the deity of Jesus* (references that show that Jesus is God, such as "I am"). Each time you note such a reference, write *Deity* in the margin, and under it, record the next reference to His deity. This will give you a good chain of cross-references.

g. *Witnesses:* Throughout his Gospel, John refers to those who bear witness to Jesus. Who are these witnesses and what is their witness? For example, John said, "I myself have seen, and have testified that this is the Son of God" (John 1:34).

3. Determine the main subject or theme of each chapter and then record it in your Bible next to the chapter number and on JOHN AT A GLANCE.

Chapters 13–17

1. This segment brings a change in Jesus' ministry as He draws away with the disciples in order to prepare them for what is to come. Make a new list of key words on a book-mark: *believe, love, works, commandments, fruit, abide, ask, truth (truly), witness,* and *devil (Satan, ruler of this world).* (Go back to chapter 12 and mark the references to *ruler of this world.)*

2. Mark in the text in a distinctive way all references, including pronouns, to the Holy Spirit. Then list in your notebook everything you learn about the Holy Spirit. This is especially important in chapters 14 through 16.

3. List in your notebook any specific instructions or commandments that Jesus gives the disciples.

4. Record the main theme of each chapter as you did before.

Chapters 18–21

1. The final chapters of John give an account of the events surrounding the arrest, trial, crucifixion, resurrection, and the postresurrection appearances of Jesus Christ. As you read each chapter:

a. Mark the following key words and their synonyms: *witness, believe, love, truth (true), life, signs,* and *king (kingdom).*

b. Record the progression of events from Jesus' arrest through His resurrection and postresurrection appearances, noting the chapter and verse. Remember that since Luke gives the chronological order of events, it becomes a plumb line for the other Gospel records.

2. Once again determine the theme of each chapter and record it as you have done previously.

3. Compile what John teaches about the King and the kingdom on the chart on pages 212–213. John 3 contains the only two references to the kingdom. The other references to Jesus as the King are in the first and last segments of John.

4. Complete JOHN AT A GLANCE by doing the following:

a. Review your chapter themes of John and determine the theme of the book. Record this in the appropriate place on JOHN AT A GLANCE.

b. You will notice a section titled "Segment Divisions" and two lines where you can record "Signs and Miracles" and "Portrayals of Jesus Christ." Review the information you have recorded in the margins. Record your observations on the appropriate segment division line. For example, in chapter 1 Jesus is referred to as "the Lamb of God." Record that fact at chapter 1 under "Portrayals of Jesus Christ." This will give you a visual picture of the structure of John.

THINGS TO THINK ABOUT

1. Do you really believe that Jesus is God and live accordingly? And what if you don't? (see John 8:24).

2. Do you know how to take another person through the Scriptures to show him that Jesus is God?

3. Do people know that you are a disciple of Jesus Christ because of your love for others and because you have continued in His Word?

4. Are you relying on the Spirit of God to comfort you, help you, bear witness through you, do the work of God through you, and guide you into all truth?

5. Do you look at other Christians and wonder why God deals differently with you than He does with them? Do you need to hear His words to Peter in John 21:22, "If I want him to remain until I come, what is that to you? You follow Me!"? Are you willing to follow Jesus wherever He leads, even if you have to do it alone? Are you telling others about Him?

Theme of John:

SEGMENT DIVISIONS

Portrayals of Jesus Christ	Signs and Miracles	Ministry		CHAPTER THEMES
			Author:	
			Date:	
		To Israel	1	
			2	**Purpose:**
			3	
			4	**Key Words:**
			5	(including synonyms)
			6	
			7	
			8	
			9	
			10	
			11	
		To Disciples	12	
			13	
			14	
			15	
			16	
			17	
		To All Mankind	18	
			19	
			20	
		To Disciples	21	

See appendix 7 for key words in the New International Version and King James Version.

207

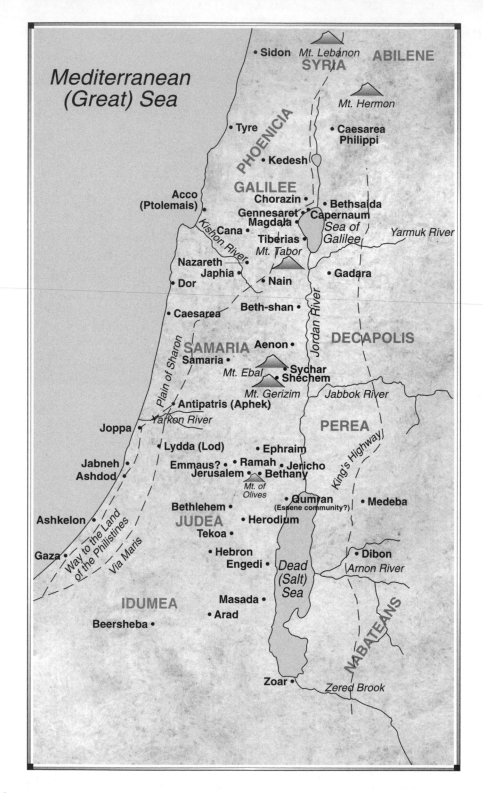

Mediterranean
(Great) Sea

• Sidon
Mt. Lebanon
SYRIA
ABILENE

Mt. Hermon

• Tyre
PHOENICIA

• Caesarea
Philippi

• Kedesh

Acco
(Ptolemais)

GALILEE

Chorazin •
• Bethsaida
Gennesaret
Capernaum
Magdala
Sea of
Galilee
Yarmuk River

Cana •
• Tiberias
Mt. Tabor

Nazareth
Japhia •
• Nain
• Gadara

• Dor

• Caesarea

Beth-shan •

Jordan River

DECAPOLIS

Plain of Sharon

SAMARIA
Aenon •
Samaria •
Mt. Ebal
Sychar
Shechem
Mt. Gerizim
Jabbok River

• Antipatris (Aphek)
Yarkon River

Joppa •

PEREA

Lydda (Lod) •

• Ephraim

Emmaus? •
• Ramah
• Jericho
Jabneh •
Jerusalem •
Bethany
Ashdod •
Mt. of
Olives

King's Highway

Bethlehem •
• Qumran
(Essene community?)
• Medeba

Ashkelon •

JUDEA
• Herodium

Tekoa •

Gaza •

Way to the Land of the Philistines

Via Maris

• Hebron
Engedi •
Dead
(Salt)
Sea
• Dibon
Arnon River

IDUMEA
Masada •
• Arad

Beersheba •

NABATEANS

Zoar •
Zered Brook

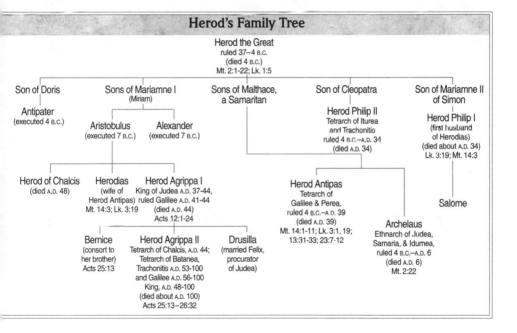

Herod's Family Tree

Herod the Great
ruled 37–4 B.C.
(died 4 B.C.)
Mt. 2:1-22; Lk. 1:5

Son of Doris

Antipater
(executed 4 B.C.)

Sons of Mariamne I
(Miriam)

Aristobulus
(executed 7 B.C.)

Alexander
(executed 7 B.C.)

**Sons of Malthace,
a Samaritan**

Son of Cleopatra

Herod Philip II
Tetrarch of Iturea
and Trachonitis
ruled 4 B.C.–A.D. 34
(died A.D. 34)

**Son of Mariamne II
of Simon**

Herod Philip I
(first husband
of Herodias)
(died about A.D. 34)
Lk. 3:19; Mt. 14:3

Herod of Chalcis
(died A.D. 48)

Herodias
(wife of
Herod Antipas)
Mt. 14:3; Lk. 3:19

Herod Agrippa I
King of Judea A.D. 37-44,
ruled Galilee A.D. 41-44
(died A.D. 44)
Acts 12:1-24

Herod Antipas
Tetrarch of
Galilee & Perea,
ruled 4 B.C.–A.D. 39
(died A.D. 39)
Mt. 14:1-11; Lk. 3:1, 19;
13:31-33; 23:7-12

Salome

Archelaus
Ethnarch of Judea,
Samaria, & Idumea,
ruled 4 B.C.–A.D. 6
(died A.D. 6)
Mt. 2:22

Bernice
(consort to
her brother)
Acts 25:13

Herod Agrippa II
Tetrarch of Chalcis, A.D. 44;
Tetrarch of Batanea,
Trachonitis A.D. 53-100
and Galilee A.D. 56-100
King, A.D. 48-100
(died about A.D. 100)
Acts 25:13–26:32

Drusilla
(married Felix,
procurator
of Judea)

Life of Christ Showing Coverage by Luke (Shaded Area)

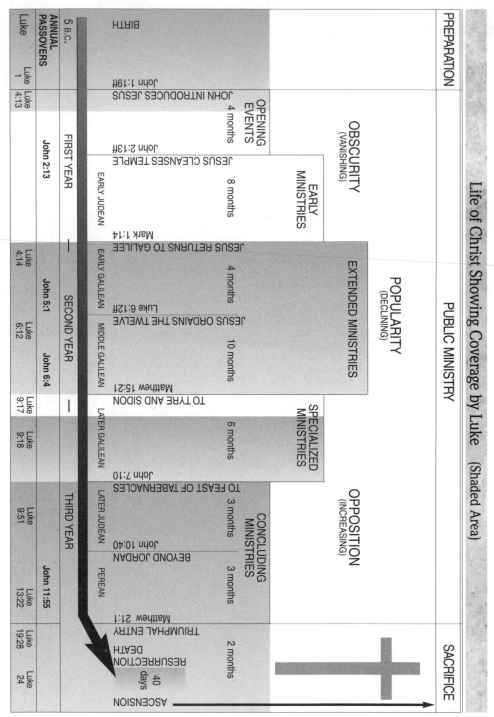

			PREPARATION	PUBLIC MINISTRY			SACRIFICE

BIRTH

John 1:19ff
JOHN INTRODUCES JESUS

John 2:13ff
JESUS CLEANSES TEMPLE

Mark 1:14
JESUS RETURNS TO GALILEE

Luke 6:12ff
JESUS ORDAINS THE TWELVE

Matthew 15:21
TO TYRE AND SIDON

John 7:10
TO FEAST OF TABERNACLES

John 10:40
BEYOND JORDAN

Matthew 21:1
TRIUMPHAL ENTRY

RESURRECTION
DEATH
40 days

ASCENSION

OBSCURITY
(VANISHING)

OPENING EVENTS
4 months

EARLY MINISTRIES
EARLY JUDEAN
8 months

POPULARITY
(DECLINING)

EXTENDED MINISTRIES
EARLY GALILEE
4 months

MIDDLE GALILEAN
10 months

SPECIALIZED MINISTRIES
LATER GALILEAN
6 months

OPPOSITION
(INCREASING)

CONCLUDING MINISTRIES
LATER JUDEAN
3 months

PEREAN
3 months

2 months

5 B.C.

FIRST YEAR

SECOND YEAR

THIRD YEAR

ANNUAL PASSOVERS

Luke	John 2:13	John 5:1	John 6:4	John 7:10	John 11:55	John 10:40

Luke 1
Luke 4:13
Luke 4:14
Luke 6:12
Luke 9:17
Luke 9:18
Luke 9:51
Luke 13:22
Luke 19:28
Luke 24

Used by permission. Jensen, Irving L. *Luke: A Self-Study Guide.* Chicago: Moody Press, 1970.

The Arrest, Trial, and Crucifixion of Jesus Christ

Matthew	Mark	Luke	John
		Luke gives consecutive	
		order of events in	
		Jesus' life	
		(Luke 1:3)	

MATTHEW	MARK

LUKE	JOHN

ACTS

I'm going away."

The 11 heard nothing else. The promise of another Helper, the Holy Spirit, fell on deaf ears. The thought that they could do the works that Jesus had done—and even greater—must have seemed preposterous to them.

Jesus had died and been buried. But three days later He arose from the dead! For more than 40 days the disciples saw, heard, and touched the Word of Life as He spoke with them of things concerning the kingdom of God. He commissioned His disciples to reach the world, and then once again He was gone, taken away before their very eyes! Before He left, He promised to send the Spirit to empower them, to teach them, and to guide them.

Then came Pentecost and the acts of the apostles. Luke wrote Theophilus all about it in the book of Acts, which was probably written about A.D. 63.

THINGS TO DO

General Instructions

1. In a distinctive way mark in the text every occurrence of the key words (along with their synonyms and pronouns) listed on the ACTS AT A GLANCE chart. Record these key words on an index card that you can use as a bookmark while studying Acts.

2. Mark every reference to time with the symbol of a green clock 🕐. Do this throughout the book of Acts whether the time is indicated by an event (such as a feast) or by mentioning a certain period of months or years. Also, double-underline in green every geographical location.

Chapters 1–2

In the first two chapters of the book of Acts, Luke gives an account of Christ's ascension and the Holy Spirit's coming.

1. Read chapter 1, looking for Jesus' instructions and promises to the apostles.

   a. In your notebook list everything you learn from the references to the Holy Spirit.

   b. Note the main events that occur in this chapter by either marking these events within the text or listing them in the margin.

2. Acts 1:8 gives an outline for the book of Acts. Remember this as you read Acts. Observe when the gospel goes from Jerusalem and Judea to Samaria and the outermost parts of the world.

3. As you read chapter 2:

   a. Keep in mind that in the NASB any Scripture printed in small caps indicates that the Scripture is either an Old Testament quotation or an allusion to an Old Testament text. Observe how much is taken from the Old Testament.

   b. List in the margin the main events that occur. As you note them, ask the "5 W's and an H": Who? What? When? Where? Why? and How? For example, ask: Who was present on the day of Pentecost? What happened? Whom did it affect? What was their response? Why did they respond as they did? How did they hear?

   c. As you mark key words, watch the word *promise* and note its relationship to the Spirit. Compare this with Acts 1:4-5.

d. Observe the main points in Peter's sermon on the day of Pentecost. Note what he emphasized in his sermon and the result.

4. Determine the theme of each of these chapters. Then record the themes on ACTS AT A GLANCE and in your Bible.

Chapters 3–7

1. As you study, do the following:

a. Read each chapter in the light of the "5 W's and an H." What happens in that chapter? Where and when did it happen? Who is involved? How are things done or said?

b. Mark every reference to the Holy Spirit and then list what you learn about the Holy Spirit, His ministry, and the results. Also mark in the text the other key words listed on ACTS AT A GLANCE. Remember to use your bookmark.

c. If a message is proclaimed in these chapters, you may want to record in your notebook the main points of that message and the effect of the message on those who hear it.

2. Determine the theme of each chapter and then record the theme as before.

Chapters 8–12

1. Read Acts 8:1-8 and then Acts 1:8. What do you see happening in Acts 8 that is a change from the first seven chapters? Note this in the margin of chapter 8.

2. Read chapters 8 through 11 carefully, as significant events occur in these chapters. As you read:

a. List the main events in each chapter. Who does what? When? Where is it done? What is said? What is the result? Who is affected? How does it happen? Don't add to the text, but simply observe it and record in your notebook what you learn.

b. Mark key words and list everything you learn about the Holy Spirit in your notebook. This is crucial to chapters 8, 10, and 11. Note to whom the Holy Spirit comes.

c. Record the theme of each chapter in your Bible and on ACTS AT A GLANCE.

3. As you read and study chapter 12, keep in mind that this is a pivotal chapter. At this point the focus of the book turns from Peter's ministry to that of Paul (Saul).

Chapters 13–28

1. Included in these chapters is an account of Paul's missionary journeys: Paul's first missionary journey in 13–14; Paul's second missionary journey in 15:36–18:22; and Paul's third missionary journey in 18:23–21:17.

For easy reference, write and color code in the margin where each journey begins.

2. As you study these chapters, mark the key repeated words. Add the word *synagogue* to your list. Also keep in mind what you learned from Acts 1:8 and watch carefully the work of the Spirit throughout these chapters. In your notebook, note your insights.

a. Examine each chapter with the "5 W's and an H." Note in the text who accompanies Paul, where they go, and what happens. Trace each of Paul's journeys on the map on page 216.

b. Carefully observe each time the gospel is proclaimed, whether to an individual or a group. Watch how Paul reasons with Jews and Gentiles. Also, note what their response is and how Paul handles it.

3. In several instances you will notice Paul giving his testimony. Compare each of these instances with Acts 9 and the account of Paul's conversion. This will give you a more complete picture of all that happened on that significant day.

4. Record the theme of each chapter on ACTS AT A GLANCE and in your Bible. Then determine the main subject for the book of Acts and record it. Complete the chart and record the ways you might segment the book of Acts according to its themes.

THINGS TO THINK ABOUT

1. What have you learned from Acts about the Holy Spirit and your responsibility to be a witness for the Lord Jesus Christ?

2. Based on what you saw in the sermons that were preached and the personal witnesses that were given, what would you include in your witness? Where would the emphasis be?

3. As you studied the lives of the early apostles and the commitment of the early church, how has God spoken to your heart? Stop and think about how they lived, and then think about how you are living. Do you have the Holy Spirit living inside you? Isn't He the same today, yesterday, and forever? If you are filled with the Holy Spirit and are not quenching Him, what should be happening in your life?

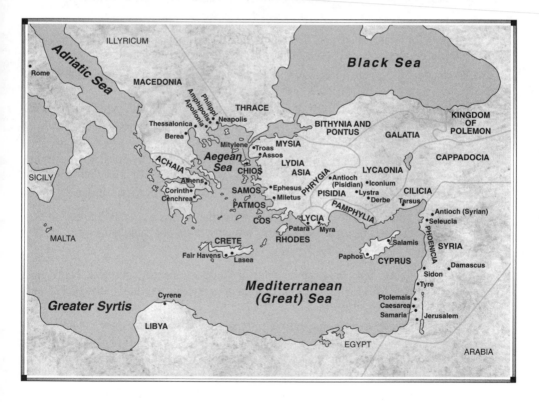

Theme of Acts:

SEGMENT DIVISIONS

			CHAPTER THEMES
			1
			2
			3
			4
			5
			6
			7
			8
			9
			10
			11
			12
			13
			14
			15
			16
			17
			18
			19
			20
			21
			22
			23
			24
			25
			26
			27
			28

Author:

Date:

Purpose:

Key Words:

believe

baptized (baptism)

Holy Spirit

witness (witnesses)

word (word of God, scriptures)

gospel

saved

church

pray (praying, etc.)

raised from the dead (any reference to the resurrection)

His name (the name of Jesus)

any reference to persecution, suffering, affliction

repent (repentance)

See appendix 7 for key words in the New International Version and King James Version.

ROMANS

*T*he gospel Paul preached, justification by faith alone, was under siege. While many directly opposed this gospel, others twisted it to suit their own preferences. The Judaizers said salvation might be by grace but the believer is "kept" by the law. They insisted that circumcision was necessary for salvation. At the other extreme, the antinomians taught that you could be saved by grace and still live any way you wanted—even continue in sin.

Only a clear explanation of the gospel could refute such errors. Eager to prove the gospel's power to save and sanctify both Jew and Gentile, Paul, like a wise lawyer, calls the gospel to the witness stand and examines it from every angle. The result is the book of Romans, a theological masterpiece written around A.D. 56 or 57.

THINGS TO DO

1. Romans is the constitution of the Christian faith. If you understand Romans you will have a plumb line for correctly interpreting any teaching on the gospel. It is a book you need to observe over and over until you are so familiar with the text that its meaning is obvious.

   a. Ideally it would be helpful to read Romans in one sitting and color every reference to Paul. If that is not possible, read it a chapter at a time. Every time you see the word *gospel*, mark it in a distinctive way so you can easily spot it in the text.

   b. Paul gives his reasons for writing Romans in the first and the last two chapters. Record these reasons on the ROMANS OBSERVATIONS CHART on page 221.

   c. Watch for and color every reference to the recipients that answers the "5 W's and an H" (who, what, when, where, why, and how). Record on the OBSERVATIONS CHART what you learn about them. Note whether Paul is writing to Gentiles, Jews, or both. Also record your insights about Paul on the same chart.

2. The book of Romans can be divided into five segments, each building on the previous one: chapters 1–3:20; 3:21-5; 6–8; 9–11; and 12–16. As you complete each segment, return to these instructions so you can see what you are to do.

3. Make a key word bookmark.

   a. Mark each of the following key words and their synonyms: *grace, faith, law, justified (justify, just), righteous (righteousness), wrath, judge (judgment), gospel, believe, sin, hope, Gentiles, Jesus Christ,* and *Spirit.* Mark references to time with a green clock ⏰.

   b. List these words on an index card and use it as a bookmark when you study. As you begin each new segment of Romans, add the next group of key words to your card. Mark or color code them on the card in the same way you plan to mark them in your Bible.

4. Watch for the word *therefore* and see what it is "there for." Several chapters have this word in the first verse. When Paul uses *therefore* he is making a point you will not want to miss.

Chapters 1–3:20

1. Read through Romans 1. As you mark the references to the gospel, list in your notebook all you learn about the gospel. Then note how Paul describes the unrighteousness of man. Mark *exchanged* and *God gave them over.* Then observe the progression of events shown by marking these two things.

2. In chapters 2–3:20, observe how Paul shows that all men—Jews and Gentiles—are under sin. Watch the references to the judgment of God.

3. Add the phrase *may it never be* to your key word list.

4. List in your notebook what you learn from this segment about sin, wrath, and the judgments of God.

5. From chapters 3 through 11 of Romans, Paul periodically asks an important question and then answers it. Mark each of Paul's questions. You might put a cloud like this ⌢⌣ around each question throughout the book. Carefully read each question and note how Paul answers it.

6. When you finish observing each chapter, record the theme of that chapter in your Bible next to the chapter number and on the ROMANS AT A GLANCE chart.

7. What do you see as the theme in this first segment of Romans? Write it (in pencil) on ROMANS AT A GLANCE in the first column under "Segment Divisions."

Chapters 3:21–5

Having established that "both Jews and Greeks [all people] are under sin" (3:9), Paul proceeds to show how God saves sinners.

1. As you read through these chapters, you will find words or phrases unique to each chapter. In chapter 4, mark *credited* and note what you learn from marking it. In chapter 5, mark and observe *death (die, died)* and *gift.*

2. List in your notebook what you learn from marking these chapters' key words, such as *righteousness* and *justified.*

3. Once again record your chapter themes on the ROMANS AT A GLANCE chart. Also write out the theme of this segment of Romans. You may want to do it in pencil to begin with.

Chapters 6–8

1. Follow the same procedure as you did in the previous segment. Add the following words and their synonyms: *flesh, life, reign, master, slaves,* and *freed from sin.*

2. Make a list of everything you learn from marking *law* and *Spirit.*

3. Mark Paul's questions and, in your notebook, list the main points of his answers.

4. Record the theme of each chapter and of this segment as you did before.

5. The ROMANS OBSERVATIONS CHART includes a place to record everything you learn from chapters 5 through 8 regarding our position in Adam (before we were saved) and our position in Christ (after we were saved). Do not read anything into the text; simply record what you learn.

Chapters 9–11

1. Follow the same pattern you used in the first segment and mark the same key words you marked in chapters 1 through 8. Also mark the following key words in this segment of Romans: *covenant (promise), foreknew,* predestined,* choice (chosen), Israel* (and its pronouns), *unbelief, saved (salvation*—go back and mark it in Romans 1:16), and *mercy.*

*These words are used in Romans 8:29-30. Go back and mark them, and in your notebook record what you learn from the text.

2. In this section it is critical that you follow Paul's reasoning by marking each question that he poses along with the main points of his answers. Do not read into the text meanings that aren't there. Simply let God speak as you listen. Meditate on Romans 11:33-36.

3. Record chapter and segment themes as before.

Chapters 12–16

1. At this point Paul makes a transition from explaining the doctrinal aspect of the gospel to describing how the gospel is to be lived out practically. As Paul turns from doctrine to duty, note the *therefore* (12:1) and how it relates to what has been written in the first 11 chapters of Romans. Think about what Paul is asking you to do. Is it reasonable? Why? What do you need to do?

2. Read Romans chapters 12 through 16 and identify the main topic or subject of each chapter. Also, mark the following: *love, authority (rulers), brethren (brother), Lord, Gentiles, minister (service, serving, servant), judge (judgment),* and *weak (weaknesses).*

3. Complete ROMANS AT A GLANCE. Fill in the chapter themes and segment divisions and then record the theme of Romans. (Do not forget to record your chapter themes in your Bible, too.)

THINGS TO THINK ABOUT

1. From your study of Romans, how is a person saved? Write this out.

2. Suppose someone accused you of not being a Christian. What proof could you give of the fact that you are a true child of God?

3. Do you know how to share the gospel with someone? Outline or write your testimony, incorporating the gospel into it.

4. How will your relationships to those in authority over you and to those who are your brothers and sisters in the faith change as you apply the truth of Romans to your life?

5. Are you ready to defend the gospel? Can you refute modern-day Judaizers and/or antinomians?

ROMANS OBSERVATIONS CHART

ABOUT PAUL

WHY HE WROTE

ABOUT THE RECIPIENTS

IN ADAM *(According to the flesh)*	IN CHRIST *(According to the Spirit)*

Theme of Romans:

Author:

Date:

Purpose:

Key Words:

SEGMENT DIVISIONS

			CHAPTER THEMES
			1
			2
			3
			4
			5
			6
			7
			8
			9
			10
			11
			12
			13
			14
			15
			16

See appendix 7 for key words in the New International Version and King James Version.

1 CORINTHIANS

Sin abounded in the cosmopolitan city of Corinth, the chief commercial city of Greece. Corinth overlooked the narrow isthmus that connected the Greek mainland with Peloponnesus and received ships in its two harbors. The Corinthians were intrigued by Greek philosophy and captivated by the disciplined training and athletic events held at the Isthmus. At one time the city was home to at least 12 pagen temples. The people, then, desperately needed to hear the good news of Jesus Christ, the One crucified for sinners.

The worship ceremonies carried out by a thousand temple prostitutes connected with the temple of Aphrodite (the goddess of love) bred blatant immorality throughout Corinth—so much so that the Greek verb translated "to Corinthianize" meant to practice sexual immorality.

Prostitutes openly plied their wares, and meat markets thrived on sales from the sacrifices offered in the temples. The Corinthians ate well, satisfied their sexual urges without condemnation, flirted with the wisdom of men, and did all they could to keep their bodies as beautiful as those of the Greek gods. They loved to listen to great orators. For the 250,000 citizens there were almost two slaves per person. What more did Corinth need? Freedom. Freedom from sin and death. God met that need by blocking Paul at every hand on his second missionary journey until he received the Macedonian call, "Come and help us."

After establishing the Corinthian church, Paul eventually went to Ephesus, where he stayed for three years. From there he wrote his first epistle to the Corinthian believers, who so desperately needed help and correction. It was sometime between A.D. 52 and A.D. 56.

THINGS TO DO

Chapters 1–6

1. Read through these chapters and color every reference to the author in one color and every reference to the recipients in another color. Note what you observe about each from doing this.

2. Read chapters 1 through 6, one chapter at a time. As you read, keep in mind what you read in the introduction to this book. Do the following:

a. Watch for the problems Paul deals with in his letter. You can notice these problems in one of several ways.

1) As you read, ask the "5 W's and an H": Who? What? When? Where? Why? and How? Especially concentrate on the problems, subjects, or people mentioned. Ask questions such as: Why would Paul mention specific people by name in this chapter? Who is causing the problem? How did the Corinthians get this way? Why does Paul say what he does about himself or his ministry?

2) Mark the following key words in the text along with *all* synonyms and pronouns: *call (calling,* etc.), *wisdom (wise), power, foolish, boast, spirit, arrogant, immorality, body, do you not know,* and *temple.*

Write the key words for this segment on an index card and use it as a bookmark.

b. As you read each of the first six chapters, note the problems Paul deals with in each chapter. In the margin make a list of these with the heading "Problems."

3. As you read, look for and note on the OBSERVATIONS CHART what you learn about the Corinthians, any commands directed to them, and the warnings Paul gives them.

4. As you finish each chapter, summarize the theme (subject) of that chapter and record

it on 1 CORINTHIANS AT A GLANCE and in your Bible.

5. Two things prompted Paul to write to the Corinthians, and these two things create a natural division in his epistle. Read 1 Corinthians 1:10-11, where Paul states his reason for writing. Record this reason on the 1 CORINTHIANS AT A GLANCE chart in the space under "Major Segment Divisions."

Chapters 7–16

1. The second division of 1 Corinthians is noted by a phrase that is repeated throughout the last segment of this book: *now concerning....* Read 7:1 and notice the transition. From this point on Paul deals with matters the Corinthians had questions about or issues that they needed to be instructed in.

2. Look up the following verses and underline or mark in a distinctive way the phrase *now concerning.* As you mark that phrase, mark along with it the subject matter Paul is about to deal with. The verses are 7:1; 7:25; 8:1; 12:1; 16:1. In the same way also mark in 15:1 the words *Now I make known to you, brethren, the gospel which I preached to you.* Marking these wordings will give you the topical divisions of this second segment of 1 Corinthians.

3. As you read through this last segment of 1 Corinthians, mark the following key words: *Spirit, body, love, sin (sinning), unbelieving (unbelievers), think (thinks, thinking), church (churches), idols (idolaters, idolatry), knowledge, preach, death (dead),* and *gospel.* Mark *raised* (*resurrection* in chapter 15). Make a new list of key words to use as a bookmark in this segment. (*Divisions* and *factions* are used in chapter 11. This is significant, since Paul again deals with problems while giving further instruction to the church.)

4. As you deal with each topic, ask questions such as: Why does the church have this question or problem? How are they behaving? What is their thinking? What are Paul's instructions regarding this subject? Why are they to do this? What are the consequences if they don't?

5. As Paul moves through these final matters of concern, he intermittently explains his position and ministry. Watch for these explanations and note if and how he ties them in with his subject matter.

6. Note on the OBSERVATIONS CHART what you learn from this segment about the Corinthians and the commands and warnings Paul gives them.

7. Determine and record the theme of each chapter in your Bible and on 1 CORINTHIANS AT A GLANCE.

8. Considering 7:1, give a title to the segment division for the second half of 1 Corinthians. Record your title on 1 CORINTHIANS AT A GLANCE.

9. Record the theme of 1 Corinthians and complete the 1 CORINTHIANS AT A GLANCE chart.

THINGS TO THINK ABOUT

1. Are you having any of the same problems in your own life or in your church that the Corinthians had? Do you think this letter has the answers for your problems or questions? How can you apply what you have learned?

2. According to the context of 1 Corinthians 3, what does it mean to be a carnal or fleshly Christian? Remember, context rules over all accurate interpretation.

3. Are you untaught—ignorant—concerning spiritual gifts? Do you know about one or two of them but not the others? Have you believed or even taught others in accord with what the whole counsel of God has to say on the subject, or have you merely gone by

your experience or reasoning? Do you appreciate other people's gifts even though they may be different from yours?

4. On what do you base your beliefs about marriage, divorce, and remarriage? What did you learn from 1 Corinthians 7 about these topics? Did this change your belief?

5. Is the preaching of the cross foolishness to you, or is it a demonstration of the power of God?

DESCRIPTION OF THE CORINTHIANS

COMMANDS TO THE CORINTHIANS

WARNINGS TO THE CORINTHIANS

Theme of 1 Corinthians:

SEGMENT DIVISIONS

PROBLEMS OR TOPICS	MAJOR DIVISIONS	CHAPTER THEMES
		1
		2
		3
		4
		5
		6
		7
		8
		9
		10
		11
		12
		13
		14
		15
		16

Author:

Date:

Purpose:

Key Words:

See appendix 7 for key words in the New International Version and King James Version.

2 CORINTHIANS

*P*aul, the apostle to the Gentiles, was taught and appointed by Jesus Christ. Strong in faith, confident, and greatly used by God, Paul was loved by multitudes and hated by countless others. Determined that the grace of God poured out on him would not prove vain, Paul labored with more effort than anyone.

However, Paul's labor was not without cost. He endured conflicts without and fears within. Yet he persevered. What were his conflicts, his fears, his sufferings? Are they similar to yours? And how did he endure? What held him? As Paul writes his second epistle to the Corinthians from Macedonia, probably in the winter of A.D. 55, he provides answers to these questions.

THINGS TO DO

General Instructions

1. Second Corinthians is different from Paul's other epistles. Watch the atmosphere or tone of this epistle. Paul is defending himself, which is unusual for Paul. As you read through the book, note the issues Paul addresses and what he says to the Corinthians, and you will understand what Paul is up against.

2. Study the 2 CORINTHIANS OBSERVATIONS CHART on page 230 and see what you'll need to observe as you study 2 Corinthians chapter by chapter. Make a duplicate of this chart so you can use it as a worksheet. When you have completed it, record the information on the original chart.

   a. As you read each chapter, list everything you learn about Paul. Be sure to note the afflictions he endured: What must he do in respect to the Corinthians? What has been done to him by the Corinthians? Ask God to show you Paul's character, his heart, his joys, and his sorrows.

   b. Note what you learn about the Corinthians. Remember to ask the "5 W's and an H": What are they like? What is their relationship with Paul like? What is going on in the Corinthian church at this time? What have they said about Paul? What problems has Paul had to deal with in respect to them?

   c. What is Paul's desire or goal for the Corinthians?

   d. Titus is mentioned several times in this letter. Record what you learn about him.

3. As you read 2 Corinthians chapter by chapter, do the following:

   a. Mark in the text in a distinctive way the key words (and their synonyms and pronouns) listed on the 2 CORINTHIANS AT A GLANCE chart. Write these on an index card that you can use as a bookmark while you study 2 Corinthians. (Hint: If you mark every reference to Satan with an appropriate symbol he will be easy to spot.)

   b. As you come to specific chapters you will notice other key words which are not listed on 2 CORINTHIANS AT A GLANCE. Mark these also.

   c. If there are several truths you learn from the use of a key word within a chapter, list in your notebook what you learn from that word. For example, list all you learn about *affliction(s)* and *sufferings*. Write the heading "Affliction/Suffering" in the margin of each chapter that has these key words. Mark the heading in a distinctive way so you can spot it easily.

4. Look for the theme (subject) of each chapter and record it in your Bible and under "Chapter Themes" on 2 CORINTHIANS AT A GLANCE.

Chapters 1–7

1. In the midst of this very personal letter, Paul gives some important insights on several subjects.

    a. Chapter 3 mentions the new covenant (which is grace) and the old covenant (which is law). These are described as ministries, and then the ministries are contrasted according to the result of each: condemnation or righteousness. Record in your notebook what you learn about each from the text.

    b. In chapter 5 Paul talks about what will happen to our earthly bodies when we die. He also discusses the judgment seat of Christ and our ministry of reconciliation. Identify how these relate to one another and what you learn about each from the text. Record any Lessons for Life ("LFL") in the margins.

    c. In chapter 7 Paul deals with two kinds of sorrow and what they produce. Don't miss this. Record your notes in your notebook.

2. What is Paul writing about in chapters 1 through 7? Is there a theme that runs through these chapters? Remember that key words reveal the themes. What key words are repeated the most in this segment?

3. How does Paul begin and end this segment?

4. Record the theme for chapters 1 through 7 on 2 CORINTHIANS AT A GLANCE under "Segment Divisions."

Chapters 8–9

1. What subject is Paul talking about in chapters 8 and 9? Note the use of the words *ministry, work,* and *service.* What ministry or work or service is he referring to?

2. Record this subject as the theme of this segment in the appropriate space on 2 CORINTHIANS AT A GLANCE.

Chapters 10–13

1. Notice when the key word *boast* first appears in the text and what happens when it appears. Note what or whom the boasting is in and what you learn.

2. In your notebook, list what you learn about Satan and spiritual warfare from these four chapters.

3. What does Paul seem to be doing in chapters 10 through 13? What opposition is there to Paul, and what is the opposition saying about him? What is his response to this opposition? Record the theme of this segment on 2 CORINTHIANS AT A GLANCE under "Segment Divisions" and complete the chart.

THINGS TO THINK ABOUT

1. What is the purpose of affliction? When you need to be comforted, do you turn to people or to God?

2. Is it always wrong to feel sorrow, to be hurt, or to have a broken heart? Is it always wrong to cause sorrow, to hurt, or to break another person's heart?

3. How do you deal with those who oppose you? How do you minister to those who are caught in the middle of a conflict and don't know who to believe?

4. Paul was human just like us; he had feelings just like we do. What can we learn from him about how we are to live and respond in spite of our feelings? When is it right to give a defense of one's self, of one's ministry?

5. Are you prepared to stand before the judgment seat of Christ?

6. What place does the ministry of giving have in your life?

7. If you were to examine yourself, would you find your Christianity genuine?

2 Corinthians Observations Chart

Paul

His character	His afflictions	His conflict with the Corinthians

The Corinthians

Their strengths	Their weaknesses	Their problems with Paul

Paul's desire for the Corinthians	Insights on Titus

Theme of 2 Corinthians:

SEGMENT DIVISIONS

		CHAPTER THEMES	
			Author:
		1	**Date:**
		2	
		3	**Purpose:**
		4	
		5	**Key Words:**
		6	comfort (comforted)
		7	afflicted (affliction, suffer, sufferings)
			sorrow(ful)
			boast
			confidence
			commend(ing)
			death
			life
			love
		8	heart
			joy (rejoice, rejoicing, rejoiced)
		9	covenant (ministry of ____)
		10	ministry
			grace
			Titus
		11	weak (weakness)
		12	mark references to the enemy (warfare, serpent, Satan, as well as pronouns and synonyms)
		13	

See appendix 7 for key words in the New International Version and King James Version.

GALATIANS

*T*he gospel introduced the Jews to a new way of life—that of grace rather than law. The old covenant, with all of its regulations, was made obsolete by the new covenant (Hebrews 8:13). This transition was difficult for some Jewish believers to handle, and a group called the Judaizers sprang up. The Judaizers embraced Christianity but said that some of the old covenant rites, including circumcision, still must be observed.

As Paul, God's apostle to the Gentiles, traveled on his missionary journeys sharing the gospel of grace, many of these Judaizers followed him, teaching the necessity of keeping the law to one degree or another. They even went to Galatia. That is why Paul wrote what he did to the churches there.

We do not know when Galatians was written, but Galatians 2:1 indicates it was after Paul's trip to Jerusalem (Acts 15). However, the date it was written does not affect the message of this critical letter. The timeless truths in this epistle will liberate you to walk in that glorious freedom of a righteous life in the Spirit—truths you can glean through careful observation.

The more you read and observe the text of this book, the more you will understand Paul's words: "It is no longer I who live, but Christ lives in me; and the life which I now live in the flesh I live by faith in the Son of God, who loved me and gave Himself up for me" (Galatians 2:20).

THINGS TO DO

1. Read Acts 13 and 14 and then look at the map on page 216 to acquaint yourself with the cities in this area. Also, review the chart on the next page showing the sequence of events in Paul's life after his conversion.

2. Read through Galatians and color every reference to the author in one color and every reference to the recipients in another. Then make a list of all you learn about each that answers any of the "5 W's and an H."

3. As you read, mark in the text the key words (and their synonyms and pronouns) that are listed on the GALATIANS AT A GLANCE chart. Mark any other key words you see as you read.

   a. After you mark the key words, it's profitable to list everything you learn from the text about the key words. This will give you additional insights into Paul's message.

   b. Mark references to time with a green clock ⏲ so that they stand out distinctively. Double-underline in green all the geographical references.

   c. Jesus Christ is mentioned 38 times in Galatians. List everything you learn about Him from this book.

4. As you read through the book, note Paul's emphasis in the first two chapters and then how the focus changes in chapter 3. In chapter 3, mark *promise* and note what it is.

5. Look for the questions Paul asks the recipients of this letter. Watch for words such as *brethren, you,* and *foolish Galatians.*

   a. Think about why Paul said all he did about himself in those first two chapters. What does this have to do with what follows in the rest of his epistle?

   b. Notice the progression of events in Paul's life as presented in these chapters.

6. Record the chapter themes on GALATIANS AT A GLANCE and in your Bible. Record the theme of the book and complete the chart, filling in the segment divisions.

THINGS TO THINK ABOUT

1. Are you living under grace or under law? Have you accepted the grace of God for your salvation but still put yourself under the law for daily living?

2. According to Galatians 5:16-21, if you live under grace, under the control of the Spirit of God, you will not be able to live a life habitually controlled by the flesh, producing the works of the flesh. Evaluate your walk according to these verses.

3. What do you boast in?

4. As you look at Paul's life, what do you learn for your own life?

Sequence of Events in Paul's Life After His Conversion*

There are differing opinions on these dates.

Scripture	Year A.D.	Event
Acts 9:1-25	33–34	Conversion, time in Damascus
	35–47	Some silent years, except we know that Paul:
Gal. 1:17		1. Spent time in Arabia and Damascus ⎤ 3 years
Acts 9:26; Gal. 1:18		2. Made first visit to Jerusalem ⎦
Acts 9:30–11:26; Gal. 1:21		3. Went to Tarsus, Syria-Cilicia area
Acts 11:26		4. Was with Barnabas in Antioch
Acts 11:30		5. With Barnabas took relief to brethren in Judea, and Paul's second visit to Jerusalem
Acts 12:23	44	Herod Agrippa dies
Acts 12:25		6. Returned to Antioch; was sent out with Barnabas by church at Antioch
Acts 13:4–14:26	47–48	**First missionary journey:** Proconsul Sergius Paulus on Paphos is datable
Acts 15:1-35; Gal. 2:1	49	Apostolic Council at Jerusalem—Paul visits Jerusalem (compare Acts 15 with Galatians 2:1) *Galatians written?*
Acts 15:36–18:22	49–51	**Second missionary journey:** *1 and 2 Thessalonians written*—1½ years in Corinth, Acts 18:11
	51–52	Gallio known to be proconsul in Corinth
Acts 18:23–21:17	52–56	**Third missionary journey:** *1 and 2 Corinthians and Romans written*—probably from Ephesus
Acts 21:18-23	56	Paul goes to Jerusalem and is arrested; held in Caesarea
Acts 24–26	57–59	Appearance before Felix and Drusilla; before Festus, appeals to Caesar; before Agrippa—datable
Acts 27–28:15	59–60	Went from Caesarea to Rome
Acts 28:16-31	60–62	First Roman imprisonment: *Ephesians, Philemon, Colossians, and Philippians written*—2 years in prison
	62	Paul's release; possible trip to Spain
	62	Paul in Macedonia: *1 Timothy written*
	62	Paul goes to Crete: *Titus written*
	63–64	Paul taken to Rome and imprisoned: *2 Timothy written*
	64	Paul is absent from the body and present with the Lord *(Others put Paul's conversion about A.D. 35, his death at A.D. 68.)*

(note in left margin: *14 years, Gal. 2:1*)

Theme of Galatians:

SEGMENT DIVISIONS

		CHAPTER THEMES
		1
		2
		3
		4
		5
		6

Author:

Date:

Purpose:

Key Words:

gospel

grace

law

Spirit

faith

promise

covenant

Christ (Jesus)

free (freedom)

circumcision

See appendix 7 for key words in the New International Version and King James Version.

EPHESIANS

*E*phesus, the fourth-largest city in the Roman Empire, was the home of the temple of the goddess called Artemis by the Greeks and Diana by the Romans. Of all the deities in Asia, none was more sought after than Artemis.

But by the time of Paul, Ephesus's position as a center of trade was lost because the harbor became unnavigable. From that point on, the worship of Artemis became the city's means of economic survival. The tourist and pilgrim trade associated with Artemis made many people in Ephesus wealthy. Silversmiths made their living selling images of this goddess and her temple. Innkeepers and restaurant owners grew rich from the large influx of worshipers who traveled great distances to see the temple of Artemis, one of the seven wonders of the world. The temple treasury even served as a bank, lending large sums of money to many, including kings. And since Artemis was the patroness of sex, prostitutes sold their bodies without condemnation in the two-story brothel on Marble Road. Although Artemis was the main attraction, all sorts of magic and sorcery were conjured up in Ephesus.

Then God sent Paul to live in Ephesus and called out for Himself a church, a light to illumine the occultic darkness of this city.

This brief glimpse into the historical and cultural setting of Ephesians should help you understand why Paul wrote what he did to the church in Ephesus. The message of this epistle is needed as much today as it was in A.D. 60 to 62, when Paul wrote it as a prisoner in Rome.

THINGS TO DO

General Instructions

1. Read Ephesians and color every reference to the author in one color, every reference to the recipients in another.

2. When you finish, read Acts 18:18-21 (Paul's first visit to Ephesus was on his second missionary journey). Then read Acts 19 for an account of Paul's second visit on his third missionary journey. This passage will help you understand why the letter to the Ephesians deals with warfare and our position in Christ more extensively than any other epistle.

Chapters 1-3

Read Ephesians 1 through 3 one chapter at a time, doing the following:

1. Mark or note each reference to God. Then make a list of everything God does.

2. Mark distinctively each reference to being *in Christ* and *in Him*. Then on the OBSERVATIONS CHART, under the heading "Our Wealth and Position in Christ," list what believers have *in Christ.* Also, pay particular attention to the phrase *in the heavenly places,* which is key to warfare. Note the chapter and verse from which the information comes when you make your list (e.g., 1:13).

3. Mark each reference to the Holy Spirit. On the OBSERVATIONS CHART, under the heading "Our Relationship with the Holy Spirit," list what is taught about the person and work of the Holy Spirit.

4. Mark the other key words (with their synonyms and pronouns) listed on the EPHESIANS AT A GLANCE chart. Put these on an index card and use it as a bookmark.

5. Mark distinctively each occurrence of *riches (rich)*. Then list what you learn about

235

these riches. Remember to ask the "5 W's and an H": Who is rich and in what? How are these riches described? What is done with the riches? And so on.

6. Mark each use of *formerly*. Then on the OBSERVATIONS CHART under the heading "Our Former Lifestyle and Walk," list what Ephesians says about how believers lived before salvation.

Chapters 4–6

1. Read Ephesians 4 through 6 chapter by chapter, doing the following:

   a. Mark each occurrence of *walk*. Then on the OBSERVATIONS CHART, under the heading "Our Walk in Christ," list what is taught about the lifestyle of a believer. Also go back to 2:2,10 and mark and list what these verses teach about the believer's lifestyle. Then ask yourself: How am I to live? Why am I able to live this way?

   b. Mark the key words listed on your bookmark. Also, mark *stand firm* in chapter 6. Observe what you learn from the uses of *former(ly)* in this section of Ephesians. Note the contrast between our former lifestyle and our walk in Christ and record any new insights.

   c. As you mark *Holy Spirit* and *in the Lord,* think about what you learn and how you are to walk in Him. Record your insights.

2. After you observe Ephesians 6:10-20, compare this with Ephesians 1:18-23. Note the references to *powers* and *rulers* (and their synonyms). Note what this tells you about the importance of spiritual warfare in this epistle and how believers can stand firm against the schemes of the devil.

3. On EPHESIANS AT A GLANCE:

   a. Record the theme of the book and of each chapter in the appropriate spaces. (Remember to go back and record each chapter's theme in your Bible.)

   b. As you have seen, there is a change of emphasis between chapters 3 and 4. Under "Segment Divisions" write what best summarizes the content of chapters 1–3 and then chapters 4–6.

THINGS TO THINK ABOUT

1. Stop and review all you observed and recorded about your position as a child of God. Go through chapter 1 again and note everything God has done for you. Watch for the personal pronoun *He*. Also note the phrase *according to* and the word *will*. Think about what God has done for you and why. Then thank Him and tell Him you want to live accordingly.

2. Ephesians 2:8-10 are extremely important verses. Think about what God is saying to you and ask God to show you whether you are trusting in His grace or in your works to get you to heaven. But don't stop there. Think about the relationship of good works to the life of a believer. How are you walking? Memorize these verses.

3. In your home do you live according to Ephesians 5:18–6:4?

4. Are you able to stand firm, or are you defeated by the devil's schemes? Don't forget where you are seated. Think about God's power, His strength, His armor. Do you have it on, and are you standing firm in truth, righteousness, peace, salvation, and faith? Are you able to use the Word of God as your offensive weapon?

OUR WEALTH AND POSITION IN CHRIST

OUR RELATIONSHIP WITH THE HOLY SPIRIT

OUR FORMER LIFESTYLE AND WALK

OUR WALK IN CHRIST

Theme of Ephesians:

SEGMENT DIVISIONS

Author:			CHAPTER THEMES
Date:			1
Purpose:			2
Key Words:			3
every reference to being in Christ (in the Lord)			
according to			
the (Holy) Spirit			
rich(es)			
in the heavenly places			4
former(ly)			
grace			
power			5
body (church)			
redemption			
walk			
the devil (including powers, rulers, authorities, etc.)			6

See appendix 7 for key words in the New International Version and King James Version.

PHILIPPIANS

*B*locked by the Spirit of God from going into Asia and Bithynia, Paul had a vision of a man from Macedonia asking him to come to Macedonia and help the churches there.

Confident that God had given him direction, Paul sailed with Timothy and Luke from Troas on a second missionary journey. Philippi, in Macedonia, basked in the fact that it was also a Roman colony, which ensured its citizens all the benefits of Roman citizenship.

As was his custom, when Paul reached a city, he sought out the Jews. Although there were not enough Jews living in Philippi to form a synagogue, the Jews met outside the gate by the river for prayer on the Sabbath. Little did Paul realize that he would end up in prison, for God knew there was a Roman jailer and his family who needed Jesus.

The events of that visit inaugurated the beginning of the church at Philippi, the church Paul addressed around the year A.D. 61 or 62.

THINGS TO DO

1. Familiarize yourself with the message of Philippians by marking every reference to the author in one color and to the recipients in another. Look for the verses in chapters 1 and 4 that tell where Paul is as he writes.

2. To understand the historical setting of Philippians, read Acts 15:35–17:1, which records Paul's first visit to Philippi. After his third missionary journey, Paul went to Jerusalem, where he was arrested. From there Paul was taken by a Roman guard to Caesarea, the Mediterranean seaport where the Roman consul often went to escape the heat and confines of Jerusalem. After remaining a prisoner in Caesarea for over two years, Paul, who as a Roman citizen had appealed to Caesar, was sent to Rome, where he lived under house arrest. Read Acts 28:14-31 and note how long Paul remained a prisoner at Rome. How does this compare with where Paul was when he wrote Philippians?

3. As you read Philippians chapter by chapter, do the following:

   a. Using the OBSERVATIONS CHART, record your insights about the author and the recipients of Philippians.

   b. In a distinctive way, mark in the text each key word (and its synonyms and pronouns) listed on the PHILIPPIANS AT A GLANCE chart. This will help you discover the themes (main subjects) of each chapter and of the book itself. Watch for other key words that are not listed but are used within each chapter.

   c. Make a list in your notebook of everything you learn from marking your key words.

   d. List each of the instructions Paul gives to the Philippian saints on the chart PAUL'S INSTRUCTIONS TO THE PHILIPPIANS on page 242. As you list these instructions, evaluate your life in the light of each one.

4. On PHILIPPIANS AT A GLANCE:

   a. Fill in the theme for the book and for each chapter. (Be sure you also record the chapter theme in your Bible.)

   b. Under "Segment Divisions" record what you see to be Paul's example in each chapter. Remember, in Philippians 3:17 Paul tells his readers to follow his example.

   c. In the next column under "Segment Divisions" write down what each chapter says about who or what Jesus Christ is in relation to the believer.

d. For another segment division, record a command to believers that correlates with the theme of each chapter.

THINGS TO THINK ABOUT

1. What have you learned from Philippians about your relationship to suffering as a Christian? How is it going to affect the way you respond to suffering?

2. Can you say with Paul, "For to me, to live is Christ and to die is gain"? If you can't, think about what has replaced Christ's rightful place in your life.

3. What have you learned from Jesus' example that you can apply to your own life? Do you have the attitude of Christ toward God and others? Do you regard others as more important than yourself?

4. Do you allow your circumstances to affect your peace? What is keeping you from His peace? After reading Philippians 4 do you see any way to handle life's anxieties?

5. What have you learned about your own needs and sharing with others in need?

AUTHOR: *Look for both pronouns and direct references*

THE RECIPIENTS: *Look for* the saints, brethren, beloved, you, *or any other ways Paul addresses those to whom he is writing. (Remember to keep asking the "5 W's and an H": How does Paul describe the Philippians? What are their problems? What is his concern for them? Why is Paul writing to the Philippians?)*

(continued)

Paul's Instructions to the Philippians

(continued)

_____
_____
_____
_____
_____
_____
_____
_____
_____
_____
_____
_____
_____
_____
_____
_____

PHILIPPIANS AT A GLANCE

Theme of Philippians:

SEGMENT DIVISIONS

	COMMAND TO:	JESUS IS:	PAUL'S EXAMPLE	CHAPTER THEMES
Author:				
Date:		1:21 MY LIFE		1
Purpose:				
Key Words:				2
imprisonment				
Christ Jesus				
joy (rejoice)	3:17 FOLLOW PAUL'S EXAMPLE			3
mind (attitude)				
gospel				
prayer			4:11 LEARNED TO BE CONTENT IN HIS CIRCUMSTANCES	4
stand firm				
day of Christ				
suffer				

See appendix 7 for key words in the New International Version and King James Version.

COLOSSIANS

*C*olossae was located 12 miles from Laodicea and about a hundred miles east of Ephesus in the valley of the Lycus River in the southern part of ancient Phrygia, the adopted home of Oriental mysticism. Many Jews, Phrygians, and Greeks came to Colossae because it was on a main trade route. The mixture of backgrounds made the city an interesting cultural center where all sorts of new ideas and doctrines from the East were discussed and considered.

With all these ungodly influences, it is no wonder that the Christians at Colossae were on Paul's heart during his imprisonment in Rome. He may never have seen their faces, but they belonged to his Christ and he was one with them in spirit. Physically he might be bound by chains, but he could reach them by letter. This was one way he could protect them from the wolves who were out to devour God's flock.

Paul wrote sometime around A.D. 62. The words he penned to the faithful saints at Colossae contained a message that would be needed down through the ages. Maybe that is one of the reasons God didn't let Paul deliver this message in person.

THINGS TO DO

1. As you read Colossians, learn all you can from the text about the author and the recipients to discover why the author writes what he does to this particular church. This will give you the key to understanding Colossians. Following this simple procedure will help:

   a. As you read, color every reference to the author in one color and every reference to the recipients in another. Make sure you mark the synonyms and pronouns that refer either to the author or the recipients.

   b. Once you've marked the author and the recipients, study what you learn from marking the text in this way. Read through Colossians chapter by chapter, looking at each reference you marked to see if it answers any of the "5 W's and an H": Who? What? Where? Why? When? and How? Ask questions such as: Who wrote this? To whom? Where were they? What were these people like? What were their situations? What were their problems? When was this written? What seemed to be going on? Why did the author say what he did?

   Look for pronouns such as *you* and note the relationship between the author and the recipients. Ask questions like these: How did the gospel get to the Colossians? Who preached the gospel to them? What was the author's main concern for the Colossians? The answers will help you understand why this letter was written.

   Asking questions like these—answered only from what the text says—will give you insight into a book of the Bible, help you to understand the context and purpose of the book, and enable you to keep its teachings and truths in their proper context.

   c. Record your insights about the author, the recipients, and the author's instructions.

2. Now read through Colossians again, a chapter at a time. As you read:

   a. Mark the key words and phrases listed on the COLOSSIANS AT A GLANCE chart. Be sure to mark the synonyms and pronouns for each key word, and to mark every reference to Jesus: *with Him, by Him, for Him, through Him,* and so on.

   b. In your notebook, list what you learn from marking *in Him* and other key words.

3. In chapter 2, note the warnings by looking for the phrases *see to it* and *let no one.*

    a. Record these warnings along with any instructions on the OBSERVATIONS CHART.

    b. With these warnings in mind, read the section titled "Understanding Gnosticism" on pages 324-325.

4. Proceed through chapters 3 and 4 in the same manner as chapters 1 and 2, adding pertinent information to your OBSERVATIONS CHART.

5. Record the theme of the book and of each chapter on the COLOSSIANS AT A GLANCE chart. Remember to record the chapter theme in your Bible. Also fill out the date the book was written, the name of the author, and his purpose for writing.

THINGS TO THINK ABOUT

1. Examine your lifestyle. What are you pursuing? Does it have eternal value? Is it drawing you closer to God or keeping you from time alone with God in prayer and in studying the Word? Are you seeking things that are above or earthly things?

2. Examine your beliefs. Are you being deluded with any modern-day philosophies or traditions that contradict the Word or aren't in the Word? Any legalistic rules that are not clearly taught in the New Testament? Any mystical teachings or prophecies that can't be supported in the Word of God or that have a tendency to add something that isn't there or that seem to be only for an elite group of people?

3. Inductive Bible study takes time. The enemy will do all he can to keep you from knowing God and His Word intimately, for truth is your major defense and offense in spiritual warfare. Are you going to make it your goal to let the Word of Christ richly dwell within you and to walk in its precepts?

4. Are you proclaiming the Lord Jesus Christ and holding firmly to all He is and all that you have in Him as He is presented in Colossians?

5. As you studied Colossians, did you see any areas in your life in which you are falling short or simply walking in disobedience to God's Word? What steps are you going to take in order to correct these?

AUTHOR

RECIPIENTS

WARNINGS AND INSTRUCTIONS

(continued)

(blank ruled lines)

COLOSSIANS AT A GLANCE

Theme of Colossians:

SEGMENT
DIVISIONS

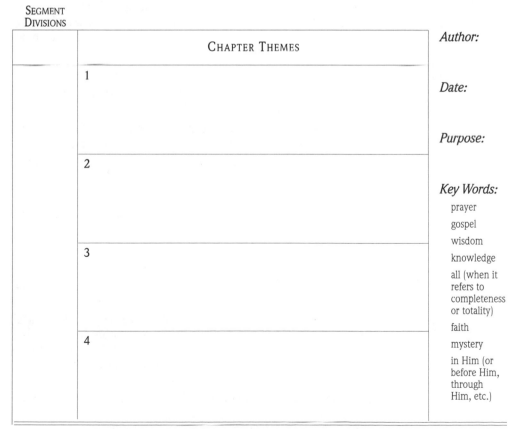

		CHAPTER THEMES
	1	
	2	
	3	
	4	

Author:

Date:

Purpose:

Key Words:
prayer
gospel
wisdom
knowledge
all (when it refers to completeness or totality)
faith
mystery
in Him (or before Him, through Him, etc.)

See appendix 7 for key words in the New International Version and King James Version.

1 THESSALONIANS

*T*imothy joined Paul and Silas (Silvanus) while they were in Lystra on Paul's second missionary journey. Since his father was a Greek, Timothy hadn't been circumcised. Not wanting to cause any unnecessary conflicts with the Jews in those parts, Paul had Timothy circumcised. Things went smoothly on their journey until Paul had a vision of a man from Macedonia appealing to him to come and help them.

Believing this call was of God, the three went to Philippi—and the persecution began. Paul and Silas were beaten with rods and thrown into prison. Undaunted and convinced of their heavenly commission, the trio traveled on through Amphipolis and Apollonia and came to Thessalonica. There they found a Jewish synagogue, where for three Sabbaths Paul reasoned with the Thessalonians from the Scriptures. Jews and Greeks, including a number of leading women, heard and believed. The Jews who didn't like this became jealous and stirred up the city. Once again there was opposition, but this time the persecution was directed not only to the trio but also to those who had believed.

Consequently, the Thessalonian believers sent Paul, Silas, and Timothy to Berea by night where again the gospel bore fruit. When the Jews of Thessalonica heard what happened in Berea, they couldn't bear it and went there to persecute the men who were upsetting the world.

From Berea Paul went to Athens and then to Corinth. But the church at Thessalonica was on his heart. How were they doing in the midst of such adamant opposition? Paul had to find out. So about A.D. 51, while in Corinth, Paul wrote his first epistle to the church at Thessalonica.

THINGS TO DO

1. If you want to understand how the church in Thessalonica was established and the events surrounding it, read Acts 16:1–17:15.

2. Read 1 Thessalonians chapter by chapter. Mark every reference to the author(s) in one color, and every reference to the recipients in another. Include synonyms and pronouns.

    a. List what you learn about the author(s). Note the relationship of the author(s) to the recipients. What example do you see that's worthy of imitation?

    b. List everything you learn about the recipients. Note whom they had been serving. What happened when they heard and believed the gospel? What were they enduring, and how?

    c. Note the different problems or concerns addressed in the letter.

3. Read through the book and mark in the text the key words (along with their synonyms and pronouns) listed on the 1 THESSALONIANS AT A GLANCE chart. When you finish, observe what you learn from marking each key word.

4. In chapters 4 and 5 are several truths about those "who have fallen asleep" and those "who are alive and remain." List what you observe about each on the OBSERVATIONS CHART. Note the progression of events in 1 Thessalonians 4:13-18. Ask the "5 W's and an H" of the text: Who is involved? What will happen? Where will they meet the Lord? When? Why are they not to sorrow? How will all this happen?

5. Record what you learn about "the day of the Lord" in chapter 5 on the chart we suggested in "Getting Started."

6. On 1 THESSALONIANS AT A GLANCE, record the theme of the book. Then record the theme of each chapter on the chart and in your Bible. Fill in any additional information under author, date, purpose, etc.

7. Often you will be able to note a turning point in an epistle as the author changes his emphasis. Such changes divide the book into segments. Where does the emphasis or content change in 1 Thessalonians? Note the topic in the first chapters of the book and when the subject changes. Title each segment of the book by thinking of the theme or subject discussed in the first three chapters and then in the last two chapters. Record your segment divisions on 1 THESSALONIANS AT A GLANCE.

THINGS TO THINK ABOUT

1. In this book Paul pours his life into other men who could carry on the work of the gospel. Are you spending time imparting the things God has done in your life to another person who can in turn minister to others? What can others imitate in you? Are you an example?

2. It is sometimes hard to give thanks in all things, yet that is the will of God. Go back over the last few days and think of the things that have happened in your life for which you have not given thanks. Determine in your heart to obey this command.

3. Are the circumstances in your life difficult? How are you responding? What will others say about your response? Can people imitate your walk with God?

4. Are you abstaining from sexual immorality? Are you defrauding others sexually in any way? Do you realize that if you are acting out your sexual passions in a way contrary to God's Word, God will act as the avenger against you?

5. Do you pray without ceasing (5:17) for those in your life who don't know the Lord? Do you boldly approach the Lord for answers to your problems? Do you pray consistently for others?

Author(s)	Recipients

(continued)

THOSE WHO HAVE FALLEN ASLEEP	PROGRESSION OF EVENTS	THE DAY OF THE LORD
THOSE WHO ARE ALIVE AND REMAIN		

1 THESSALONIANS AT A GLANCE

Theme of 1 Thessalonians:

	SEGMENT DIVISIONS	CHAPTER THEMES
Author:		
Date:	1	
Purpose:		
Key Words:	2	
gospel (word)		
tribulation (suffered, affliction)	3	
Spirit		
any reference to Jesus' coming		
faith	4	
hope		
love		
day of the Lord	5	
every reference to Satan (the tempter)		

See appendix 7 for key words in the New International Version and King James Version.

2 THESSALONIANS

*I*t had been four to six months since Paul wrote his first epistle to the church at Thessalonica in A.D. 51. Their persecution had not subsided, but much to Paul's joy, his labor had not been in vain; the beloved believers at Thessalonica had withstood the attacks of the tempter.

However, Paul was concerned about some things in the church. Once again, during his second missionary journey he had to take time to write—and put his distinguishing mark on this letter. The church had to know without a doubt that this letter was from him.

THINGS TO DO

1. If you haven't studied 1 Thessalonians, you should do so before you begin 2 Thessalonians. However, if you have worked through 1 Thessalonians, read it once again. Observe what Paul says about the coming of the Lord Jesus. Also give special attention to 1 Thessalonians 4:13–5:11.

2. Now read 2 Thessalonians. Mark every reference to the author(s) in one color and to the recipients in another. Note how 1 Thessalonians ties in with 2 Thessalonians. Look for the following information and record it on the OBSERVATIONS CHART.

   a. What do you learn about the author and the recipients of this letter? What are the circumstances of the recipients?

   b. Paul addresses several problems that need correction. List these in the margin and on the chart. This will help you see his purpose in writing. Then note the instructions or commands related to each problem addressed. List these on your OBSERVATIONS CHART.

   c. Paul also praises the Thessalonians and encourages them about the things they are doing well. List the exhortations he includes in his letter.

   d. Be certain you record what happens to those who do not obey the gospel.

   e. From what you have observed, why do you think Paul wrote this book? Record this on 2 THESSALONIANS AT A GLANCE under "Purpose."

3. Read through 2 Thessalonians again, a chapter at a time, and do the following:

   a. Mark in the text the key words (including their synonyms and pronouns) listed on 2 THESSALONIANS AT A GLANCE. Also watch for any words you feel are key but aren't listed.

   b. Now go back through the key words and observe what you learned from marking these words. You may want to write your observations in your notebook.

4. On the OBSERVATIONS CHART are two more headings: "When the Day of the Lord Comes" and "When the Man of Lawlessness Is Revealed."

   a. Carefully read 2 Thessalonians 2:1-12 and list everything the chapter says must happen *before* the day of the Lord can come.

   b. Do the same for the revelation of the man of lawlessness.

   c. Record your insights on the "Day of the Lord" chart we suggested in "Getting Started," page 25.

5. Think through each chapter and record its theme on 2 THESSALONIANS AT A GLANCE and in the appropriate place in your Bible. Also record the theme of the book, author, and date.

252

THINGS TO THINK ABOUT

1. How do you react to trials? Are you willing to suffer persecution? What does your response tell you and others about God? Do people see your faith? Is His love evident in your life?

2. Do you lead a disciplined life? Does your lifestyle encourage laziness in others? What are you doing for the furtherance of the kingdom? Or are you just waiting for Jesus to come back? Is this pleasing to God? Can you say, "Follow my example"?

3. When the good you do doesn't seem appreciated or even noticed, how do you feel? For whom are you doing it? Will you persevere?

4. Does what you believe about prophecy or any other doctrine come from a careful, personal study of God's Word, or does it come from what others teach you and books? Are you holding fast to what you know of the Word of God, or are you easily persuaded by "faddish" teaching?

Author	Recipients	Those Who Do Not Obey the Gospel

Problems/Concerns	Instructions	Exhortations

When the Day of the Lord Comes	When the Man of Lawlessness Is Revealed

Theme of 2 Thessalonians:

Author:

Date:

Purpose:

Key Words:

   affliction
(suffering,
persecutions)

   coming of
Jesus Christ (or
synonymous
references)

   God

   Spirit

   love

   faith

   glory (glorified)

   man of
lawlessness

   undisciplined
(unruly)

   day of the Lord
(and pronouns)

   truth

   example
(model)

Segment Divisions	Chapter Themes
	1
	2
	3

See appendix 7 for key words in the New International Version and King James Version.

1 TIMOTHY

*T*hirty years of labor for the gospel had taken its toll on Paul. His body bore the marks of a servant of Jesus Christ (Galatians 6:17). Yet the intensity of his suffering was minor compared to the intensity of his love and concern for the churches.

Undaunted by two years of house arrest in Rome, Paul pressed on toward the prize of the high calling in Christ Jesus. He intended to visit Asia, Macedonia, and possibly Spain. Spain had been on his heart before he became a prisoner of Rome.

Paul also was concerned about the church at Ephesus. Timothy, his faithful co-laborer, was pastoring that strategically important church. Possibly concerned that he might be delayed and that Timothy might need instructions to set before others as an ever-present reminder, Paul wrote to his beloved son in the faith an epistle that would become a legacy for the church and a pillar and support of the truth. It was around A.D. 62.

THINGS TO DO

1. Read 1 Timothy. Mark every reference to Paul in one color and every reference to Timothy in another. Include synonyms and pronouns. Note 1:3 and 3:14-15 to see why Paul wrote this epistle. On the 1 TIMOTHY AT A GLANCE chart, record Paul's purpose for writing.

2. Read 1 Timothy again, one chapter at a time. On the OBSERVATIONS CHART:

   a. List what you learn from marking the references to Paul. Observe how he refers to himself, stating his position of authority, which qualifies him to instruct Timothy in the matters described in this letter.

   b. List what you observe from marking references to Timothy. Note where Timothy is and what his relationship is to Paul.

   c. List the commands and instructions Paul gives about specific groups of people or practices. Record what you learn about overseers (elders) and deacons. Also record what you see about general groups of believers in the church. There is a designated space for each of these groups on the OBSERVATIONS CHART.

   d. Record the specific charges Paul gives Timothy as his representative in Ephesus and as the one who is organizing and instructing the church there.

3. As you read, mark in the text the key words (with their synonyms and pronouns) listed on 1 TIMOTHY AT A GLANCE. These key words give clues about the most important and most often-mentioned instructions.

4. Unless you already recorded this on your OBSERVATIONS CHART, make a list of what you learn from the text about these key words. You'll see what is important to the health of the church.

5. What do you think is the theme of 1 Timothy? Are there any problems or concerns the author must address? How does the theme relate to these concerns? Record the theme of the book on 1 TIMOTHY AT A GLANCE and then list the theme of each chapter on the chart and also in your Bible. Finally, fill in any additional information under author, purpose, and so on.

THINK ABOUT

\u operate in your own church according to the principles set forth in 1 Timothy?

vou esteem your local church leadership?

ʸ on behalf of all men, including those in authority?

PAUL	TIMOTHY

OVERSEERS (ELDERS)	DEACONS	MEN
	SLAVES	RICH (OR THOSE WHO WANT TO BE)

(continued)

1 TIMOTHY OBSERVATIONS CHART

WOMEN	CHARGES AND INSTRUCTIONS TO TIMOTHY
WIDOWS	
PRAYER	

Theme of 1 Timothy:

	SEGMENT DIVISIONS	CHAPTER THEMES
Author:		
Date:		1
Purpose:		
Key Words:		2
teach		
faith		3
doctrine		
godliness		4
money (rich, riches)		
any reference to the devil		5
all references to prayer		6

See appendix 7 for key words in the New International Version and King James Version.

2 TIMOTHY

*P*aul now found himself in a new set of circumstances. It was about A.D. 64 (some say A.D. 67), and Timothy was heavy on his heart. Paul had to write one last letter to his disciple, reminding Timothy of crucial matters concerning the ministry and urging him to make every effort to come quickly—before winter—because...

THINGS TO DO

1. Read 2 Timothy. Mark every reference to Paul in one color and Timothy in another. In chapters 1, 2, and 4, Paul refers to his circumstances: where he is and what is about to take place in his life. To help set the context of this letter, record on the OBSERVATIONS CHART anything you learn about Paul that would answer the "5 W's and an H": who, what, when, where, why, and how.

2. Read 2 Timothy again. Observe everything you marked regarding Timothy and record your insights on the OBSERVATIONS CHART.

3. As you read 2 Timothy you probably noticed the many commands and/or instructions Paul gave Timothy. These are easy to see because the verb usually comes first in the sentence and the "you" is implied. An example of this is seen in 1:13: "Retain the standard of sound words."

    a. List the instructions and/or commands Paul gives Timothy throughout the letter on the OBSERVATIONS CHART. (Note the chapter and verse in which you find each.)

    b. As you look for these instructions and/or commands, mark in the text the key words (and their synonyms and pronouns) listed on the 2 TIMOTHY AT A GLANCE chart. When you mark references to the gospel, don't miss synonyms such as *sound words, word, Scripture, sacred writings,* etc.

4. Think back over the list of instructions and commands Paul gives Timothy and keep in mind the emphasis Paul places on the gospel. What do you think Paul's main message is to Timothy in this epistle? Record this as the theme of the book on 2 TIMOTHY AT A GLANCE.

5. Look at the book one chapter at a time and summarize the main teaching or theme of each chapter on 2 TIMOTHY AT A GLANCE and in your Bible. (Note: The theme of each chapter should relate to the general theme of the book.)

6. On 2 TIMOTHY AT A GLANCE you will see space to trace two themes, "Paul's Example" and "God's Provision," that run throughout the book. Doing this will give you additional insight into the practicality of 2 Timothy for your own life. Examine each chapter in the light of these two themes and record your insights on the appropriate spaces on the chart.

THINGS TO THINK ABOUT

1. What is your responsibility toward the gospel? To what lengths will you go in order to carry out this responsibility?

2. What are you doing to make sure you handle the Word of God accurately? Do you simply repeat what you have been taught or are you carefully studying the Word systematically?

3. Are you willing to suffer for the sake of those who would come to know the Lord Jesus Christ and receive salvation?

4. What kind of men and women do you need to beware of in these last days?

5. How are you living? Are you a coward or have you fought the good fight of faith?

6. Are you ready to die? How will you feel when you see Jesus Christ face-to-face?

PAUL	TIMOTHY

PAUL'S INSTRUCTIONS TO TIMOTHY

_____

_____

_____

_____

_____

_____

_____

_____

_____

_____

_____

_____

_____

_____

_____

_____

_____

2 TIMOTHY AT A GLANCE

Theme of 2 Timothy:

SEGMENT DIVISIONS

GOD'S PROVISION	PAUL'S EXAMPLE	CHAPTER THEMES		Author:
		1		Date:
				Purpose:
		2		Key Words:
				gospel
DELIVERED PAUL OUT OF PERSECUTIONS	ENDURED PERSECUTIONS	**3**		suffer (hardships, persecutions)
				endure(d)
				faith
		4		ashamed

TITUS

When Paul sailed past Crete on his way to Rome, he was not the master of his own ship. He was Rome's prisoner. How wise the centurion guard would have been had he followed Paul's urging to put ashore in Crete! Despite the winds, they sailed on under much duress. As Paul had predicted, the ship was lost in Malta, the island 58 miles south of Sicily.

Paul's ship sank to the bottom of the sea; Crete had sunk to the depths of sin. Broken to pieces morally by the incessant pounding of a godless lifestyle, Crete needed the good news of the gospel. Unlike the sunken ship, however, Crete was not beyond redemption.

Whether Crete was on Paul's heart before his two years' house arrest in Rome, we don't know. We only know that once Paul was free from Rome's chains he apparently went with Titus to Crete and left him there.

As Paul wrote Titus, it was about A.D. 62. He didn't know he would return to Rome for one final imprisonment.

THINGS TO DO

1. Read through Titus without stopping so that you understand the general content and thrust of the letter. Mark every reference to Paul in one color and Titus in another, including synonyms and pronouns. Record what you learn about each under the designated headings on the OBSERVATIONS CHART.

2. Read Titus again, one chapter at a time. As you read each chapter:

   a. Note the groups of people mentioned in each chapter. List what you learn about each on the OBSERVATIONS CHART.

   b. Mark in the text the key words listed on the TITUS AT A GLANCE chart. Be sure also to mark the synonyms and pronouns.

3. The commands, warnings, and instructions Paul includes in his letter to Titus help define Paul's purpose for writing. Read Titus again chapter by chapter and note each command, warning, or instruction Paul gives Titus. Either mark these with a distinguishing symbol or list them on the OBSERVATIONS CHART under "Instructions to Titus."

4. Listing Paul's commands, warnings, and instructions to Titus probably has helped you see the dominant subject of Titus. Look for the verses in chapters 2 and 3 regarding what Titus is to teach. They summarize the thrust of Paul's letter. These verses will help you determine the theme of the epistle. Record it on TITUS AT A GLANCE.

   a. Now summarize the theme or main message of each paragraph and then of each chapter and record these on TITUS AT A GLANCE. Also, record the chapter theme in your Bible.

   b. Fill in author, date, and purpose on the same chart.

THINGS TO THINK ABOUT

1. The world, by its lifestyle, denies God. What about you? Do you deny ungodliness and worldly desires, or do you indulge the desires of your flesh? What do your deeds say about your beliefs?

2. It is difficult always to be considerate to everyone, isn't it? When did you last fail in this area? Have you determined afresh to be gentle and uncontentious even in the most

difficult situation with the most difficult person? Your actions often will speak louder than your words ever can.

3. Your salvation was not based on performance but on the mercy and grace of God. What has your heavenly Father saved you from? Think on His goodness that brought you from death into life and brought you out of the kingdom of darkness into the kingdom of His glorious light. Have you thanked Him lately for His mercy and grace? Why not do it now? Pray for those close to you who have yet to experience the saving grace of God.

TITUS OBSERVATIONS CHART

PAUL	TITUS

ELDERS (OVERSEERS)   **REBELLIOUS MEN**   **OLDER WOMEN**

YOUNG WOMEN

OLDER MEN

BELIEVERS IN GENERAL

BONDSLAVES

YOUNG MEN

(continued)

INSTRUCTIONS TO TITUS

_____
_____
_____
_____
_____
_____
_____
_____
_____
_____
_____

TITUS AT A GLANCE

Theme of Titus:

SEGMENT
DIVISIONS

	PARAGRAPH THEMES	CHAPTER THEMES	
	1:1-3	1	*Author:*
	1:4		*Date:*
	1:5-9		
	1:10-16		*Purpose:*
	2:1-2	2	*Key Words:*
	2:3-5		God
	2:6-8		Jesus Christ
	2:9-10		doctrine
	2:11-14		word (the truth)
	2:15		grace
			deeds
	3:1-11	3	sound
	3:12-14		speak (speech)
	3:15		sensible

PHILEMON

Slavery was a fact of life in Paul's day—a fact Paul couldn't change. But Paul could show slaves and masters how they were to behave toward one another as those redeemed by Jesus, the One who had become a bondservant on their behalf. In his epistles Paul shared these principles.

Now, however, something else had come up. Paul had to appeal to Philemon, a believer from Colossae, about a very personal matter: One of Philemon's slaves had run away, and according to Roman law he could be put to death by his master. So at about the same time Paul wrote Colossians, he wrote to Philemon from his rented quarters, where as a prisoner of Rome he also could be put to death. It was about A.D. 61 or 62.

THINGS TO DO

1. Read through Philemon and mark every reference (including pronouns and synonyms) to the author (Paul) in one color and every reference to the recipients in another.

   a. When you finish reading and marking, go back and note everything you learn about Paul on the OBSERVATIONS CHART. Watch for Paul's reason for writing and how he goes about achieving his purpose. Record his reasons on the PHILEMON AT A GLANCE chart.

   b. Also note everything you learn about the recipients of Paul's letter and record this information in the appropriate section of the OBSERVATIONS CHART.

   c. Record on the OBSERVATIONS CHART everything you learn about Onesimus.

2. Carefully read the book again, marking in the text each of the key words (with their synonyms and pronouns) listed on the PHILEMON AT A GLANCE chart. Then observe what you learn from marking these words.

3. Record the theme of Philemon on PHILEMON AT A GLANCE and also in your Bible. Because Philemon is only one chapter, it is divided into paragraphs on the chart. Read the book paragraph by paragraph and record on the chart the theme of each paragraph. Then fill in the rest of the chart.

THINGS TO THINK ABOUT

1. How much do you care about others? Enough to come to another's aid, to assume the role of an advocate?

2. What can you learn from Paul's example in the way he appealed to Philemon?

3. Is there someone you need to forgive and offer restoration?

4. Can someone appeal to you to do the right thing on the basis of your character, or does he have to force your hand through rules, regulations, or some sort of a "bribe"?

PHILEMON OBSERVATIONS CHART

THE AUTHOR	THE RECIPIENT	ONESIMUS

PHILEMON AT A GLANCE

Theme of Philemon:

Author:

Date:

Purpose:

Key Words:

love

appeal

slave

SEGMENT DIVISIONS	PARAGRAPH THEMES
	VERSES 1-3
	VERSES 4-7
	VERSES 8-16
	VERSES 17-20
	VERSES 21-22
	VERSES 23-25

See appendix 7 for key words in the New International Version and King James Version.

HEBREWS

$\mathcal{P}$ersecution increased as the gospel spread. The persecution was especially intense for Jewish believers because they had turned their back on the world and its ways, and they had abandoned the ordinances of the law, which Jews had embraced since the time of Moses. This left them in a no-man's-land. Jews as well as Gentiles who did not believe in Jesus Christ could not understand them, nor would many tolerate their newfound faith without challenge or attack.

Imagine yourself in a similar situation. What if you were wrong about Jesus Christ? What if He were not really the Messiah? And what about the new covenant? What if it didn't replace the old covenant? What if you really did need a continuing blood sacrifice for your sins? *What if...?*

So that we could be secure in our faith, God moved an unknown author to write the book we call Hebrews. No other book in the New Testament gives us what Hebrews gives us—the assurance that we have a High Priest who is touched with the feeling of our weaknesses, One who ever lives to make intercession for us, the Mediator of a new and better covenant.

Hebrews was probably written before A.D. 70 because the book makes reference to the temple as if it were still standing and the priests were still making religious sacrifices.

THINGS TO DO

1. Before you begin your study of Hebrews, read Hebrews 13:22 to discover the author's purpose for writing. Record this on the HEBREWS AT A GLANCE chart.

2. In order to grasp the awesome truths of this book and properly interpret its difficult passages, you need to understand to whom the book is written. As you read Hebrews chapter by chapter:

   a. Mark every reference to the recipients in a specific color. Obviously the words *you, beloved,* and *brethren* refer to the recipients. However, when the author addresses the recipients he often includes himself, using the pronouns *we* and *us.* When this happens, mark these as you would other references to the recipients.

   b. Also, mark every reference to the author(s) in another distinctive color.

   c. When you finish, list everything you learn about the author and about the recipients in the appropriate columns on the OBSERVATIONS CHART.

   d. As you saw in 13:22, Hebrews is a letter of exhortation. Watch for these exhortations. They are often introduced with the phrase *let us.* Therefore, mark every *let us* in a distinctive way. List the exhortations on the OBSERVATIONS CHART.

   e. Throughout the book you will come across occasional warnings. In Hebrews 2:1, in the first of the warnings, the author includes himself and writes, "We must pay much closer attention to what we have heard, so that we do not drift away from it."

      1) Mark each warning in a distinctive way and record that warning in the appropriate column on the OBSERVATIONS CHART.

      2) When you note each warning, record the consequences of not heeding it. As you note the consequence, remember to whom the book is addressed. Let the text simply speak for itself. Don't read it through your theological glasses; rather, let the text say what it says.

3. As you study each chapter, do the following:

   a. Write the key words (including their synonyms and pronouns) listed on the HEBREWS

AT A GLANCE chart on an index card. Mark each word (and its synonyms and pronouns) in a distinctive way in the text exactly as you marked it on the card. Beginning at chapter 7, mark every occurrence of the word *covenant*. You will also discover other key words (not on your list) that occur frequently in a chapter or segment of Hebrews. Mark these in a distinctive way.

b. As you finish reading a chapter, review what you learned from marking key words. Then determine the theme or subject of that chapter. Record it in your Bible and on HEBREWS AT A GLANCE.

4. To truly appreciate and understand the book of Hebrews, you need to do the following:

a. Look back through your work and note all the times you marked *Jesus* and the pronouns referring to Him. Also look for the phrase *better*. Then, using the OBSERVATIONS CHART, list what you learn from Hebrews about our Lord.

b. There is much in Hebrews about the priesthood and about Jesus as our High Priest. Make a chart entitled THE PRIESTHOOD AND JESUS and list your information in three columns: "Insights into Priests and the Priesthood," "Insights into Jesus, Our Great High Priest," and "How This Applies to Me." Record your insights on this chart.

c. Review what you learn from marking the word *covenant* and note what the text says on a chart you might want to title A COMPARISON OF THE TWO COVENANTS: LAW AND GRACE AS TAUGHT IN HEBREWS.

5. Complete HEBREWS AT A GLANCE by doing the following:

a. Look at each of your chapter themes in order to determine the theme of Hebrews and record it on the chart.

b. Fill in the section titled "Segment Divisions."

1) Segment divisions indicate a change in the thrust or topic of the book. One change in emphasis occurs at Hebrews 10:19, where the author stops dealing with the doctrinal aspects of the truth he is sharing and begins to address the practical aspects. Record this segment division on the chart in the appropriate space.

2) Look again at the chapter themes. Are there any other divisions? If so, record them. This will help you find where a specific truth is covered in Hebrews.

THINGS TO THINK ABOUT

1. Meditate on the truths you learned about Jesus. Do you see Him as "better than..."? How supreme is He in your life?

2. As you press on to Christian maturity, are you noticing a new sense of confidence in your God? Is your faith being strengthened? Are you drawing near to God? Do you think Jesus understands what you're going through? Can He really help? Have you asked Him?

3. Are you laying aside every encumbrance that is slowing you down, and every sin, and running with endurance the race set before you? If not, what is holding you back?

4. How do you deal with persecution? How do the warnings and exhortations of Hebrews apply to your life?

5. Are you continually offering up the sacrifice of praise? What are some things you can thank God for today even though they do not necessarily seem good now? Remember, it's a *sacrifice* of praise.

HEBREWS OBSERVATIONS CHART

AUTHOR	EXHORTATIONS
RECIPIENTS	

(continued)

WARNINGS	CONSEQUENCE OF NOT LISTENING/OBEYING

THE SUPREMACY OF JESUS

Theme of Hebrews:

		CHAPTER THEMES

Author:
 unknown

Date:

Purpose:

Key Words:

 Jesus (Son)

 God

 angels

 sin (sinners)

 priest
 (priests,
 priesthood)

 therefore

 faith (faithful)

 greater

 better
 (better than)

 let us

 perfect

 mark the
 reference to the
 devil

 covenant

#
1
2
3
4
5
6
7
8
9
10
11
12
13

See appendix 7 for key words in the New International Version and King James Version.

JAMES

*W*hat a turnaround from the day James told his half brother what to do if He wanted to be known publicly! Full of unbelief and convinced that Jesus was nothing more than his eldest brother, James told Jesus to take His disciples and go up to the Feast of Booths and do His works there. Jesus might have found more disciples there, but James was not to be numbered as one of them—at least, not until Jesus rose from the dead (see 1 Corinthians 15:7).

Convinced from that point on that Jesus was the Christ, James would lay claim not to his physical relationship to Jesus but to his spiritual relationship as a bondservant of the Lord Jesus Christ. He became a pillar of the church, a leader of the council of Jerusalem, and a friend of Peter and Paul. But most of all he was a friend of Jesus, a covenant friend for whom he would be martyred around A.D. 62.

Sometime before A.D. 50 or in the early 50s, James would write his one epistle to be included in the pages of Holy Scripture, an epistle that would show what the gospel is like when it is lived out in shoe leather.

THINGS TO DO

1. Read James in one sitting to familiarize yourself with the book as a whole.

2. Mark every reference to the recipients. James structures his writing distinctively. Once you see the pattern he uses, you will better understand the flow of the book.

   a. First, James introduces a subject by making a statement or giving an introduction. For example, in James 1:2 he says to consider it all joy when you encounter various trials.

   b. He then usually follows with more instructions concerning that particular subject, *or* he gives an illustration pertaining to the subject, *or* he gives an explanation of it.

3. As you read back through James, mark in the text the key words (and their synonyms and pronouns) listed on the JAMES AT A GLANCE chart. Key words help you see the subjects of the book; keep in mind that some key words only appear in a portion of a book.

   a. Watch for these, including *say (says)* and *works* in chapter 2, *tongue* in chapter 3, and so on. Mark these in their own distinctive way. Also, mark any reference to the devil and his demons.

   b. When you finish, you'll find it profitable to list everything you learn from marking a key word.

4. Read James chapter by chapter:

   a. List the subjects introduced by the author on the JAMES SUBJECT BY SUBJECT chart. Be sure to include the chapter and verse from which you took the information.

   b. Next, if the author gives instructions or illustrations regarding a particular subject, record that information in the appropriate column.

5. After you list the subjects in each chapter, determine the theme of each chapter and record these themes on JAMES AT A GLANCE and in your Bible.

6. Finally, look for the theme of James. Determine if one subject is predominant or if there is a common denominator among the subjects. The more dominant or common subject

will be the theme of James and points to the author's reason for writing. Record the theme of James on JAMES AT A GLANCE and complete the chart.

THINGS TO THINK ABOUT

1. How are you handling the trials in your life?
2. Are you a doer of the Word or a hearer only?
3. Do you show partiality in dealing with people? Are you a respecter of persons?
4. Is your faith seen by your works? If not, what should that tell you?
5. Are you a friend of the world? What do you need to do?

SUBJECT	INSTRUCTION	ILLUSTRATION/EXPLANATION
		(continued)

SUBJECT	INSTRUCTION	ILLUSTRATION/EXPLANATION
		(continued)

Subject	Instruction	Illustration/Explanation

James at a Glance

Theme of James:

Author:

Date:

Purpose:

Key Words:
  brethren

  faith

  perfect
  (perfected)

  sin

  rich (riches)

  judge(s)
  (judged,
  judgment)

  law

	Segment Divisions	Chapter Themes
		1
		2
		3
		4
		5

See appendix 7 for key words in the New International Version and King James Version.

1 PETER

*T*he hour had come for the Shepherd to be smitten and for the sheep to be scattered. Jesus chose to spend His final hours with His eleven, preparing them for the tribulation that would come. Yet, after Jesus' resurrection and ascension, the tribulation seemed to be relatively mild. The disgruntled Pharisees wanted to shut up the men who were turning Jerusalem upside down with their teaching and miracles, but nothing seemed life threatening.

Then the first stone was thrown, and Stephen, the first martyr, was brought to the ground. Saul watched him die. In hearty agreement with Stephen's death, Saul went to the high priest to gain permission to round up those who were spreading this gospel. However, Saul's purge was short-lived, for Jesus saved him on the road to Damascus and changed his name to Paul. Yet the persecution of Christians continued. Herod, the Jewish king, became the adversary of believers; consequently, Jews who confessed Jesus as the Messiah were scattered abroad to other Roman provinces.

However, it wasn't until the Roman emperor Nero that the persecution of Christians reached beyond the confines of Judah. Rumor had it that Nero had burned Rome so he could rebuild it as he wanted. Needing a scapegoat to divert attention from himself, Nero blamed the fire on the Christians and began the systematic persecution of God's children.

Jesus had prepared Peter for the world's tribulation; now Peter would prepare others. His first epistle was written on the eve of Nero's persecution, about A.D. 63 or 64. Nero died in A.D. 68, but not before Rome put Peter to death.

THINGS TO DO

1. Read through 1 Peter and do the following:

   a. In the initial verses of the book, Peter describes himself and states to whom he is writing. In the last verses of the book, he tells why he wrote this epistle. Mark every reference to the author in a distinctive color and every reference to the recipients in another color. Record your insights about the author and his purpose in writing on the 1 PETER AT A GLANCE chart.

   b. Pay close attention to the recipients of 1 Peter. What is their condition? What is going on in their midst? Record what you learn on the OBSERVATIONS CHART.

2. Look for and mark in a distinctive way the key words (and their synonyms and pronouns) listed on 1 PETER AT A GLANCE. Also remember to mark key words that you are marking throughout your Bible, including references to the devil. On a separate sheet of paper, list the truths you learn from every mention of key words. This is imperative if you want to understand 1 Peter. (Because God and Jesus Christ are each mentioned so much, you may want to mark only the instances in which you learn something new or important to remember.)

3. Peter gives the reader many commands and instructions. You notice these by the construction of the sentence. The verb usually comes first and the "you" is implied. An example is seen in 1:13: "Prepare your minds for action."

   a. In a distinctive way, mark Peter's instructions or commands. Then list these under "General Instructions" on the OBSERVATIONS CHART.

   b. First Peter was written not only for the recipients but also for you. Think about how Peter's instructions and commands apply to your own life.

4. Peter also instructs specific groups of people such as servants, wives, husbands, etc. List his instructions to each group under the headings on the OBSERVATIONS CHART.

5. From what you have read, why are the believers to do these things? Or what future event is the motivation for living life in accordance with Peter's exhortations?

6. Finally, summarize the theme of each chapter and record it on 1 PETER AT A GLANCE and in your Bible.

THINGS TO THINK ABOUT

1. What have you learned about the way you are to live? How are you to respond to others, even when they are not living properly or treating you properly? What is Jesus' example in 1 Peter 2:21-25? Will you follow it?

2. As you think about what those believers were suffering, should you be surprised if you undergo the same? What will suffering accomplish in your life?

3. Even if you don't have a Nero in your life, is your adversary the devil still prowling about like a lion, seeking whom he may devour? What are you to do, according to 1 Peter?

4. When Jesus returns, will you be found standing firm in the true grace that has been provided you? What must you do or change in order to be prepared to see Him face-to-face?

Author	Recipients
General Instructions	
	(continued)

1 Peter Observations Chart

INSTRUCTIONS TO

Wives   Husbands

Elders   Young men   Servants

1 Peter at a Glance

Theme of 1 Peter:

SEGMENT
DIVISIONS

	CHAPTER THEMES
1	
2	
3	
4	
5	

Author:

Date:

Purpose:

Key Words:
suffering, trials (and all synonyms)
grace
glory
salvation
any reference to Jesus' future revelation
love
Holy Spirit
called
chosen
holy
precious
perishable (imperishable)

See appendix 7 for key words in the New International Version and King James Version.

2 PETER

A fisherman by trade, Peter had been captured and transformed by the Great Shepherd. Is it any wonder that even in Peter's darkest hour, the welfare of God's sheep was uppermost in his mind?

Ever since the day he stood with Jesus by a fire, the morning air full of the aroma of roasting fish, Peter had known the way he would die. But Peter would be faithful. His concern about his death and the way he would die would not override his concern for the sheep Jesus had commissioned him to feed and shepherd. And so, sometime around A.D. 63 or 64, Peter writes "to those who have received a faith of the same kind as ours."

In A.D. 64, according to tradition, Peter was crucified upside down for the Lord he once denied knowing. How Peter had grown in the grace and knowledge of his God!

THINGS TO DO

1. Read 2 Peter, marking every reference to the author in a distinctive color and every reference to the recipients in another color. Then on the OBSERVATIONS CHART note everything you learn about each. Observe what the author says about himself. When in his life is he writing? Who are the recipients? How are they described? Why is he writing?

2. In a distinctive way, mark in the text the key words (and their synonyms and pronouns) listed on the 2 PETER AT A GLANCE chart. Then list on a piece of paper the truths you learn by marking these key words. Be thorough because the lists will help you see the flow of the book.

3. Read through 2 Peter again and look for specific instructions that Peter gives the readers concerning their behavior and belief. Record these on the OBSERVATIONS CHART under "Instructions." Also look for and note any people or groups of people of which Peter warns them to beware.

4. In this book, Peter states specifically why he is writing. Look for and underline the verse in which Peter says, *"I am writing to you."* Also, underline any other verses that indicate his purpose in writing. Record his purpose for writing on 2 PETER AT A GLANCE.

5. Summarize the message of each paragraph and record its theme on 2 PETER AT A GLANCE. Then determine the chapter themes and the book theme and record these in the appropriate places on the chart and in your Bible.

6. Mark every reference to God (and Lord, if it refers to the Father). Then list what you learn about God from this short but much-needed epistle.

7. There is a reference to the day of the Lord in 2 Peter. If you are keeping a record of what the Bible teaches about the day of the Lord as suggested in Getting Started," page 25, record these insights there.

THINGS TO THINK ABOUT

1. What would it take to live your life so that you may be found spotless and blameless at Christ's coming? Are you willing?

2. Is there a danger today that false teachers will arise among the brethren, as in Peter's day? What do you need to know to be able to detect them? What is your protection?

3. How can you keep from falling from your own steadfastness? Practically, what do you need to do in order to grow in the grace and knowledge of Jesus Christ?

PETER	INSTRUCTIONS
RECIPIENTS	
	WARNINGS

Theme of 2 Peter:

	SEGMENT DIVISIONS	PARAGRAPH THEMES	CHAPTER THEMES
Author:			
		1:1-11	1
Date:			
		1:12-15	
Purpose:			
		1:16-18	
Key Words:			
		1:19-21	
prophecy (prophet, prophetic)			
		2:1-3	2
knowledge (know, knowing, known)			
		2:4-10	
remind (reminder)			
		2:11-16	
true (truth)			
		2:17-22	
diligent (diligence)			
		3:1-7	3
false teachers			
		3:8-10	
mockers			
destroyed			
		3:11-13	
promise			
day of the Lord			
		3:14-18	

See appendix 7 for key words in the New International Version and King James Version.

1 JOHN

*A*s a boy, John thought of Jesus as just a cousin, one of the sons of Aunt Mary, his mother Salome's sister. Little did John realize that someday he would be chosen by God to be one of Jesus' twelve apostles.

John had been known as a "son of thunder" (Mark 3:17), but a transformation had taken place. Now he was called "the disciple whom Jesus loved."

Even though John's name is not mentioned in this epistle, there is much evidence that he is the author. John had been with Jesus. He had seen Him, heard Him, touched Him, and been filled with His love. This is evident as you hear John's fatherly heart for those who belong to Jesus. He loves the fathers, the young men, the dear children. Yet as he writes about the antichrists and deceivers, you can hear the rumble of thunder in the background.

We don't know when John wrote this first epistle. It may have been between A.D. 85 and 95, when he was in Ephesus before being exiled to the Isle of Patmos. Love—and thunder—compelled him to write. He had to protect his children from a deception that could darken their understanding. He had to warn them about the brewing storm of gnosticism—a teaching that could keep them from having fellowship with him and thus with the Father and the Son (1 John 1:3).

THINGS TO DO

1. Begin your study by reading through 1 John and marking every reference to the author in one color and every reference to the recipients in another.

2. If you want to handle a passage of Scripture accurately you must always interpret it in the light of its context. Context simply means that which goes "with" *(con)* the "text." Context rules when it comes to interpretation. Identifying the author's purpose for writing will help you discern the context of a passage. What the author says, he says in the light of his purpose for writing.

In this letter the author tells us his purpose in seven different verses: 1:4; 2:1,12-14,21, and 26. Then in 1 John 5:13 he concludes by summarizing his purpose for writing. Read these verses and record his reasons for writing on the chart I AM WRITING TO YOU. Record on the 1 JOHN AT A GLANCE chart the author's purpose for writing.

3. One of the major heresies the church would face was gnosticism. Gnosticism wasn't in full bloom in John's time, but the seeds had been sown. Understanding gnosticism will help you better understand why John concentrated on the truths contained in his writing. Therefore, before you go any further, read the article "Understanding Gnosticism" on pages 324-325.

4. Now read 1 John chapter by chapter:

   a. Mark each of the key words (and their synonyms and pronouns) listed on 1 JOHN AT A GLANCE. When you finish, go to the chart 1 JOHN KEY WORDS and record the number of times each key word is used in each chapter. Then determine the number of times each word is used in 1 John. Doing this will help you see the main themes of 1 John.

   b. John uses contrasts in order to make his point: light/darkness, children of God/children of the devil, etc. Watch for these contrasts; observe what you learn from them.

5. Remember, 1 John was written "so that you may know." When you finish reading

287

all five chapters, trace throughout 1 John the repeated use of the word *know* and record what you learn from the text on the chart WHAT I CAN KNOW and HOW I CAN KNOW IT. Watch the matters John deals with in respect to wrong behavior or wrong belief.

6. You may want to keep a running list of everything you learn about God, Jesus Christ, and the Spirit from this book.

7. Record the theme of each chapter on 1 JOHN AT A GLANCE and in your Bible next to the chapter number. Fill in any remaining information called for on the chart.

THINGS TO THINK ABOUT

1. Based on the criteria given in this book, how can you know whether or not you have eternal life?

2. What have you learned about sin from 1 John? Do you practice sin or righteousness?

3. Do you love the things of the world? Are you caught up in the pride of life, in boasting, or in desiring whatever your eyes see?

4. According to 1 John 3, what are you to do when your heart condemns you?

5. Does your belief about Jesus Christ match what 1 John teaches about Him?

1 John Observations Chart

I Am Writing to You

1:4	
2:1	
2:12	
2:13	
2:14	
2:21	
2:26	
5:13	

1 John Key Words

Chapter	Fellowship	Abide	Sin	Know	Love	Born of God	Write	Light	Truth
1									
2									
3									
4									
5									
Total									

What I Can Know	How I Can Know It

(continued)

1 JOHN OBSERVATIONS CHART

WHAT I CAN KNOW	HOW I CAN KNOW IT

1 JOHN AT A GLANCE

Theme of 1 John:

SEGMENT
DIVISIONS

		CHAPTER THEMES
	1	
	2	
	3	
	4	
	5	

Author:

Date:

Purpose:

Key Words:
 fellowship
 abide
 sin
 know
 love
 born of God
 light
 truth (true)
 write (writing)
 world
 mark every
 reference to the
 devil (or evil one)

See appendix 7 for key words in the New International Version and King James Version.

2 JOHN

A caring father can't ignore something that threatens his children. So around A.D. 90 the paternal apostle John sat down to write yet another epistle. It is short, to the point, and needful—even today.

THINGS TO DO

1. Read through 2 John as you would a letter you had just received. Mark every reference to the author in one color and the recipients in another. Then read it again and:

   a. Mark the key words listed on the 2 JOHN AT A GLANCE chart.

   b. List all you learn about the recipients of this letter in your notebook. Note John's feelings toward them, his instructions (or commands), his warnings, and the reason for his warnings.

2. Record the theme of 2 John in the appropriate space on 2 JOHN AT A GLANCE. Then record the theme of each paragraph and fill in any other pertinent information.

THINGS TO THINK ABOUT

1. What does this book say about someone who does not abide in the teaching of Christ? Do you know someone who could fit that description? What should you do?

2. You probably noted that verse 4 says "some" of the children are walking in truth (see also John 17:17). Are you careful to walk in all the truth you know? Do you realize that before God, you are responsible to live out the truth that has been entrusted to you?

3. According to this little epistle, what does it mean to walk in love? Are you doing this?

Theme of 2 John:

SEGMENT
DIVISIONS

	PARAGRAPH THEMES	Author:
		Date:
	VERSES 1-3	
		Purpose:
	VERSES 4-6	
		Key Words:
	VERSES 7-11	truth
		love
		commandment(s)
	VERSE 12	teaching
		walk
	VERSE 13	abide(s)
		deceiver(s)

See appendix 7 for key words in the New International Version and King James Version.

3 JOHN

*L*ove cares about the individual. Love encourages. Love rebukes. Love walks in truth. And so, in love, John wrote a third epistle before he was exiled to Patmos, where he penned the book of Revelation. It was around A.D. 90.

THINGS TO DO

1. Read this short letter through once. Mark every reference to the author in one color and every reference to the recipients in another. When you finish, list on a paper what you learn about each.

2. Read the book again, marking each of the key words listed on the 3 JOHN AT A GLANCE chart.

3. Other names are mentioned. Note who they are and what is said about each person. See what you learn as you observe the contrast between these people.

4. Make a list of (or mark distinctively) the instructions and warnings John gives in this epistle.

5. Complete 3 JOHN AT A GLANCE.

THINGS TO THINK ABOUT

1. What is your testimony before others? Are you known for your love of others or for your love of yourself? Do you share what you have with others? Do you listen to others? Do you have to be first?

2. According to what John says in this epistle, what does the way you live have to do with your relationship to God?

3. Are you quick to love, to exhort, and to stand for truth? What do you need to do?

Theme of 3 John:

SEGMENT
DIVISIONS

	PARAGRAPH THEMES	Author:
	VERSE 1	Date:
	VERSES 2-4	Purpose:
	VERSES 5-8	Key Words:
	VERSES 9-10	truth
		good
	VERSES 11-12	evil
	VERSES 13-15	

JUDE

*J*ude had to speak up. He wasn't an apostle and he wasn't a pillar in the church, like his brother James. Although he was the half brother of the Lord Jesus Christ, Jude did not claim any relationship to Jesus Christ other than that of being His bond-servant.

Initially Jude didn't believe in Jesus (John 7:5), but finally he understood who Jesus was—the Son of God. Jude had grown up in the presence of the One who came to save His people from their sins (Matthew 1:21). No wonder Jude had to write what he did!

THINGS TO DO

1. Though only one chapter in length, Jude is a pertinent book. Read it to familiarize yourself with the content.

2. Read through Jude again. This time mark every reference to the author in one color and every reference to the recipients (including all synonyms and pronouns) in another color. When you finish, list everything you learn about the author and about the recipients in the appropriate columns on the JUDE OBSERVATIONS CHART.

3. Now review the list of what you observed about the author and the recipients to discern the author's purpose in writing this epistle. Record this purpose on the JUDE AT A GLANCE chart.

4. When you read through Jude, you will notice a third category of people mentioned in verse 4: the "certain persons [who] crept in unnoticed."

    a. Read through Jude a third time and mark in a distinctive color or way every reference to these people. Watch for and mark the pronouns and various synonyms used to describe these people.

    b. Record on the OBSERVATIONS CHART all you learn about these ungodly people. When you do, it will become obvious why Jude was moved to write what he did.

5. There is a pattern in this letter. First, Jude refers to "these [ungodly] men," and then he uses Old Testament examples or illustrations to make a point. Read through Jude again and watch for this pattern. You may want to underline every Old Testament incident or reference that Jude uses. As you study, watch what the Old Testament people do and note how God deals with them. Be sure not to miss any contrasts and comparisons Jude is making between these Old Testament people and "these [ungodly] men."

6. Now read through Jude again and mark in the same way every reference to *condemnation* and *judgment,* whether it pertains to the ungodly persons or to those mentioned in the Old Testament examples. Various synonyms are used to refer to their condemnation, so watch for and mark them carefully—all in the same way.

7. Jude contains specific instructions for the recipients of his letter, whom he calls *beloved.* In the margin of the text, note the occurrence of each instruction either by writing *Instruction* in the margin or noting it with a symbol. You might want to record these instructions on the OBSERVATIONS CHART, along with what God promises or undertakes to do on the recipients' behalf.

8. Determine what you believe to be the theme of Jude and write it down on JUDE AT A GLANCE.

9. Finally, look at Jude paragraph by paragraph, determine what you believe to be the theme for each paragraph, and then record it in the designated place on JUDE AT A GLANCE. Fill in any other information requested.

10. If you want to study Jude further, look up the cross-references in the margin of your Bible to the Old Testament characters and illustrations and see what you learn from each. This will deepen your insight into these ungodly men.

THINGS TO THINK ABOUT

1. Think about the promises to the "beloved in God." Spend time in prayer, praising God for what He will do on your behalf. Then think of the responsibilities that are yours and talk with God about how you are to fulfill these.

2. Review the characteristics of the ungodly. Do you know of anyone who fits this description? How does knowing this help you? What are you to do in respect to these people? Are you willing?

Jude Observations Chart

The Author	The Recipients
The Ungodly	

JUDE OBSERVATIONS CHART

JUDE'S INSTRUCTIONS TO THE BELOVED	GOD'S PROMISES TO THE BELOVED

JUDE AT A GLANCE

Theme of Jude:

Author:

Date:

Purpose:

Key Words:

	SEGMENT DIVISIONS	PARAGRAPH THEMES
		VERSES 1-2
		VERSES 3-4
		VERSES 5-7
		VERSES 8-13
		VERSES 14-16
		VERSES 17-23
		VERSES 24-25

See appendix 7 for key words in the New International Version and King James Version.

REVELATION

*J*ohn, one of the sons of Zebedee, identifies himself throughout his Gospel not by his name but as "the one whom Jesus loved." John walked in faith, taking Jesus at His word, and consequently was secure in His love.

Therefore, when John was banished to the barren Isle of Patmos (and, according to tradition, submerged in a cauldron of hot oil), he remained steadfast in Jesus' love. He was faithful to his calling even in the midst of Nero's persecutions of Christians in A.D. 54 through 68 and then Domitian's in A.D. 81 through 96.

While John was exiled on Patmos, God unveiled to him the coming of the Lord Jesus Christ and what soon would come to pass—a revelation unparalleled, the last to be given. It was about A.D. 95. With John's revelation the New Testament canon of Scripture would be complete. The church could be secure. Every prophecy would be fulfilled, just as God had said.

THINGS TO DO

Chapters 1–3

1. To familiarize yourself with the first two segments of the book of Revelation, carefully read 1:1–4:1 in one sitting. (*Revelation* is a translation of the Greek word *apokalupsis,* which means "an unveiling.")

2. Mark the following key words (along with their synonyms and pronouns) in chapter 1, and then list in your notebook everything you learn from the text about these words: *Jesus Christ, God (the Father), Spirit (seven Spirits),* and *write.*

3. Revelation 1:19 gives an outline of the book of Revelation.

   a. List the three things John was to write:

   1) _____

   2) _____

   3) _____

   b. Now look at Revelation 4:1 and note how it relates to 1:19. Revelation 4 begins the third segment of Revelation. Chapter 1 describes what John saw, and chapters 2 and 3 are "the things which are." What is the third segment that begins in 4:1?

   c. Using the terminology found in Revelation 1:19, record these three segments in the space for segment divisions on the REVELATION AT A GLANCE chart. (The lines to divide the book into these sections are already drawn.)

4. Read Revelation 1–3 and do the following:

   a. Watch for key repeated phrases or words listed on REVELATION AT A GLANCE. Mark these in the text in a distinctive way so you can spot them immediately. Watch for a pattern in Jesus' messages as He addresses each church.

   b. Now concentrate on Jesus' messages to the churches, one church at a time. Record what you learn about each church on the chart JESUS' MESSAGES TO THE CHURCHES beginning on page 302. When you see what is said regarding those who overcome, note how John describes overcomers in 1 John 5:4-5. Add what you learn to the chart.

5. Record the main theme of each chapter in the text next to the chapter number and on REVELATION AT A GLANCE.

Chapters 4–22

1. In the last 19 chapters of Revelation Jesus shows John "the things which must shortly take place." Read Revelation 4–22 one chapter at a time and do the following:

   a. As you read, ask the "5 W's and an H": Who? What? Why? When? Where? and How? For example, if it is an event, ask: What is happening? Who is involved? When will this happen and where? Why is this happening? How will it happen? If it is a person or a personage: Who is this? What is this person like? What does he do? When? Where? Why? What are the consequences? How will he accomplish it? These are very critical questions. If these are answered carefully after thoroughly observing the text and apart from preconceived ideas, you will learn much. Make a list of what you learn. Record your insights in your notebook.

   b. Mark key repeated words (along with their synonyms and pronouns—*he, she, it, we, they, us,* and *you*) in a distinctive way. Some key words are listed on REVELATION AT A GLANCE. Since it is a long list, write these on an index card, color code the words as you intend to mark them in the text, and use the card as a bookmark. When you finish marking these, record in your notebook what you learn from each one (unless you have been told to record that information on a chart).

   c. As you go through Revelation, let the text speak for itself. Remember, truth is revealed gradually, so don't become impatient. Simply observe what is being said without adding your own interpretation. Stay in an attitude of prayer, ask God to open the eyes of your understanding, and put away any preconceived ideas you might have.

2. Mark in a distinctive way all references to time. Observe what happens during that time. In biblical reckoning 42 months, 1260 days, and time, times and half a time all refer to a period of 3 1/2 years. Note all that happens within the framework of 3 1/2 years.

Give careful attention to *when* something begins and ends: for example, the great day of God's wrath, when the mystery of God is finished, when God begins to reign. Observe carefully the three woes and the events surrounding them. Noting the timing of these will help you understand Revelation better.

3. As you observe what happens during each of the seals, trumpets, and bowls, record your insights on the chart on page 305, THE SEVEN SEALS, TRUMPETS, AND BOWLS. Then consider whether the seals, trumpets, and bowls happen at the same time or follow one another.

4. Babylon intermittently plays an important role from Genesis to Revelation. As you mark every reference to Babylon, carefully note whether it is referring to "the woman" or to the city. Then discern whether they are one and the same or two separate but somehow related entities. In chapters 17 and 18, where Babylon is preeminent, list what you learn from marking each reference to Babylon.

5. As you study Revelation, you may want to consult any notes you have made on the chart THE DAY OF THE LORD as recommended in "Getting Started," page 25, to see if there are any parallels between what you have observed in other books and what you see in Daniel and in Revelation.

6. There is much to learn about the Godhead in this book that you will want to remember and meditate on. Record what you learn in your notebook.

7. When you finish going through Revelation, record the chapter themes in the text and on REVELATION AT A GLANCE, along with other pertinent information called for on the chart.

8. Finally, see how various chapters of the book group according to events, places, or

persons. Use your chapter themes as a guide to see when these groupings occur. Record these groupings under "Segment Divisions" on REVELATION AT A GLANCE, placing them at the chapter numbers in which they occur.

THINGS TO THINK ABOUT

Chapters 1–3

1. As you look at the Lord's message to each church, do you think the message could be for the church today? Look back through Jesus' messages to the churches in chapters 2 and 3 and note what the Spirit is saying to him who has "an ear." To whom is the Spirit speaking? What does He want you to hear? To do?

2. Think about what you have learned about Jesus Christ from these three chapters and then spend some time worshiping Him for who and what He is.

3. According to 1 John 5:4-5, and Revelation 2–3, are you an overcomer? How does it show? Is there anything you need to do that you are not presently doing so that when Jesus appears you won't be ashamed?

Chapters 4–22

1. Revelation gives insight into God's judgment upon the wicked because of what they worship. It also gives a glimpse of the way the righteous worship. How would you compare your worship with the worship described in Revelation? You might want to go back and look at the scenes where God is worshiped and use them as a pattern for worship.

2. Now that you have a better understanding of the wrath to come upon the unbeliever, what priority needs to be placed on sharing the gospel? Is witnessing a priority in your personal life?

3. Has your life been changed by Jesus Christ? Do you no longer live in habitual sin? If not, you need to be saved. Will you acknowledge the Lord Jesus Christ as God, receive His forgiveness for your sins, and let Him take full control of your life? If so, record the date in the margin. Surely you have seen that He is worthy—and trustworthy.

4. Revelation 22:12 tells us Jesus is coming, and His reward is with Him to give to everyone according to what he has done. Are you living in the light of that day?

	DESCRIPTION OF JESUS	COMMENDATION TO THE CHURCH	REPROOF GIVEN TO THE CHURCH	WARNINGS AND INSTRUCTIONS TO THE CHURCH	PROMISE TO THE OVERCOMERS
EPHESUS					
SMYRNA					

(continued)

Jesus' Messages to the Churches

	Description of Jesus	Commendation to the Church	Reproof Given to the Church	Warnings and Instructions to the Church	Promise to the Overcomers
PERGAMUM					
THYATIRA					

(continued)

	DESCRIPTION OF JESUS	COMMENDATION TO THE CHURCH	REPROOF GIVEN TO THE CHURCH	WARNINGS AND INSTRUCTIONS TO THE CHURCH	PROMISE TO THE OVERCOMERS
SARDIS					
PHILADELPHIA					
LAODICEA					

THE SEVEN SEALS, TRUMPETS, AND BOWLS

	SEALS	TRUMPETS	BOWLS
1st			
2nd			
3rd			
4th			
5th			
6th			
7th			

Theme of Revelation:

SEGMENT DIVISIONS

Author:

CHAPTER THEMES

Date:

				1	

Purpose:

				2	
				3	
				4	
				5	

Key Words:

   God

				6	

   Jesus (Christ)

   in the Spirit

				7	

   church(es)

				8	

   throne

   mystery

				9	

   repent

   overcome(s)

				10	

   mark every
reference to
Satan (demons,
devil, dragon)

				11	
				12	

   after these
things

				13	

   and I saw
(looked)

				14	

   angel(s)

   seal(s)

				15	

   nations

				16	

   trumpet(s)

   bowl(s),
plague(s)

				17	

   woe

				18	

   wrath

   beast

				19	

   Babylon

				20	

   earthquake,
voices,
thunder,
lightning

				21	
				22	

See appendix 7 for key words in the New International Version and King James Version.

APPENDIX 1: UNDERSTANDING THE VALUE OF GOD'S WORD

WHAT IS THE BIBLE?

The Bible is comprised of 66 separate writings or books. It was written over a period of approximately 1400 to 1800 years by more than 40 authors from various walks of life. While many of the authors are identified, some remain unknown.

The Bible is divided into the Old Testament, comprised of 39 books, and the New Testament, comprised of 27 books. The Old Testament, the Bible of the nation of Israel, was divided into three segments: the Law or Torah, the Prophets or Nebi'im, and the Writings or Kethubim. While the Old Testament was originally written in two Semitic languages, Hebrew and Aramaic, the vast majority of it is in Hebrew.

With the growth of the Greek Empire came the spread of the Greek language, and the Old Testament was translated into Koine (common) Greek around 250–100 B.C. This translation is referred to as the Septuagint or the LXX. It contains the same books as the Hebrew Old Testament, but the order and breakdown of the books was changed to the form now used in the Old Testament.

By the time of the Lord Jesus Christ, Koine Greek had become the popular language used throughout most of the Mediterranean world. Therefore, the New Testament was written in Koine Greek. However, a few Aramaic phrases are found in the New Testament because Aramaic was the vernacular of the people of Israel. Jesus and His disciples spoke Aramaic as well as Koine Greek. Much of the Old Testament was translated into Aramaic, and these works are referred to as the Targums.

HOW WAS THE BIBLE WRITTEN AND TRANSLATED?

The Bible itself tells us how it was written:

"All Scripture is inspired by God" (2 Timothy 3:16). Men "moved by the Holy Spirit spoke from God" (2 Peter 1:21). The Greek word for inspired, *theopneustos*, means "God-breathed." The Holy Spirit carried men along, moving and guiding them as they wrote in their own words what God wanted them to say. Thus we have *verbal* inspiration, because the words of the original text were inspired by God. And because all Scripture was given by inspiration we have *plenary* inspiration, which means total or complete inspiration. Every part of the Bible is inspired. The Bible does not merely contain the words of God, but it actually is the Word of God. Thus the original writings, often called *autographs*, are infallible—without error. This concept is called the verbal, plenary inspiration of the autographs.

Autographs

In early history, writing was done on stone, clay tablets, leather (animal skins), and papyrus scrolls. The New Testament autographs were probably written on papyrus. Papyrus, made from the inner bark of a reed plant, was formed into a paper-like material which was glued together and rolled into a scroll. Normally the writing was done on only one side of the scroll, so that as it was read it was unrolled with one hand and rolled up with the other. The scrolls were kept in a cylindrical box called a *capsa*.

According to the Jewish Talmud, the Scriptures were to be copied only on the skins of what God deemed as clean animals, such as sheep, calves, and goats. Parchment (dried animal skin) was costly but more durable and permanent than papyrus.

The Accuracy of the Copies

Eventually the scrolls were replaced by the *codex*. The codex (plural *codices*) was made from folded sheets, *quires*, which were stitched together like a book. Copies of the Old Testament were transcribed by hand under the strictest measures. The men who copied the manuscripts were called *scribes*. If one error was found the entire copy was destroyed. Thus the accuracy of the Old Testament is phenomenal. This accuracy has been confirmed by the large number of copies, by the Septuagint, and by the Dead Sea Scrolls.

More than 5000 ancient Greek copies of all or portions of the New Testament have been found. Although there are minor variances in the copied manuscripts, none affect doctrinal issues.

The Canon

The same omnipotent Sovereign who inspired men to write the Word of God led other men to recognize that these were the books which would comprise the *canon* of Scripture. The canon is the group of books which are recognized to be inspired by God. This group comprises the Old and New Testaments. The Old Testament canon of 39 books was fairly widely accepted in the days of Jesus Christ. Jesus Himself, who is one with the Father, always affirmed and never contradicted the Old Testament. Revelation, the last of the New Testament books to be written, was completed before the end of the first century A.D. By A.D. 367 Bishop Athanasius compiled the first known list of the current 27 books of the New Testament.

Translations

The Hebrew/Aramaic and Greek copies of the 66 books of the Bible are the basis of the translations made in the various languages of the world. A translator will study the original words of these copies, determine what those words mean, and then select the best way to faithfully transmit the meaning of the original words in their context into the language of their translation. This is called a *primary translation*.

A *secondary translation* occurs when a translation is made from a primary translation of another language, say English, into a third language. Thus a secondary translation is not made from a copy of the original language but from a second language translated from the original language (the primary translation).

HOW DO WE KNOW THE BIBLE IS WHAT IT CLAIMS TO BE—THE WORD OF GOD?

Believing the Bible is ultimately a matter of informed faith. You either believe what the Word of God says about itself or you don't. You either believe the testimony of Jesus Christ regarding the Word of God or you don't.

There are several areas of objective evidence that test and support the veracity of the verbal, plenary inspiration of the autographs.

First, there is *bibliographic evidence* for the Bible's authenticity. No other ancient writings have as much manuscript evidence as does the Bible. Aside from 643 copies of Homer's works, which were written about 850 B.C., the other classical works written between 450 B.C. and 10 B.C. have anywhere from 3 to 20 copies each, but the New Testament has over 5000. And not only is there more than an ample *quantity* of copies of the Bible, but the *quality* of the biblical manuscripts surpasses that of other manuscripts as well.

The passage of time is also a factor. The Dead Sea Scrolls, which date from 200 B.C. to A.D. 68, greatly reduce the time span between the writing of the Old Testament books to our earliest existing copies of the Old Testament. The time span between the autographs of the New Testament and its existing copies is between 100 and 200 years, a very low figure.

Second, there is *internal evidence* for the authenticity of the Bible. The Bible not only claims to be the Word of God, but it also states that not the smallest letter or stroke will pass away from the law (the Old Testament) until all is accomplished (Matthew 5:17,18). Many of the writers claimed to be eyewitnesses who wrote what they saw, heard, or experienced. Although there were so many different authors who wrote over such a long time span, there are no contradictions in what they wrote. Also, what was written in the Old Testament, sealed and canonized, is often seen fulfilled in the New Testament. Thus there is the internal evidence of fulfilled prophecy.

OVERVIEW OF THE BIBLE

PRE-EXILIC	EXILIC	POST-EXILIC	NEW TESTAMENT
(Before the Babylonian Exile of Judah)	*(During the Babylonian Exile of Judah)*	*(After the Babylonian Exile of Judah)*	

PRE-EXILIC	EXILIC	POST-EXILIC	NEW TESTAMENT
TORAH	**PROPHETIC BOOKS**	**HISTORICAL BOOKS**	**GOSPELS**
(the Law, Moses, the Pentateuch)	Daniel	1 and 2 Chronicles (written)	Matthew
	Ezekiel		Mark
Genesis	Lamentations	Ezra	Luke
Exodus		Nehemiah	John
Leviticus		Esther	
Numbers			
Deuteronomy			
HISTORICAL BOOKS		**PROPHETIC BOOKS**	**HISTORY**
Joshua		Haggai	Acts
Judges		Zechariah	
Ruth		Malachi	
1 and 2 Samuel			
1 and 2 Kings			
1 and 2 Chronicles			
PROPHETIC BOOKS			**PAUL'S EPISTLES**
(in parentheses is the kingdom to which prophesied)			Romans
			1 Corinthians
			2 Corinthians
Obadiah (Southern)			Galatians
Joel (Southern)			Ephesians
Jonah (Northern)			Philippians
Amos (Northern)			Colossians
Hosea (Northern)			1 and 2 Thessalonians
Isaiah (Southern)			1 and 2 Timothy
Jeremiah (Southern)			Titus
Micah (Southern)			Philemon
Nahum (Southern)			
Zephaniah (Southern)			
Habakkuk (Southern)			
POETRY AND WISDOM			**GENERAL EPISTLES**
Job			Hebrews
Psalms			James
Proverbs			1 and 2 Peter
Ecclesiastes			1, 2, and 3 John
Song of Solomon			Jude
			PROPHECY
			Revelation

Finally, there is an abundance of *external evidence* that supports the Bible's infallibility. When the Bible speaks on matters of history or science, it speaks accurately. There were times when it was supposed that science or history contradicted the Bible; however, later it was discovered that all the facts had not yet been uncovered.

More recent archaeological evidence has affirmed the historicity of the Bible in a multitude of ways as it speaks regarding rulers, nations, languages, battles, customs, geographic locations, tragedies, and other events. Extra-biblical writings also affirm what the New Testament teaches about the historicity of Jesus Christ and other New Testament characters.

Have you accepted the Bible as the inerrant Word of God, profitable for teaching, reproof, correction, and training in righteousness, that you may be adequate, equipped for every good work? (2 Timothy 3:16). As you study the Bible, you will discover that it is a supernatural book ... the very words of life.

APPENDIX 2: MAJOR EVENTS IN ISRAEL'S HISTORY

The Word of God takes on new life when a person understands the major events in Israel's history between the years of Abraham and the birth of Christ. Old and New Testament prophecies regarding Israel and her relationship to various world powers are seen in a new dimension.

Once you are acquainted with the religious, cultural, and political setting of Bible times, you will better understand God's plan for mankind and you will have a greater appreciation of the times in which our Lord lived and gave birth to His church.

FROM ADAM TO ABRAHAM
(The Beginning to About 2000 B.C.)

In the beginning there was no sin. Adam and Eve lived in unbroken fellowship with their Creator until they believed a lie and chose to disobey the explicit command of God. From that time on all mankind would be born in sin and bear its consequence: death.

Yet a merciful and loving God did not leave mankind in despair; He promised a Redeemer, born of a woman's seed. With the passing of time man's iniquity increased until every intent of his heart was only evil. God was grieved in His heart and "sorry that He had made man." And with that He determined to "blot out man...from the face of the land." But Noah found favor in the eyes of the Lord, for he was a righteous man, blameless in his time.

When the flood came, only those in the ark were preserved: Noah and his family, eight people in all. However, the basic sin nature of those who survived had not changed, and it wasn't long before they too were in rebellion against God. And God knew that because they were one society and had the same language, nothing which they purposed to do would be impossible for them.

So once again God intervened, though this time He didn't destroy man from the face of the earth, for He had put a rainbow in the heavens and had made a covenant which He would not break. God intervened by confusing mankind's language and scattering them over the face of the whole earth.

Then around 2000 B.C. God called a man to leave Ur of the Chaldees and go to a land which He would show him. That man's name was Abram. From Abram God would not only make a great nation, but through him He would bless all the families of the earth. Thus God made a covenant with Abram and his descendants forever, and with that covenant He changed Abram's name to Abraham, "Father of a Multitude." With that covenant also came the promise of the land of Canaan as the eternal possession of Abraham's descendants.

The Seed that God promised Adam and Eve, the One who would redeem mankind, would come not only through the seed of the woman, but also through the loins of Abraham and his descendants, Isaac and Jacob. To Isaac would be born Jacob, and to Jacob 12 sons. As God confirmed His covenant with Jacob, He changed Jacob's name to Israel, the one who fathered the heads of the 12 tribes of Israel. A covenant nation had been brought into existence by God. In the fullness of time the Redeemer, the messenger of the covenant, would come from the tribe of Judah.

But all was not well among Jacob's sons, for they were jealous of Joseph, Jacob's favorite, his firstborn by Rachel. As they plotted to take Joseph's life, Reuben and Judah intervened, and Joseph was sold into slavery and taken to Egypt. While Joseph's brothers meant this for evil, God meant it for good. Joseph went from being a slave in Potiphar's house to being a vice-regent in Pharaoh's palace via a prison. In His sovereignty God used Joseph's position in

311

Egypt to deliver Israel's family from famine in Canaan. They lived in Egypt for 430 years, 400 of those years as slaves. Then around 1525 B.C. a son by the name of Moses was born to two of these Hebrew slaves.

FROM THE EXODUS UNDER MOSES TO THE MONARCHY UNDER SAUL
(1445 B.C. to 1051 B.C.)

About 80 years after the birth of Moses, the sons of Israel cried out to the God of Abraham, Isaac, and Jacob because of their great affliction. God heard their cry and appeared to Moses in a burning bush. The great I AM would deliver them from the house of bondage, from the land of Egypt, and take them to the land He promised to Abraham. Moses would serve as God's spokesman, as their human deliverer, and as the one to whom God would give the pattern for the tabernacle. In the tabernacle God would give the Israelites not only the means of worshiping Him, but a picture of the Redeemer who was yet to come.

After the Israelites wandered in the wilderness for 40 years because of their unbelief, Joshua took them across the Jordan River into the promised land. The people served the Lord all the days of Joshua and the elders, and then there arose a generation who did not know Joshua, and the children of Israel served the gods of the people of Canaan and did evil in the sight of the Lord. So the Lord delivered them into the hands of their enemies. But when the people cried out to the Lord in their distress, God raised up judges from among the people. And God was with each judge all the days of his life. But when the judge died, the cycle of sin and slavery repeated itself. There was no visible king in Israel and everyone did what was right in his own eyes. Israel was to be a theocracy, with God as King, but the people did not obey their God.

Finally, in the days of Samuel, the prophet and judge, the people insisted on having a king over them like the other nations. Although this request grieved Samuel, God gave them what they wanted, for they had rejected Him.

FROM UNITED KINGDOM TO DIVIDED KINGDOM
(1051 B.C. to 931 B.C.)

Saul, Israel's first king, gave God sacrifice rather than obedience, and so God raised up a man after His own heart. David, the son of Jesse from the tribe of Judah, was anointed by God to become king.

David reigned from 1011 to 971 B.C. During that time his passion was to build a permanent dwelling for God in Jerusalem, the city of David. God saw the intent of David's heart, but because David had been a man of war, the building of the temple would be the task of David's son and successor, Solomon, born to Bathsheba.

On the day when the ark of the covenant was brought into the temple and the temple was dedicated to the Lord, Solomon fell on his face before God and reminded Him of His covenant promises. Fire came from heaven and devoured the burnt offerings, and the glory of the Lord filled the temple.

But Solomon disobeyed God. He married foreign wives and set up their idols on high places in Jerusalem. When Solomon was old, his wives turned his heart away after other gods and his heart was not wholly devoted to serving God, as the heart of his father, David, had been.

After Solomon died, God tore the kingdom of Israel in two.

FROM 931 B.C. UNTIL THE BIRTH OF CHRIST

In 931 B.C. the tribes of Judah and Benjamin formed the southern kingdom of Judah, with Jerusalem as their capital. The remaining ten tribes formed the northern kingdom of Israel and eventually made Samaria their capital. The northern kingdom immediately began to worship idols, so in 722 B.C. God allowed the Assyrians to take them captive.

Although the southern kingdom was warned by the prophets of God that they too would go into captivity if they did not repent of their disobedience and idolatry, Judah did not listen. In 605 B.C., just before Nebuchadnezzar became king of Babylon, he attacked Jerusalem and took the king and some of his nobles captive to Babylon. Among them was Daniel (Daniel 1:1,2). In 597 B.C. Nebuchadnezzar again attacked Judah, this time taking about 10,000 captives to Babylon, Ezekiel among them. Then in 586 B.C. Babylon, now the predominant world power, conquered Judah and destroyed not only the city of Jerusalem but the magnificent temple built by Solomon during his reign over Israel.

Separated from Jerusalem and their temple, the exiles established **synagogues** as a means of preserving their faith. The synagogues became centers of learning and worship where the Jews recited the **Shema** (Deuteronomy 6:4), read from the law and the prophets, prayed, and delivered messages.

Men trained in writing who recorded events and decisions were called **scribes**. They assumed the responsibility of copying, preserving, and even teaching the Word of God in the synagogues. By New Testament times the scribes were considered experts in interpreting and teaching the law and were referred to as lawyers.

Having experienced firsthand the cursings of disobedience as promised in the book of Deuteronomy, the exiled Jews seemed to gain a new respect and appreciation for the Word of God. They saw that God meant what He said and would not alter it even for His covenant people.

It was sometime after the kingdom divided and Judah went into captivity that the exiles became known as **men of Judah** or **Jews**.

The Persian Period
(539 to 331 B.C.)

When the Medes and the Persians conquered Babylon in 539 B.C., they became the predominant world power in Babylon's stead. Daniel 5 records this invasion.

Approximately 175 years before Cyrus (the king of Persia) was born, Isaiah prophesied that God would raise up Cyrus to perform His desire (Isaiah 44:28). Second Chronicles 36:22, 23 records the fulfillment of God's plan: Cyrus issued a decree allowing the exiles of Judah to return to Jerusalem and rebuild their temple. Just as Jeremiah had prophesied (Jeremiah 29:10; Daniel 9:2), exactly 70 years from the

time of Babylon's first attack on Jerusalem, the Israelites returned to their land.

The group which returned is referred to in Scripture as the **remnant**. *Diaspora*, the Greek word for scattering, became the term used to describe the Jews who remained in exile among the nations.

The book of Ezra records the return of the remnant and the building of the **second temple** during the time of Haggai and Zechariah. The book of Nehemiah records the rebuilding of the walls of Jerusalem. Nehemiah and Ezra were contemporaries. Ezra is referred to as a **scribe**.

The book of Malachi records the last Old Testament prophecy given by God. After this prophecy God did not inspire canonical Scripture again for 400 years.

This 400 years of silence which followed the book of Malachi is called the **intertestament period**. Although God was silent in that He did not speak through His prophets during this time, the events of these 400 years testify to the fulfillment of much that was written by Daniel the prophet.

These years could be divided into three periods: the Greek, the Maccabean, and the beginning of the Roman period.

The Greek Period
(331 to 63 B.C.)

The Greek period encompasses three different rulerships over Jerusalem.

Under Alexander the Great
(331 to 323 B.C.)

As the Persian Empire grew and threatened the security of the city-states of Greece, Philip of Macedonia sought to consolidate Greece in an effort to resist attack from Persia.

In 336 B.C. Philip was murdered, and his son, Alexander, who was about 20 years old, became king. Within two years Alexander set out to conquer Persia, whose empire now extended westward as far as Asia Minor (modern-day Turkey).

Over the next two years Alexander conquered the territory from Asia Minor to Pakistan and to Egypt, which included the land of the Jews. Although the account is not universally accepted by other historians,

Josephus, a Jewish historian who lived about A.D. 37–100, wrote that as Alexander marched into Jerusalem he was met by Jaddua and other Jewish priests dressed in their priestly garments and by the people of Jerusalem wearing white robes.

In a dream Jaddua had been told to put wreaths on the city walls in order to greet Alexander. Alexander also had a dream which coincided with this event. When Alexander was escorted into Jerusalem and shown the prophecy in Daniel 8 which described the destruction of the Medo-Persian Empire by a large horn on a goat (which represented Greece), Alexander felt the prophecy pertained to him and offered the Jews whatever they wanted. Alexander treated the Jews well and did not harm Jerusalem or their rebuilt temple.

When Alexander built the city of Alexandria in Egypt, he encouraged many Jews to settle there in order to help populate the city. Whenever Alexander conquered an area he established Greek cities and colonies, bringing in his Greek culture, ideas, and language. His goal was to consolidate his empire through a common way of life and thinking which became known as **Hellenization. Koine Greek** became the common language in the countries ruled by Greece and continued to be the primary language of civilization through the time of Christ. The New Testament was written in Koine Greek.

Alexander and his war-weary army returned from the Indus River Valley to Babylon in 323 B.C. History tells us he sat down and wept because there were no more territories to conquer. He died in Babylon that year at the age of 33.

Because Alexander died without an appointed heir, his kingdom fell into chaos. After 22 years of struggle among his generals, it was divided among four of them: Lysimachus, Cassander, Ptolemy I Soter, and Seleucus I Nicator. (See chart below.)

Under the Ptolemies of Egypt
(323 to 204 B.C.)

Ptolemy I Soter, who took Egypt, was given Jerusalem and Judea. The Jews fared well; they were allowed to govern themselves and practice their religion without interference. Under his leadership Jews were permitted to go to Egypt. Some Jews were invited to go to Alexandria and become scholars. The Ptolemies moved Egypt's capital from Memphis to Alexandria and made it the center of learning and commerce. There the Jews were encouraged to use the Greek library, at that time the most extensive and best in the world. As a result many were caught up in philosophy and logic and drank deeply from the cup of Hellenism.

It is believed that Ptolemy II Philadelphus commissioned the translation of the Pentateuch into the Koine Greek. The Greek translation of the entire Old Testament, eventually completed about 100 B.C., was referred to as the **Septuagint** (meaning 70), or abbreviated as the **LXX**. Many of the New Testament writers quoted from the Septuagint.

Other writings produced during this intertestament period are the **Apocrypha**, the **Pseudepigrapha**, and the **Qumran Scrolls** (also called the **Dead Sea Scrolls**). The **Apocrypha** are composed of a variety of writings, including apocalyptic, wisdom, and historical literature. It is from the apocryphal book of First Maccabees that historians gained insight into the period from the Maccabean revolt through the time of John Hyrcanus. The

---

The Division of Alexander the Great's Empire

Lysimachus	Cassander	Ptolemy I Soter	Seleucus I Nicator
took	took	took	took
Thrace and Bithynia	Macedonia	Egypt	Syria

*Ptolemy I Soter and Seleucus I Nicator began a succession
of competing dynasties for which the land of Israel became a pawn.*

Apocrypha were included in the Septuagint, although they were not part of the Hebrew Scriptures.

The **Pseudepigrapha** are a collection of writings even more extensive than the Apocrypha, but scholars cannot entirely agree on which writings comprise this group. These writings are attributed to noted people such as Adam, Abraham, Enoch, Ezra, and Baruch—but scholars agree that these claims are not authentic.

The **Qumran** or **Dead Sea Scrolls** were manuscripts apparently written or copied between 200 B.C. and A.D. 70 by a Jewish religious sect called **Essenes**. The particular community of Essenes who lived close to the Dead Sea seem to have practiced celibacy and a strictly disciplined communal lifestyle, separating themselves from others. The Dead Sea Scrolls describe the lives and beliefs of this group which lived in the last two centuries before Christ; they also include the oldest known manuscripts of the Old Testament. The scrolls are so named because they were hidden and preserved in some caves near an archaeological excavation called Khirbet Qumran on the western side of the Dead Sea.

Under the Seleucid Kings of Syria (204 to 165 B.C.)

Those ruling Syria, referred to as the kings of the north in Daniel 11, wanted the beautiful land of Israel. When Antiochus III the Great conquered Ptolemy V Epiphanes of Egypt, Jerusalem and Judea were brought under Syrian dominance.

After gaining dominance over the Jews, Antiochus was defeated by the Romans and ended up having to pay Rome a large sum of money for a period of years. To make sure he complied, Rome held his son, Antiochus IV, hostage in Rome.

Antiochus III the Great was succeeded by his son Seleucus IV Philopator, who ruled from 187–175 B.C. In 175 B.C. Antiochus IV Epiphanes (the son who had been held hostage in Rome) usurped the throne by killing his brother. He ruled until 163 B.C. He was called *Epiphanes*, which means "manifest" or "splendid."

Until this period in Israel's history, the priesthood had been a matter of birthright and the office was held for life. However, during his reign Antiochus IV Epiphanes sold the priesthood to Jason, the brother of the high priest. Jason also paid Antiochus a high price in order to build a Greek gymnasium near the temple. During this time many Jews were lured into a Hellenistic way of life. All this brought a great conflict among the orthodox Jews and the "Hellenistic" Jews. During this period the land of Israel was referred to by different regions: Judea, Samaria, Galilee, Perea, and Trachonitis.

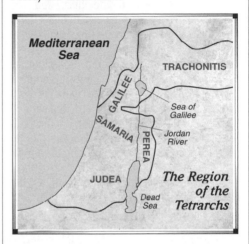

The conflict was heightened when Antiochus IV Epiphanes sought to take the throne of Egypt but was rebuffed by Rome. Because of that and because of what he surmised as a revolt in the priesthood, Antiochus unleashed his anger on those Jews who wouldn't curry his favor or fully adopt Hellenism. He was determined to destroy Judaism. Circumcision was forbidden; those who disobeyed were put to death. Copies of the law were desecrated with heathen symbols or burned, while anyone found with a copy of the law was to be put to death. The Jews were also forbidden to celebrate the Sabbath. Then Antiochus sacrificed a pig on the altar in the temple and erected a statue of Zeus, an abomination of desolation, in the holy place (Daniel 11:31).

Finally, Antiochus sent his officers throughout the land to compel Jews to make sacrifices to Zeus.

The Maccabean Period
(165 to 63 B.C.)

When Antiochus IV Epiphanes's officer arrived in the village of Modein (which lies halfway between Jerusalem and Joppa) and commanded the aged priest Mattathias to make a sacrifice to Zeus, the officer didn't know it was the last official duty he would perform in his life. As Mattathias refused, a younger Jew stepped forward to take his place. When he did, a furious Mattathias plunged his knife not only into the Jewish volunteer but also into the Syrian officer. Mattathias fled with his five sons to the hills, and the Maccabean revolt, led by Mattathias's third son, nicknamed Maccabeus (the Hammerer), began.

Three years after Antiochus IV Epiphanes defiled the temple, the Jews recaptured Jerusalem. They removed the statue of Zeus and refurbished the temple and reinstituted Jewish sacrifices. On December 25 the Jews celebrated with a feast of dedication (John 10:22), which from then on became the annual feast of lights or Hanukkah.

Thus began what is referred to as the **Hasmonean Dynasty** as the descendants of Mattathias ruled Israel until Rome conquered Jerusalem in 63 B.C.

When Simon, the last surviving son of Mattathias, was murdered, Simon's son, John Hyrcanus, named himself priest and king. He ruled from 134–104 B.C. He destroyed the Samaritan temple on Mount Gerizim, and from that time on the Jews had no dealings with the Samaritans. After that Hyrcanus moved southeast and conquered the land of the Idumeans, who came from the ancient kingdom of Edom. The peoples of this land were given the choice of emigrating or converting to Judaism. This was the land of Herod the Great, who would someday become Rome's appointed king of the Jews.

During the reign of John Hyrcanus, the **Pharisees**, a religious sect of the Jews, arose from the Hasidim. The **Hasidim**, a militant religious community dedicated to the obedience of the law and the worship of God, began around 168 B.C. and was active during the Maccabean revolt. The word *Pharisee* means "separated one" and was probably used to describe these men because they separated themselves from the strong influence of Hellenism. During New Testament times the

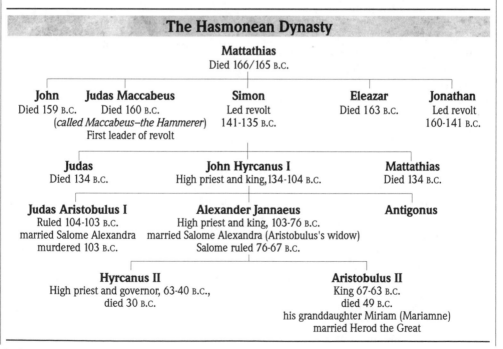

The Hasmonean Dynasty

Mattathias
Died 166/165 B.C.

John	Judas Maccabeus	Simon	Eleazar	Jonathan
Died 159 B.C.	Died 160 B.C.	Led revolt	Died 163 B.C.	Led revolt
	(*called Maccabeus–the Hammerer*)	141-135 B.C.		160-141 B.C.
	First leader of revolt			

Judas	John Hyrcanus I	Mattathias
Died 134 B.C.	High priest and king, 134-104 B.C.	Died 134 B.C.

Judas Aristobulus I	Alexander Jannaeus	Antigonus
Ruled 104-103 B.C.	High priest and king, 103-76 B.C.	
married Salome Alexandra	married Salome Alexandra (Aristobulus's widow)	
murdered 103 B.C.	Salome ruled 76-67 B.C.	

Hyrcanus II	Aristobulus II
High priest and governor, 63-40 B.C.,	King 67-63 B.C.
died 30 B.C.	died 49 B.C.
	his granddaughter Miriam (Mariamne)
	married Herod the Great

majority of the scribes were Pharisees.

Doctrinally the Pharisees viewed the entire Old Testament as authoritative; however, they also accepted the oral tradition as equally authoritative. To the Pharisee, to study the law was true worship. They believed in life after death, the resurrection, and the existence of angels and demons. Although the Pharisees taught that the way to God was through keeping the law, they were more liberal in their interpretation of the law than were the Sadducees. The Pharisees represented the largest religious sect, but their numbers declined when they fell into John Hyrcanus's disfavor.

The **Sadducees**, a smaller religious sect comprised mostly of the upper classes, were often of the priestly line and were usually more wealthy than the Pharisees. For the most part the Pharisees were of the middle-class merchants and tradesmen. The Sadducees accepted only the **Torah** (the first five books of the Old Testament) as authoritative. While they were rigid in the observance of the law and held to its literal interpretation, they denied divine providence, the resurrection, life after death, the existence of angels and demons, and any reward or punishment after death. They opposed the oral law as obligatory or binding and were materialistic.

The Sadducees controlled the temple and its services. However, because the Sadducees leaned toward Hellenism, they were unpopular with the majority of the Jewish populace.

Aristobulus I, who succeeded his father, John Hyrcanus, married Salome Alexandra. However, when Aristobulus died, Salome married his brother Alexander Jannaeus, who became high priest and king in 103 B.C. This marriage created many enemies for Alexander Jannaeus because the high priest was to marry only a virgin.

When he died in 76 B.C., his wife, Salome Alexandra, took the throne, but as a woman she could not hold the office of high priest, so her oldest son, Hyrcanus II, assumed that position.

Civil war broke out when Salome died, because her younger son, Aristobulus II, who was supported by the Sadducees, sought to take the throne from Hyrcanus II. He was willing to give up that position, but Antipater (an Idumean and the father of Herod the Great) befriended Hyrcanus and persuaded him to seek outside help in order to regain his position as the rightful heir. Hyrcanus's forces came against Aristobulus and defeated him. He had to flee and made the temple in Jerusalem his fortress, but he was besieged by Hyrcanus's forces.

Early in this period the Hasmoneans had made a treaty with Rome in order to keep Syria, their northern neighbors, in check. Now the Roman army under Scaurus was in Syria because Seleucid rule had collapsed. Scaurus heard about the civil war in Judea and went there. Both Aristobulus and Hyrcanus sought his help. Scaurus sided with Aristobulus and had the siege lifted from Jerusalem, but the fighting continued. An appeal was made to the Roman general Pompey, who said he would settle the dispute and urged them to keep peace until he arrived. However, Aristobulus went back to Jerusalem to prepare resistance, which caused Rome's support to turn to Hyrcanus. Pompey arrived and took Aristobulus and his family captive, besieging the city for three months.

The Period of Roman Rule
(63 B.C. to A.D. 70)

In 63 B.C. Pompey conquered Jerusalem and with some of his soldiers walked into the holy of holies. Although they didn't touch any of the furnishings, they alienated the Jews, who never forgave Pompey. About 12,000 Jews died during this Roman siege of Jerusalem, a supposed attempt to settle a civil war.

Rome broke up the Hasmonean dynasty and their territory. Judea was now reduced to smaller borders and its independence lost. It was now a territory of Rome. Hyrcanus II could be the rightful priest but not king. He was now under the governor of Syria, a Roman province. Scaurus was appointed governor. Aristobulus and many Jews were taken to Rome. Not much later Gabinius, a Roman governor of Syria, took control. He entrusted the temple to Hyrcanus and changed the government of Judea.

The Jewish state was divided into five

districts governed by a council that remained under the jurisdiction of the governor of Syria; Hyrcanus, the high priest, was made ruler over Jerusalem. Antipater was his chief magistrate.

The high priest presided over the **Sanhedrin**, a 71-member council comprised of both Sadducees and Pharisees, which governed the Jews under the authority of Rome. Although the Sanhedrin seemed to have autonomy in the matters of the civil and criminal government of the Jews, apparently the Sanhedrin was not allowed to put people to death without the permission of the Roman procurator. The Sanhedrin is often referred to as "the council" in the Gospels and Acts.

In 55 B.C. three men—Pompey, Crassus (the governor of Syria), and Julius Caesar—controlled Rome. Crassus, considering himself another Alexander the Great, set out to conquer the world. However, just before this he stole the treasures from the temple in Jerusalem. Crassus and his army were later destroyed by the Parthians.

Parthia, southeast of the Caspian Sea and part of the Persian Empire, had been conquered by Alexander the Great. But Rome would not conquer them until A.D. 114.

After Crassus's death, Julius Caesar took Italy and then set out to destroy Pompey. Pompey fled to Egypt, where he was assassinated. During this time Antipater supported Caesar, so out of gratitude Caesar gave him the official title of Procurator of Judea.

Antipater made his son Phasael governor of Judea and his son Herod governor of Galilee. Hyrcanus II remained high priest, although Antipater and his two sons robbed him of his authority.

In 44 B.C. Caesar was murdered by Brutus and Cassius. Civil war broke out in Rome. Cassius took control of the east. Because of the instability of Rome, Hyrcanus's rivals made a bid for power.

Antipater was murdered in 43 B.C. Antigonus, Aristobulus's son (who was supported by the Parthians), invaded the country.

At that time Herod came to the aid of Hyrcanus, who out of gratitude gave Herod a beautiful woman named Miriam. They were not married until five years later.

After that Brutus and Cassius were defeated by Mark Antony and Caesar's nephew Octavian (who would later become Caesar Augustus). Mark Antony became ruler of the east. In 40 B.C., when the Parthians invaded Palestine, Herod fled to Rome.

That year, at the urging of Antony and Octavian, Herod was made king of the Jews. It took him three years to rid the area of the Parthians and establish his rule in Judea. Just before laying siege to Jerusalem, Herod married Miriam (also called Mariamne), hoping that his marriage into the Hasmonean family would make him more acceptable to the Jews.

In 20 B.C. Herod began rebuilding the temple. The one built by Zerubbabel after the Babylonian exile was so pitifully small in comparison to the first temple that Herod was determined to make it larger and more magnificent than Solomon's. Although the temple itself was completed in a year-and-a-half, the construction and decoration of its outer courts continued for years, so in A.D. 26 the Jews would say, "It took forty-six years to build this temple" (John 2:20).

Herod, whose people (the Idumeans) had been forced to convert to Judaism under John Hyrcanus, was only a Jew in practice when he lived in Judea. Although Rome gave Herod the title "King of the Jews," he was never accepted by those he ruled over.

Then "in the days of Herod the king, magi from the east arrived in Jerusalem, saying, 'Where is He who has been born King of the Jews?'" (Matthew 2:1, 2).

The true King had come...the Ruler who would shepherd God's people Israel (Matthew 2:6).

Herod died in 4 B.C. But those living in Judea and Galilee saw a great light and heard with their own ears the voice of God, the King of kings.

The 400 years of silence had been broken.

Why Jesus' Birth Is Shown as 4 B.C.

The designation of years as A.D. or B.C. did not begin until the sixth century, and was not widely adopted until the eighth century. This designation was created by a highly regarded scholar named Dionysius Exiguus, who was skilled in mathematics, astronomy, and theology. Dionysius was born in Scythia, and went to Rome in 496. In the year 523, the papal chancellor Bonifatius (under Pope John I) asked Dionysius to compile a table of the dates of Easter. An existing table that covered the nineteen-year period denoted 228–247 counted the years from the beginning of the reign of the Roman emperor Diocletian, which was the custom of the time. Rather than honor Diocletian, the persecutor of Christians, Dionysius fixed the birth of Christ relative to Diocletian's reign in such a manner that it fell on 25 December (or 25 March) in the 753rd year since the founding of Rome. Thus he designated these same 19 years as *Anno Domini Nostri Jesu Christi* 532–550. Thus, Dionysius's *Anno Domini* 532 is equivalent to *Anno Diocletian* 248. Under Dionysius's scheme of dating, the year starting one week after the birth of Christ was year 1 of the era "of the Lord," or *Anno Domini* 1. According to Dionysius's calculations, A.D. 1 would have been the year of our Lord's birth. There is no "zero" year, so the preceding year is 1 B.C. (before Christ).

Research since Dionysius's time, however, indicates Christ must have been born earlier than A.D. 1. We know from the book of Matthew that Jesus was born under the reign of Herod the Great. History confirms that Herod the Great died in the year we now call 4 B.C., which means Jesus could not have been born any later than that. There is no universally accepted year of Christ's birth, but 4 B.C. is a frequently used figure, and it's the date used in all the timelines in this book.

FROM CHRIST TO MODERN TIMES

Many Jewish leaders were religious, but they did not know God. When Jesus came to explain the Father, they rejected Him. They rejected God's precious cornerstone. Consequently, once again they would be banished from their land.

Jesus warned, "When you see Jerusalem surrounded by armies, then recognize that her desolation is near....for there will be great distress upon the land and wrath to this people; and they will fall by the edge of the sword, and will be led captive into all the nations; and Jerusalem will be trampled under foot by the Gentiles until the times of the Gentiles are fulfilled" (Luke 21:20,23,24). God had spoken. Had the people listened, they wouldn't have been caught unawares—but they refused to hear.

The Destruction of Jerusalem
(A.D. 70)

The conflict between the Jews and their Roman ruler intensified. Tacitus, the Roman historian, said the Jews put up with things until the procuratorship of Gessius Florus. When the Jews rose up against Florus's army, war became inevitable. Nero commanded T. Flavius Vespasian to subdue the Jews. Vespasian reduced the Galilee and secured Judea, except for Jerusalem, Masada, and two other fortresses.

During this time, Nero committed suicide and civil war broke out in Rome. Galba, Otho, and Vitellius succeeded one another as emperor. Then the eastern legions of Rome proclaimed Vespasian emperor, and Vitellius was murdered. Vespasian put his son Titus in charge of the war and sailed for Rome. In A.D. 70 Titus besieged Jerusalem. Over one million Jews died in five months. On August 6, the ninth of Ab, Roman forces invaded the temple and, just as Jesus prophesied, not one stone was left upon the other. Jerusalem was burned. Titus went to Rome to celebrate his victory with his father.

Although some of the Jews fled to Masada, the Jewish state no longer existed. Sometime between A.D. 72–74 Masada fell to the Roman governor Flavius Silva.

Hadrian and Aelia Capitolina

In A.D. 132 the Emperor Hadrian banned circumcision and the observance of the Sabbath. He also made plans to build a temple to Zeus. These actions spurred Simon bar Kochba to lead another revolt. After Hadrian crushed the Bar Kochba revolt, Hadrian rebuilt Jerusalem in A.D. 136, named it Aelia Capitolina, and forbade the Jews entrance to the city on pain of death. That edict was enforced for about 500 years.

The Byzantine Period
(A.D. 324 to 638)

In A.D. 324 Constantine became sole emperor of Rome. In A.D. 330 the capital was moved from Rome to Byzantium, which was renamed Constantinople (present-day Istanbul, Turkey) in his honor. According to some traditions, Constantine became a Christian after seeing a vision of a cross and hearing the words, "By this sign thou shalt conquer." What is fact is that he proclaimed Christianity as the official religion of the Roman Empire.

Constantine's mother, the empress Helena, began restoring the city of David (Jerusalem), locating Christian sites and building shrines over the places associated with Christianity. Helena and the city's bishop, Macarius, built the Church of the Holy Sepulchre on the site where they believed Jesus had been buried. Byzantine churches could be seen across the land. By the fifth century the Roman Empire divided and the eastern half became the Byzantine Empire, with its capital in Constantinople. Rome became the capital of the western Roman Empire.

In the fifth century the Jews were permitted to pray on the temple mount on Tisha B'Av, the anniversary of the destruction of the temple. By the middle of the century Jerusalem was recognized as a patriarchal territory equal in status to Constantinople, Alexandria, Rome, and Antioch.

In A.D. 614 the Persians conquered the land, massacred the people, and destroyed the churches. In A.D. 629 the Byzantine emperor Heraclius reconquered Jerusalem.

The Early Muslim Period
(A.D. 638 to 1099)

Nine years later the Muslims were ruling. During this time Christians and Jews were permitted to worship freely. Jews returned to Jerusalem. The Umayyad dynasty reigned from 660–750. The prophet Mohammed's journey from Mecca to Jerusalem on his winged horse Al-buraq was linked to the temple mount, thus making it a holy site for the Muslims. In the seventh century, Caliph Abd al-Malik commissioned the building of the mosque, the Dome of the Rock, on the temple mount.

Thus Jerusalem became the third-holiest city for Islam. The Arabs built only one new city, Ramle, which Suleiman made his capital in the eighth century.

The Crusader Period
(A.D. 1099 to 1244)

In 1099, at Pope Urban II's appeal, the Crusaders crossed Europe to liberate the Christian holy places from the Muslims. The city was theirs after a five-week siege. Jerusalem became the capital of the Crusader kingdom. European Christian noblemen and bourgeoisie came to settle in Jerusalem. Mosques were turned into churches, and new churches and monasteries were built. For the next 88 years, Jews and Muslims were not permitted to live in Jerusalem, but only visit it.

The Ayyubid Interlude
(A.D. 1187 to 1192)

In 1187 Saladin, the founder of the Ayyubid dynasty, took Jerusalem, destroyed the cross on top of the Dome of the Rock, and turned churches into mosques. The Jews were now allowed to return to Jerusalem. They came from North Africa, France, and England to settle alongside the Jews of Jerusalem.

Then in 1192 Richard the Lion Hearted and Phillipe Auguste of France restored the Crusader kingdom which had been conquered by Saladin. Jerusalem was divided. The temple mount and its mosques remained in Muslim hands while the other parts of the city came under Christian rule. In 1244 the Crusaders lost the city.

The Mamluk Period
(A.D. 1260 to 1517)

In 1260 Jerusalem was conquered by the Mamluks, military regiments from central Asia who were the new rulers of Egypt. The Mamluks established **madrasas** (institutes of religious instruction) and hostels for Muslim scholars and pilgrims.

The Ottoman Period
(A.D. 1517 to 1917)

The Ottoman Empire, comprised of Constantinople, Asia Minor, parts of Europe and the Balkans, Egypt, and Syria, added Israel and Judea in 1517. Jerusalem was taken from the Mamluks by Ottoman Turks. Sultan Suleiman the Magnificent had the walls which still surround Jerusalem built at this time. After his death the Jewish community became more firmly entrenched as they built the Jewish quarter along the Zion Gate. Jewish scholastic centers were established in Jerusalem and Safed. The Christians split into various eastern communities.

In 1832 the Pasha of Egypt, Mohammed Ali, denuded the Holy Land of trees as he set out to build his ships. However, his approval of Christian missions and schools, foreign consulates, and archaeological expeditions opened up Jerusalem to Western influence. In the late 1800s a political movement called Zionism sprang up in Europe. Its goal was to create a homeland for Jewish people in Palestine. Jews fleeing eastern Europe and Russia and arriving in Abraham's land were quick to adopt Theodor Herzl's vision for a free state for Jews. In 1897, the first Zionist Congress was held.

The British Mandate
(A.D. 1917 to 1948)

Four hundred years of Ottoman rule came to an end on December 9, 1917. Two days later British Field Marshal Allenby entered the Citadel and Jerusalem was pronounced the capital of the country. The Balfour Declaration promised the establishment of a national home for the Jews. In 1920 and 1929 Jews and Arabs had violent clashes. The Arabs rebelled in 1936-1939, and open war erupted as Arabs and Jews fought for control over Jerusalem.

From 1939 to 1945 six million Jews were systematically murdered under the direction of Adolf Hitler. After World War II, world opinion strongly favored the establishment of a Jewish homeland. By November 1947 the tension between Jews and Arabs was so great the United Nations decided to intervene, end the Mandate, and make Jerusalem an international city. The United Nations voted 33 to 13 to partition the country west of the Jordan River into two parts—one for Arabs, one for Jews. The Jews agreed, but the Arabs rejected the plan.

The State of Israel
(May 14, 1948)

On May 14, 1948, when the British withdrew, the Jews proclaimed the independent State of Israel. The next day Israel was attacked by Iraq, Lebanon, Syria, Jordan, and Egypt. By December Israel won its independence. Jordanian soldiers, however, remained in the West Bank (biblical Judea and Samaria). Egypt held the Gaza Strip. When a cease-fire was declared in January 1949, the city was divided. Jordan held all the shrines encompassed by Suleiman's walls; the old city of Jerusalem was out-of-bounds for the Jews.

Israel prepared for the influx of more than 800,000 immigrants from 102 countries during the next seven years. Living conditions were austere, but the Jews were home! By 1957 the malarial swamps of the Hula Valley were drained and the waters of the Sea of Galilee flowed south through pipelines, bringing life to the arid Negev.

The Sinai Campaign
(1956)

In 1956 Israel executed a swift victory over Egypt in the Sinai Campaign. On the guarantee of freedom of navigation in the Straits of Tiran and the Gulf of Elath, Israel withdrew her troops from the Sinai. Then later, once again, Egyptian troops moved to Israel's borders.

The Six-Day War
(1967)

The Six-Day War broke out on June 5, 1967. During that war Israel gained control of Judea, Samaria, the Golan Heights, Gaza, and the Sinai peninsula, and reunited Jerusalem under Jewish sovereignty for the first time since the Bar Kochba revolt, more than 1800 years earlier. The Jews could finally weep at the holy wall of Jerusalem, the western wall of the sacred temple mount.

The Yom Kippur War
(1973)

In 1973, on Yom Kippur, the highest of holy days, Israel was attacked on the Golan Heights by Syria and across the Suez Canal and into Sinai by Egypt. After three weeks the Israeli defense forces finally drove the attackers back. Disengagement agreements were signed between Israel and Egypt and between Israel and Syria.

The Peace Treaty Between Israel and Egypt
(1979)

In March of 1979 Israel and Egypt signed a historic peace treaty returning the Sinai to Egypt.

On June 6, 1982, Israel launched Operation Peace for Galilee in order to remove from Lebanese territory the Palestine Liberation Organization's threat to its northern settlements.

The Middle East Gulf War
(1991)

In January 1991, when war broke out between Iraq and a coalition of nations headed by the United States of America, Iraq responded with missile attacks on Israel—although Israel was not part of the conflict and remained out of the conflict at the United States's urging. The Middle East Gulf Crisis came to an end approximately six weeks later.

The Peace Treaty Between Israel and the PLO
(1993)

In September 1993, Israel and the Palestine Liberation Organization (PLO) signed an agreement in which Israel was to give administrative control of the Gaza Strip and portions of the West Bank to the PLO by May 4, 1999, in exchange for peace. An armed Palestinian police force was to replace the Israeli Defense Forces to ensure continued security in the regions, Israel was to release some prisoners, and the PLO was to arrest terrorists who acted against Israel. Since the signing of this agreement (known as the Oslo Accord because it was negotiated in Oslo, Norway), the scheduled withdrawal of Israeli forces has proceeded more slowly than planned, and terrorism against Israeli citizens has not ended.

The words of Leviticus 25:23 seem poignant in our day: "The land, moreover, shall not be sold permanently, for the land is Mine; for you are but aliens and sojourners with Me."

The words of Zechariah the prophet remain unfulfilled, but because of all that is transpiring, they are read with new insight and great anticipation:

> *Behold, a day is coming for the LORD when the spoil taken from you will be divided among you. For I will gather all the nations against Jerusalem to battle, and the city will be captured, the houses plundered, the women ravished, and half of the city exiled, but the rest of the people will not be cut off from the city. Then the LORD will go forth and fight against those nations, as when He fights on a day of battle.*
>
> *In that day His feet will stand on the Mount of Olives, which is in front of Jerusalem on the east; and the Mount of Olives will be split in its middle from east to west by a very large valley, so that half of the mountain will move toward the north and the other half toward the south....*
>
> *Then the LORD, my God, will come, and all the holy ones with Him!...*
>
> *And the LORD will be king over all the earth; in that day the LORD will be the only one, and His name the only one* (Zechariah 14:1-4,5,9).
>
> *Amen. Come, Lord Jesus* (Revelation 22:20).

Appendix 3: Historical and Grammatical Helps

The information in this section will provide you with additional tools for your inductive study of God's Word.

Take some time to familiarize yourself with the basic content of each part of this section so you will know what is at your fingertips when you need it.

THE ARK OF THE COVENANT

The one piece of furniture that is the most holy to the Jews is the Ark of the Covenant. The following information will help you understand why it is so important to them and why Orthodox Jews are still looking for it.

The Ark, a box about 4 feet long by 2 1/2 feet wide by 2 1/2 feet high, was constructed of acacia wood and overlaid with gold inside and out. Because it symbolized God's presence, no one was allowed to touch it. Four gold rings were attached to the feet of the Ark. Poles, made of acacia wood and overlaid with gold, were slipped through these rings so that the Ark could be carried from place to place (Exodus 25:10-22). Only the Kohathites (a division of the Levites) were allowed to move the Ark.

When the Ark was in the tabernacle the cloud of God's presence hovered over the mercy seat (Leviticus 16:2; 1 Samuel 4:4). The mercy seat, made of pure gold with a gold cherub attached at each end, covered the Ark of the Covenant. On the day of atonement the high priest sprinkled the blood of sacrifice on the mercy seat as a covering for the sins of the people. (The Hebrew word for mercy is *kapporeth*, a covering.)

Inside the Ark was the testimony, the stone tablets bearing the ten commandments (Exodus 40:20; Deuteronomy 10:2). For a period of time the Ark also contained Aaron's rod which budded (Numbers 17:10) and a gold jar of manna (Hebrews 9:4).

The tabernacle, where the Ark resided in the most holy place, and the furniture were made according to the pattern of God's throne in heaven. God gave Moses this pattern when He instructed him to build the tabernacle (Hebrews 8:1-5).

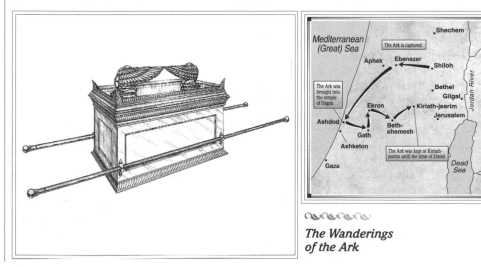

The Wanderings of the Ark

323

The Ark journeyed before the children of Israel as they moved from Sinai to Canaan. It went before them as they crossed the Jordan River and conquered Jericho. It rested at Gilgal, Shechem, Bethel, and Shiloh. Then the Philistines at Ebenezer captured it and kept it for seven months. They took it to Aphek, Ashdod, Gath, and Ekron. From Ekron they sent it back and it ended up in Beth-shemesh. It was at Beth-shemesh that some people were killed because they looked into the Ark. From there the Ark was taken to Kiriath-jearim (Gibeath) and the house of Abinadab.

When David became king he wanted to move the Ark to Jerusalem. The Israelites broke God's command by moving it on a cart rather than carrying it by the poles. When the Ark started to fall off the cart, a man named Uzzah touched the Ark and was killed by God. This incident occurred on the threshing floor of Nacon (also referred to as Chidon) (2 Samuel 6:6-7; 1 Chronicles 13:9). The Ark remained in the house of Obed-edom the Gittite, a Philistine from Gath, for three months until David had the Kohathites move it to Jerusalem. There the Ark was placed in the midst of a tent (2 Chronicles 1:4).

When Solomon became king and built the temple, the Ark was moved from the tent in Jerusalem to the temple, which was built on the threshing floor of Ornan (1 Chronicles 21:18; 2 Chronicles 3:1). There the Ark was placed in the most holy place (1 Kings 8:6; 2 Chronicles 5:2-14).

There is no record of the whereabouts or fate of the Ark since the destruction of the temple by the Babylonians in 586 B.C.

The last mention of the Ark is in Revelation 11:19: "The temple of God which is in heaven was opened; and the ark of His covenant appeared in His temple, and there were flashes of lightning and sounds and peals of thunder and an earthquake and a great hailstorm."

UNDERSTANDING GNOSTICISM

Much like the church today, many members of the early church were significantly influenced by a prevailing philosophy of the day. While some of the New Testament was being written, the church in Asia was being threatened by gnosticism, a philosophy which became the major opponent of the gospel in the early apostolic church.

A familiarity with the teachings of gnosticism will give you a greater understanding of and appreciation for some of the warnings and teachings given in the epistles.

Many members of the early church were seeking enlightenment, and were easily deceived by Gnostic teachers and led astray from the simplicity and purity of devotion to Christ. Some had apparently left the church to form their own community, teaching a different gospel from what the apostles had preached. This movement away from the church caused those who remained to question what was true, and thus confusion crept in.

The term *gnosticism* comes from the Greek word *gnosis*, meaning "knowledge." Gnosticism is a philosophy which centers on a search for higher knowledge. The Gnostics taught that this knowledge was not intellectual knowledge but a knowledge which the ordinary Christian was incapable of attaining. Once a believer came into possession of this extraordinary knowledge, according to Gnostic thought, he had "salvation."

Although Gnostic philosophy took many strange and divergent turns, two axioms were basic to its teaching:

∾ *The first major Gnostic doctrine was the supremacy of knowledge.*

> Certain *pneumatikoi* or "spiritual ones" claimed to have special knowledge of the truth.

> Ordinary Christians did not or could not possess this secret of higher knowledge.

∾ *The second major doctrine of gnosticism was the separation of spirit and matter.*

> All matter was considered to be evil and the source of evil.

> The spirit was considered to be good and impervious to defilement by anything the body (matter) did.

Claiming a so-called higher knowledge beyond that revealed by God in Christ Jesus and through the prophets, gnosticism had its origins in the philosophies of the Greeks and the Romans, in the creeds of Plato and Philo, and in the religions of the East, especially those of Persia and India. As long as Christianity kept its Judaic roots, it was free from these heresies. However, when Christianity spread to Gentile territory, an attempt was made on the part of Eastern philosophical religion to form an alliance with it.

Many Gnostics allegorized the Old Testament and did not interpret its teachings literally. They strayed from the veracity of the Word, which would have exposed their erroneous teaching regarding creation, sin, and the restoration of all things. They failed to see how a supreme God, pure in spirit and essentially good, could create a universe of matter which they considered evil.

When the Gnostics embraced Christianity, they split into factions on the subject of Christ's deity. Two of the major factions taught as follows:

∾ The Docetic Gnostics denied the humanity of Jesus. The word *docetic* comes from the Greek word *dokeō*, "to seem." According to the Docetists, it was impossible for God, who was spirit and good, to become flesh, which was matter and evil, in the person of Jesus Christ. They believed that Jesus was a phantom; He didn't possess a real flesh-and-blood body. He only seemed to have a body.

∾ The Cerinthian Gnostics (followers of Cerinthus) separated the man Jesus from the *aeon*, the power of Christ. They believed that when the dove came on Jesus at His baptism, the power of Christ came and rested on the man Jesus. This power then departed before His death on the cross. So it was simply the "man" Jesus who died, not Jesus Christ, God in the flesh.

These Gnostic heresies denied that God became man and walked this earth in the person of Jesus Christ to bring redemption and salvation to mankind. Having eliminated Jesus Christ as the only way to God, the Gnostics believed they could make their own way to God through their inquiry and knowledge. Faith and one's deeds were viewed as having no significance in salvation or the life of a believer.

Understanding the basis of gnosticism and the forms of thought that it took in the early days of the Christian church will enable you to better understand the doctrinal heresy which some of the New Testament writers addressed.

GUIDELINES FOR INTERPRETING PREDICTIVE PROPHECY

From Genesis to Revelation the Bible is filled with prophecy. If you want to handle the prophecies in the Word of God accurately, the following guidelines will give you some important parameters.

The Greek word for prophecy, *propheteia*, comes from two Greek words, *pro*, meaning "forth," and *phēmi*, meaning "to speak." It means to speak forth the mind and counsel of God. According to this definition, all Scripture is in a sense prophecy.

Predictive prophecy points to a future fulfillment and is of divine origin. In *Understanding and Applying the Bible*, Dr. Robertson McQuilkin says: "There are two purposes for predictive prophecy. The chief purpose is to affect the conduct of those who hear the prophecy. Another purpose is met only when the prophecy is fulfilled. That purpose is to build faith, to establish confidence in the God who miraculously foretold events (John 13:19; 14:29; 16:4)" (p. 215).

Some scholars divide predictive prophecy into two categories: forthtelling and foretelling. Forthtelling prophecies contain a message about the present or immediate time. (Often this is a call to godly living in the light of prophecy yet to be fulfilled.) Foretelling prophecies contain a message about what God will do in the future.

When a prophet spoke for God, the prophecy could refer to the following:

• a present or near fulfillment

• a future fulfillment

• a twofold fulfillment: a near fulfillment and then a later, future fulfillment

As you read the prophecies of the Bible, keep in mind the following guidelines and discern whether the prophecy refers to:

• the prophet's own time and/or a future time

- the captivity and/or restoration of Israel or Judah

- the first coming of Christ and any events connected with it

- the second coming of Christ

- the last days or end times

∾ *As you study prophecy, it is important to remember that the prophets did not always indicate intervals of time between events, nor did they always write their prophecies in chronological order.* For example, an Old Testament prophecy could include the first and second comings of Christ without any indication of the time span between the two comings. One such prophecy is found in Isaiah 65:17-25. In this prophecy, Isaiah first talks about the new heavens and the new earth (in which we know there is no death), and then in verses 18-25 he refers to a time when a youth dies at age 100 and the wolf and lamb lie down together. Chronologically, verse 17 will be fulfilled *after* verses 18-25 become a reality.

∾ *Always approach a prophecy as literal (in its usual, ordinary meaning) unless one of the following occurs:*

- The grammatical context shows that it is figurative language by the use of similes, metaphors, parables, allegories, symbols, or types.

- A literal interpretation violates common sense, is contrary to what the author is saying, or is contrary to what the rest of Scripture teaches.

∾ *When a prophetic passage cannot be taken literally, look for what the author is trying to convey through his figurative or symbolic language.* To discern what the author is saying, look for answers in the following places:

- within the context of the book in which the passage appears

- in any other writings of that author

- in any other prophetic writings to which the author had access (for example, other prophetic books or passages in the Word of God)

∾ *Remember that often when a prophet refers to future events, he does not use the future tense.*

∾ *When you interpret Scripture, consider the historical context of that writing, remembering that God was delivering His prophecy to a particular people at a particular time.* Granted, it might have been a prophecy with a future fulfillment, but it would still be delivered in a way that was comprehensible to those receiving that prophecy—even though they might not understand the details, the symbolism, or the full implications of the prophecy.

Make a careful historical and cultural analysis of the text. Determine the identity of all historical events, proper names, and geographical locations before you attempt to interpret the text.

∾ *Remember that the meaning of a specific prophecy could not always be understood by*

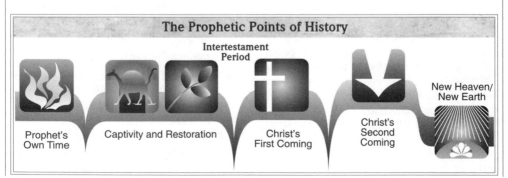

The Prophetic Points of History

Intertestament Period

Prophet's Own Time

Captivity and Restoration

Christ's First Coming

Christ's Second Coming

New Heaven/ New Earth

the prophet or by the people who heard the message. For example, Daniel could not understand what he had written, since it was to remain sealed until the end time (Daniel 12:8-9).

However, many prophecies will come to light through the following:

a fulfillment as recorded in history

a fulfillment as recorded in the New Testament

an explanation given by an Old Testament or a New Testament writing (for example, Acts 4:24-28)

∽ *Remember that many New Testament prophecies include Old Testament quotations and allusions.* Scholars estimate that at least 350 Old Testament quotations or allusions appear in the book of Revelation alone. Revelation is replete with the language of Isaiah, Jeremiah, Ezekiel, Daniel, and the minor prophets. It is obvious that the author of Revelation was steeped in the Old Testament, for he talks in Old Testament phraseology. So to correctly interpret New Testament prophecy, check Old Testament cross-references.

∽ *When you study prophecy, watch for phrases which indicate periods of time.* For example, look for *in the last days, day of the Lord, day of wrath,* and *end of the age.* When you come across phrases such as these, carefully observe the things which occur during that particular time period. Then ask the following questions:

• Have these events ever occurred in history?

• Do these events coincide with any other particular period of time?

• Do these events parallel any events mentioned in another place in the Word of God?

FIGURES OF SPEECH

Although the Bible is to be interpreted literally, it is important to remember that, as with other writings, it contains figures of speech which must be interpreted for what they are and in the light of their intended purpose. As you seek to handle the Word of God accurately,

you will find it helpful to understand the definitions of the different types of figures of speech.

A *figure of speech* is a word, a phrase, or an expression used in an imaginative rather than a literal sense.

Discerning the use of figures of speech is important in biblical interpretation. For example, there has been much controversy in the church over Jesus' statement regarding the bread at the Last Supper: "When He had taken some bread and given thanks, He broke it and gave it to them, saying, 'This is My body which is given for you'" (Luke 22:19). Some believe that the bread actually becomes His body (the doctrine of transubstantiation); others believe that Jesus was simply using a metaphor and that the bread is representative of His body.

Three principles for dealing with figurative language are:

• Identify the fact that the author is using figurative language.

• Identify the type of figurative language in use: simile, metaphor, hyperbole, and so on.

• Follow the guidelines for interpreting what the author meant by his use of that particular figure of speech.

You will be aided in your study of Scripture if you are able to identify when the author is using a figure of speech. The following are brief definitions of the types of figurative language used in the Bible.

∽ A *metaphor* is an implied comparison between two things which are different. In a metaphor the words of comparison—*like, as, as...so is,* and *such as*—are *not* used. An example is John 6:48, where Jesus says, "I am the bread of life."

∽ A *simile* is an expressed comparison of two different things or ideas that uses the words *like, as, as...so is,* and/or *such as.* An example is Revelation 1:14b, "His eyes were like a flame of fire."

∽ *Hyperbole* is a deliberate exaggeration for effect or emphasis. Hyperboles are found in all languages, and they are frequently used among Semitic peoples. For example, "My soul is crushed with longing" (Psalm 119:20).

∽ *Metonymy* is used when the name of one object or concept is used for that of another to which it is related. This is a figure of association. An example of a metonymy is found in the statement, "All the country of Judea was going out to him" (Mark 1:5). The metonymy is *country*, which refers to the people rather than the region itself. Note also the hyperbole: *all* the country.

∽ *Synecdoche* is another figure of association where the whole can refer to the part or the part to the whole. This is often found in the use of the term *the law*, which can refer to the Pentateuch (the first five books of the Old Testament), the ten commandments, or the whole Old Testament.

A synecdoche can also be a singular for a plural or a plural for a singular. An example is in Jeremiah 25:29. God says He is going to summon "a sword against all the inhabitants of the earth." The singular sword represents many swords.

∽ In *personification* an object is given characteristics or attributes that belong to people—for example, when the trees clap their hands and the mountains sing for joy (Isaiah 55:12).

∽ *Irony* is a statement which says the opposite of what is meant. Irony is used for emphasis or effect. When it is not easy to discern if a statement is ironic, then examine it first as a true statement. As such, does it make sense in its context? Second, examine it as figurative irony. If this makes sense and fits with the context, then accept it as irony. Otherwise, treat it as a truth.

Here are two examples of irony:

1. In 1 Kings 22:1-23, a true prophet tells the king what he wants to hear, but it is a lie. It's obvious he is using irony because the king tells him to stop prophesying falsely and to tell the truth.

2. In 1 Corinthians 4:8 Paul says to the Corinthians, "You are already filled, you have already become rich, you have become kings without us; and indeed, I wish that you had become kings so that we also might reign with you." When you read this, it is obvious the Corinthians are not kings, nor does Paul desire to reign with them.

Parables

A *parable* is a story which, although not usually factual, remains true to life and teaches a moral lesson or truth. Every detail of a parable will reinforce the main theme, but you shouldn't always attempt to ascribe a specific spiritual meaning and application to each point.

Jesus frequently used parables in His teaching for two reasons: to reveal truth to believers and to hide truth from those who had rejected it and/or hardened their hearts against it.

To correctly interpret a parable:

• *Determine the occasion of the parable.* Since parables clarify or emphasize a truth, discover why the parable was told. What prompted it?

• *Look for the intended meaning of the parable.* The meaning will sometimes be stated. If not, it can usually be determined by the application of the parable to the hearer.

• *Don't impose any meaning beyond what is clearly stated or applied to the hearers by the speaker of the parable.*

• *Identify the central or focal idea of the parable.* Every parable has one central theme or emphasis. No detail of the story is to be given any meaning that is independent of the main teaching of the parable.

Since a parable has one central point of emphasis, identify relevant details. To attach meaning that is not in the context of the occasion or relevant to its central emphasis is to go away from the meaning of the parable. A detail is relevant only if it reinforces the central theme of the parable.

How many sermons have you heard on the parable of the prodigal son? Many teachers violate the occasion and meaning of this parable, attaching all sorts of meanings to the details of this story. Jesus told this parable because He wanted the Pharisees to see what their hearts were like as they grumbled, "This man receives sinners and eats with them"

(Luke 15:2). In order to make His point Jesus told three consecutive parables about three things which were lost: a sheep, a coin, and a son. In each of the parables Jesus uses the following words: *lost, found, sin,* and *joy (rejoice)*. When He gets to the story of the prodigal son, He shows them the kindness of the father's heart versus the hardness of the elder brother's, and in doing so, shows the Pharisees that their hearts are like the elder brother's, not the father's.

• *Interpret parables in the context of the culture of Bible times rather than the culture of today.* For example, in the parable of the wise and foolish virgins, the central emphasis of the parable is, "Be on the alert then, for you do not know the day nor the hour" (Matthew 25:13). Understanding Eastern wedding traditions would give insight into the parable and explain why some were ready and others were not.

• *Do not establish doctrine when parables are the primary or only source for that teaching.* Parables should amplify or affirm doctrine, not establish it.

Allegory

An *allegory* is a description of one thing using the image of another—a story with an underlying meaning different from the surface facts of the story itself. Some refer to an allegory as an extended metaphor, which is an implied comparison between two different things. An allegory is a realistic or nonrealistic story created to teach one or more truths which may or may not be related.

The chart below comparing parables and allegories will help you distinguish one from the other.

When interpreting an allegory, follow these guidelines:

• List the features of the allegory.

• Note any interpretation given within the text of the allegory.

• Study the allegory's features according to sound principles of biblical exegesis. Do not contradict the clear teaching of the Word of God by interpreting an unexplained detail in an allegory in a way contrary to other truths.

• Do not try to identify all the features of an allegory.

Types

A type is a prophetic symbol designated by God.

The word *type* comes from the Greek word *tupos*. A *tupos* was a mark formed by a blow or an impression, creating a figure or an image on the object that was struck. Therefore, a type prefigures something or someone to come. That which it prefigures is called an *antitype*.

Parable	Allegory
1. Has one central point	1. Can have more than one central point
2. Teaches one truth	2. Can teach a number of truths
3. Every relevant detail reinforces the central theme or point of emphasis	3. The details of an allegory may be many and varied, relating to more than one theme
4. Can have irrelevant details; all features of the parable do not have to be identified	4. Can have irrelevant details; all the features of an allegory do not have to be identified
5. Usually the story is separate from its interpretation and application	5. Intertwines the story and the meaning
6. Interpretation usually follows the parable	6. Interpretation is found within the allegory

A type prefigures only one antitype, although it may parallel many points in the antitype. An illustration of this is the tabernacle, a type of man's redemption. According to Hebrews 10:20, the veil that separated the holy place from the holy of holies prefigured the flesh of Jesus Christ.

When determining types, although it may not be formally stated, there should be some evidence of divine affirmation of the corresponding type and antitype. For example, in Romans 5:14 we read, "Nevertheless death reigned from Adam until Moses, even over those who had not sinned in the likeness of the offense of Adam, who is a type of Him who was to come." The word translated *type* is the Greek word *tupos*. Adam was a type or figure of Christ, who was to come. In 1 Corinthians 15:45, Christ is referred to as "the last Adam." If the Word does not designate something as a type, then the Bible expositor should simply show the parallels without calling it a type.

Symbols

A symbol is a picture or an object that stands for or represents another thing. For example, the seven candlesticks mentioned in Revelation 1:20 represent the seven churches described in Revelation 2 and 3.

When noting symbols it is important to remember the following:

• *The item used as a symbol can symbolize different things.* For example, water is used to symbolize the Word of God (Ephesians 5:26) and the Holy Spirit (John 7:37-39).

• *Although a symbol can represent many things, when it does symbolize something in a given passage, a single parallel is intended.* For instance, in John 7:37-39 water symbolizes the Holy Spirit, not the Word.

• *Interpret symbols in the light of a biblical setting and culture rather than the culture of the current interpreter.*

• *Symbols are timeless and can symbolize something past, present, or future.*

LAWS OF COMPOSITION

A literary composition is an arrangement of thoughts which conveys meaning to a reader.

An understanding of the laws of composition will help you discern what the author is saying.

The following laws of composition can help you in your study of the Word of God.

1. **Comparison**—to compare in order to show similarities. A comparison is the association of like things.

2. **Contrast**—to compare in order to show differences. A contrast is the association of opposites.

3. **Repetition**—to use the same word or phrase a number of times.

4. **Progression**—to extend a specific theme throughout a portion of Scripture. Many times the author will amplify what he is saying as he progresses in his writing or adds to what he has said.

5. **Climax**—a high point built by a progression from the lesser to the greater. A climax is simply an extension of the law of progression until it reaches a peak of intensity.

6. **Pivotal point**—a changing or a turning so that the elements on each side of the point differ in some way. In the Gospel of John the pivotal point comes in 11:54, when Jesus turns from ministering mainly to the public to ministering to His disciples. (Read John 11:54.) In Genesis the pivotal point of the book comes in chapter 12, where Moses turns from recording major events to tell us of major characters.

7. **Radiation**—the central or single point from or to which other truths point. An illustration of this is 1 Corinthians 15, where the truths of that chapter all radiate to resurrection.

8. **Interchange**—to alternate, in sequence, at least two main thoughts, subjects, or characteristics. This is most apparent in the Gospel of Luke. Luke opens with the announcement of the birth of John the Baptist, then moves to the announcement of Jesus' birth. He then returns to John the Baptist's birth, then to the birth of Christ. This is alternation or interchange.

9. **General to particular (or vice versa)**—to move from the extensive or general to the specific or particular. This is beautifully seen in Genesis 1 and 2. Genesis 1 gives the general overview of creation, including the creation of man, male and female, on the sixth day.

Genesis 2 moves from the general to the particular, giving more details of the creation of woman.

10. **Cause and effect (or vice versa)**—to move from the source to the consequence of it. An example of this is found in John 11. Verse 4 states that the cause of the death of Lazarus, the beloved friend of Christ, was to glorify the Son. The effect is seen in verse 45, where the people believed on Christ after seeing His power in raising Lazarus. The effect is also seen in John 12:17-18, where once again the Son is glorified.

11. **Explanation or analysis**—the presentation of an idea or event followed by its explanation. This is expertly done by our Lord in John 6, where He multiplies the loaves and the fishes and then brings forth His discourse stating that He is the bread who gives us life.

12. **Interrogation**—the presentation of a question, usually followed by its answer. Paul masterfully uses this technique in writing Romans. Paul anticipates his readers' questions or objections, states them usually in the form of a question, and then proceeds to answer the very questions he has raised. Romans 6 beautifully demonstrates this technique.

13. **Preparation or introduction**—the presentation of background information to prepare the reader for that which follows. The purpose of the Gospel of John is to prepare the reader to believe that Jesus is the Christ, the Son of God. In John 1:1-18 the writer thoroughly introduces his subject and prepares his readers for what is to come.

14. **Summarization**—to restate the main points, to sum up, or to briefly restate particular truths. Moses does this in chapters 1 to 4 of the book of Deuteronomy as he rehearses before the children of Israel those things that took place following the exodus from Egypt. Acts 7 provides a masterful summarization by Stephen of Israel's history.

TENSE, VOICE, AND MOOD OF GREEK VERBS

There are many excellent study tools which can help you examine the text more deeply through Greek word studies. If you would like to pursue Greek word studies further, a highly recommended book is *The Complete Word Study New Testament*, by Spiros Zodhiates.

The following explanation of the tense, voice, and mood of Greek verbs will help those who do not know Greek but want a better understanding of the implications of the kind of action indicated by the verbs.

Because verbs express action, they are often the most significant element in the expression of thought. Therefore, understanding the Greek verb is a key to correct interpretation and application of Scripture. (Context is the most important key to correct interpretation and application, since the Greek words get their meaning from the context.) Three major features of Greek verbs are tense, voice, and mood.

Part of the beauty of the Greek language is that the construction of the verb clearly shows who does the action, whether the statement is a command or the passage is speaking of reality or possibility.

By thinking through a simple, concise explanation of tense, voice, and mood, new vistas of insight will be opened to you. Keep in mind that the following is a simplified and nonexhaustive summarization of a complex subject. The purpose of this information is to give you an overview of terms that are frequently used in the more technical commentaries.

Tense
(Shows the Kind of Action)

Greek verb tenses differ from English verb tenses in that the kind of action portrayed is the most significant element, and time is a relatively minor consideration.

∾ **Action as continuous**

Present tense—continuous action. It is primarily progressive or linear; it shows action that is continuing.

Examples:

Jeff *is studying* the Bible.

John 15:4b—"As the branch *cannot bear* fruit of itself unless it *abides* in the vine, so neither can you unless you *abide* in Me."

John 15:6—"If anyone *does not abide* in Me."

Imperfect tense—continuous action, usually in the past.

Examples:

Jeff *was studying* the Bible.

John 15:19a—"If you were of the world, the world *would love* its own." (Literally, "would have been loving" its own.)

∾ **Action as completed**

Perfect tense—punctiliar action in the past with the results continuing into the present. Punctiliar action is action that happens at a specific point in time.

Examples:

Jeff is being transformed by *having studied* the Bible.

John 15:3—"You are already clean because of the word which I *have spoken* to you."

John 15:10b—"Just as I *have kept* My Father's commandments and abide in His love."

Pluperfect tense—punctiliar action in the past with the results continuing in the past.

Examples:

Jeff was transformed because he *had studied* the Bible.

John 9:22—"For the Jews *had* already *agreed*."

∾ **Action as occurring**

Aorist tense—punctiliar action. The aorist tense states an action as completed without regard to its duration; that is, it denotes the fact of an action without any reference to the length of that action. Compared to the present tense, the aorist tense expresses the action like a snapshot while the present tense action is like a moving picture, continuing on.

Examples:

Jeff *studied* the Bible.

John 15:4a—"*Abide* in Me, and I in you."

Future tense—indefinite action to occur in the future. Indicates continuing or punctiliar action in the future.

Examples:

Jeff *will be studying* his Bible.

John 15:7—"It *will be done* for you."

John 15:8—"*So* prove to *be* My disciples."

Voice
(Shows How the Subject Is Related to the Action)

∾ **Active voice—indicates that the subject produces the action.**

Examples:

Jeff *hit* the ball.

John 15:2b—"And every branch that bears fruit, He *prunes* it."

∾ **Passive voice—indicates that the subject is acted upon.**

Examples:

Jeff *was hit* by the ball.

John 15:6—"And they *are burned*."

∾ **Middle voice—indicates that the subject initiates the action and also participates in the results of the action.** (This voice is unique to Greek construction.)

Examples:

Jeff *hit* himself with the ball.

John 15:26—"That is the Spirit of truth who *proceeds* from the Father, He will testify about Me."

One note of interest when looking up a verb in a Greek study tool: The middle and passive voices will have identical forms, but the context will show you if the subject is receiving the action (passive voice) or if the subject initiated the action and participated in it (middle voice).

Also, some verbs are *deponent verbs*. This means that their form in a Greek study tool may be listed as a passive or middle voice verb but their function or action is active. Usually your Greek study helps will list these as deponent verbs.

Mood

(Shows How the Action Is Related to Reality from the Speaker's Point of View)

ꙮ **Indicative mood—the declarative mood or mood of certainty.** It is a statement of fact which assumes reality from the speaker's point of view. This mood simply states a thing as being a fact.

Examples:

Bible study *has changed* Jeff's life.

John 15:6—"He *is thrown* away as a branch and *dries* up; and they *gather* them, and *cast* them into the fire and they *are burned*."

ꙮ **Imperative mood—usually a command or entreaty.** It is the mood of volition or will. The imperative mood in the Greek makes a demand on the will of the reader to obey the command; it is used to indicate prohibition and authority.

Examples:

Jeff, *study* your homework.

John 15:4—"*Abide* in Me."

John 15:7—"*Ask* whatever you wish."

John 15:9—"*Abide* in My love."

John 15:20—"*Remember* the word that I said to you."

One aspect which will help your study of God's Word is the understanding of the combination of the present tense and the imperative mood that is stating a negative command (a prohibition). The *present imperative prohibition* demands cessation of some act already in progress.

Example:

John 20:17—"Jesus said to her, '*Stop clinging* to Me.' " In other words, Mary was already clinging to Jesus, and Jesus was telling her to stop clinging and to go on refusing to cling to Him.

ꙮ **Subjunctive mood—the mood of probability.** It implies some doubt regarding the reality of the action from the speaker's point of view. It expresses an uncertainty or an action which may or should happen. This is the mood used for conditional clauses, strong suggestions, or "polite" commands.

Examples:

Jeff *may have done* his homework. Jeff, if you do not do your homework, you cannot participate in the class discussion.

John 15:2—"That it *may bear* more fruit."

John 15:4b—"As the branch cannot bear fruit of itself unless it *abides* in the vine, so neither can you unless you *abide* in Me."

John 15:6—"If anyone *does not abide* in Me."

John 15:7—"If you *abide* in Me, and My words *abide* in you."

Something else which may help you in your study of God's Word is an understanding of the combination of the aorist tense and the subjunctive mood that is stating a negative command (a prohibition). The *aorist subjunctive prohibition* is a warning or an exhortation against doing a thing not yet begun.

Example:

John 13:8a—"Peter said to Him, '*Never shall* You *wash* my feet!' " In other words, Peter was telling Jesus that He was not to wash his feet and Jesus was not even to start washing his feet.

ꙮ **Optative mood—the mood of possibility.** This mood presents no definite anticipation of realization but merely presents the action as conceivable from the speaker's point of view (used less frequently than the other moods).

Examples:

I *wish* my neighbor, Jeff, would take the Precept Bible Studies.

2 Thessalonians 3:5—"May the Lord *direct* your hearts."

TENSE, MOOD, AND VOICE OF GREEK VERBS

MOOD

The mood expresses the relationship of the action to reality from the speaker's point of view.

Mood	Relation to Reality	Usage or Meaning	Example
Indicative	Mood of certainty (reality)	Used to declare a statement of fact as something which is true. Expresses that which is actual, factual, or real from the speaker's point of view.	Bible study has changed Jeff's life.
Imperative	Mood of volition or will (potential reality)	Usually used to express a command or entreaty. Denotes intention, authority, permission, or prohibition.	Jeff, study your homework.
Subjunctive	Mood of probability (probable reality)	Used to express an action which may or should happen but which is not necessarily true at the present, from the speaker's point of view. Expresses conditional or uncertain actions.	Jeff may have done his homework.
Optative	Mood of possibility (possible reality)	Merely presents an action as conceivable from the speaker's point of view, with no definite anticipation of realization.	I wish my neighbor, Jeff, would take the Precept Bible Studies.

TENSE, MOOD, AND VOICE OF GREEK VERBS

TENSE

The emphasis is on the *kind* of action, not the time of action.

Tense	Kind of Action	Example
Present	Continuous action	Jeff is studying the Bible.
Imperfect	Continuous action in the past	Jeff was studying the Bible.
Perfect	Punctiliar action in the past with the results continuing into the present	Jeff is being transformed by having studied the Bible.
Pluperfect	Punctiliar action in the past with the results continuing in the past	Jeff was transformed because he had studied the Bible.
Aorist	Punctiliar action (The time can be past, present, or future but is generally past.)	Jeff studied the Bible.
Future	Generally continuous action in the future, but on occasion it can be punctiliar.	Jeff will be studying his Bible.

TENSE, MOOD, AND VOICE OF GREEK VERBS

VOICE

The voice expresses the relationship of the subject to the action.

Voice	How the Subject Is Related to the Action	Example
Active	Indicates that the subject produces the action	Jeff hit the ball.
Passive	Indicates that the subject is acted upon	Jeff was hit by the ball.
Middle	Indicates that the subject initiates the action and participates in the results of the action	Jeff hit himself with the ball.

TENSE, MOOD, AND VOICE OF GREEK VERBS

PROHIBITIONS

This is when the speaker states a negative command.

Prohibition	Definition	Example
Present imperative (used with a negative)	This prohibition demands cessation of some act already in progress.	John 20:17
Aorist subjunctive (used with a negative)	This prohibition is a warning or exhortation against doing a thing not yet begun.	John 13:8

APPENDIX 4: READ THROUGH THE BIBLE IN ONE YEAR

Weekly Reading Plan

WEEK	READING	WEEK	READING
1	Genesis 1–24	27	Psalms 110–150; Proverbs 1–4
2	Genesis 25–43	28	Proverbs 5–31
3	Genesis 44–Exodus 14	29	Ecclesiastes; Song of Solomon; Isaiah 1–9
4	Exodus 15–34		
5	Exodus 35–Leviticus 14	30	Isaiah 10–35
6	Leviticus 15–Numbers 4	31	Isaiah 36–57
7	Numbers 5–22	32	Isaiah 58–66; Jeremiah 1–10
8	Numbers 23–Deuteronomy 4	33	Jeremiah 11–30
9	Deuteronomy 5–27	34	Jeremiah 31–49
10	Deuteronomy 28–Joshua 12	35	Jeremiah 50–52; Lamentations; Ezekiel 1–12
11	Joshua 13–Judges 8		
12	Judges 9–21; Ruth; 1 Samuel 1–4	36	Ezekiel 13–31
13	1 Samuel 5–24	37	Ezekiel 32–48; Daniel 1–2
14	1 Samuel 25–2 Samuel 15	38	Daniel 3–12; Hosea
15	2 Samuel 16–1 Kings 7	39	Joel; Amos; Obadiah; Jonah; Micah; Nahum
16	1 Kings 8–22		
17	2 Kings 1–18	40	Habakkuk; Zephaniah; Haggai; Zechariah; Malachi
18	2 Kings 19–1 Chronicles 12		
19	1 Chronicles 13–2 Chronicles 8	41	Matthew
20	2 Chronicles 9–32	42	Mark
21	2 Chronicles 33–36; Ezra; Nehemiah 1–8	43	Luke
		44	John 1–14
22	Nehemiah 9–13; Esther; Job 1–10	45	John 15–21
23	Job 11–42	46	Acts 1–12
24	Psalms 1–38	47	Acts 13–28
25	Psalms 39–76	48	Romans; 1 Corinthians
26	Psalms 77–109	49	2 Corinthians; Galatians; Ephesians
		50	Philippians; Colossians; 1 and 2 Thessalonians; 1 and 2 Timothy; Titus; Philemon
		51	Hebrews; James; 1 and 2 Peter; 1 and 2 John
		52	3 John; Jude; Revelation

Each week's reading has roughly the same number of verses. One suggestion for using this plan is to try to accomplish the week's goal, and not necessarily follow a precise day-by-day schedule. Use a bookmark to keep your place, and if you miss a day, on the next day just pick up where you left off, and press on toward your goal. In a year, you'll have read the Bible from Genesis to Revelation!

APPENDIX 5: THREE-YEAR BIBLE STUDY PLAN
A Plan to Help You Study the Bible

For many beginning Bible students, their first question is "Where do I start?" Many reading plans are available, but there are few plans for systematic study.

One approach is to start with Genesis and work your way through Revelation. Or, you could start with Matthew and work your way through the New Testament first, and then the Old Testament. There are many Old Testament references in the New Testament that will make more sense if you study the Old Testament before the New Testament, but the option is yours. Whichever place you start, the following plan can help you make sense of how the books fit together and determine the pace at which you progress through the Bible.

Old Testament Study

Studying history usually makes the most sense if you work chronologically. In the Bible, the historical books not only teach history, but also an ongoing revelation of God to man. They progressively reveal God's plan for the redemption of mankind, from creation and the fall up to the appearing of Messiah, the Lord Jesus Christ.

The prophetic books fit into a specific chronology with the historical books. As the Old Testament reveals the history of God's people Israel, we see various prophets bringing messages from God to the kings of Israel and Judah, to the exiles, and to those who return from exile. Integrating the messages of the prophets with the messages of the historical books can help you to grasp the whole of God's message. Or, you can study the prophets after you study the historical books, so you don't interrupt the flow of your historical study. The wisdom literature can be studied separately because it is timeless and somewhat independent of

the time period in which it was written, but there is still a link to the overall progressive revelation of God in time and history.

In general, we recommend studying a book of the Bible as a unit. The *New Inductive Study Bible* gives a set of directions at the beginning of each of the 66 books. Genesis through 2 Kings are in chronological order; however, 1 and 2 Chronicles and the prophets overlap these books. First Chronicles 1–9 detail the genealogies from Adam through the returning exiles from Babylon. Then starting with 1 Chronicles 10, the history of the southern kingdom, Judah, is given, and the story parallels 1 Samuel 31 through 2 Kings 25. So as you study Chronicles, you can go back and compare your reading with what you learned in previous books.

New Testament Study

In general, the study of the New Testament can also proceed chronologically, but only to a point. The gospels are first, Acts gives us the development of the church, and Paul's letters overlap Acts. When reading the letters, the strict chronological order is critical only when it's obvious that one letter clearly follows the other, such as 1 and 2 Corinthians, 1 and 2 Thessalonians, 1 and 2 Timothy, and 1 and 2 Peter. The main point of these letters is the theology that is taught, not the sequence. And, of course, Revelation comes last. So the New Testament can be studied straight through.

If you have chosen to study the New Testament before the Old Testament, we would recommend that when you get to the book of Revelation, you study Daniel first, then 1 and 2 Thessalonians. You'll find many references to the Day of the Lord in Old Testament prophecy, so familiarity with the Old Testament will help.

THREE-YEAR BIBLE STUDY PLAN

A Plan to Help You Study Through the Bible

Studying the Bible thoroughly can take time. An adaptation of the plan to read through the Bible in one year is to *triple* the time—that is, using three weeks to study what you would have read in one week:

WEEKS	READING
1-3	Genesis 1–24
4-6	Genesis 25–43
7-9	Genesis 44—Exodus 14
10-12	Exodus 15–34
13-15	Exodus 35—Leviticus 14
16-18	Leviticus 15—Numbers 4
19-21	Numbers 5–22
22-24	Numbers 23—Deuteronomy 4
25-27	Deuteronomy 5–27
28-30	Deuteronomy 28—Joshua 12
31-33	Joshua 13—Judges 8
34-36	Judges 9–21; Ruth; 1 Samuel 1–4
37-39	1 Samuel 5–24
40-42	1 Samuel 25—2 Samuel 15
43-45	2 Samuel 16—1 Kings 7
46-48	1 Kings 8–22
49-52	2 Kings 1–18
1-3	2 Kings 19—1 Chronicles 12
4 6	1 Chronicles 13—2 Chronicles 8
7-9	2 Chronicles 9–32
10-12	2 Chronicles 33–36; Job
13-15	Psalms 1–38
16-18	Psalms 39–76
19-21	Psalms 77–109
22-24	Psalms 110–150
25-27	Proverbs
28-30	Ecclesiastes; Song of Solomon; Obadiah; Joel; Jonah
31-33	Amos; Hosea; Isaiah 1–7
34-36	Isaiah 8–31
37-39	Isaiah 32–53
40-42	Isaiah 54–66; Micah; Nahum; Zephaniah
43-45	Jeremiah 1–18
46-48	Jeremiah 19–37
49-50	Jeremiah 38–52
51-52	Habakkuk; Daniel

WEEKS	READING
1-3	Ezekiel 1–23
4-6	Ezekiel 24–42
7-9	Ezekiel 43–48; Lamentations; Ezra
10-12	Haggai; Zechariah; Esther
13-15	Nehemiah; Malachi
16-18	Matthew
19-21	Mark
22-24	Luke
25-27	John 1–10
28-30	John 11–21
31-33	Acts 1–13
34-36	Acts 14–28
37-39	Romans
40-42	1 and 2 Corinthians; Galatians
43-45	Ephesians, Philippians; Colossians; 1 and 2 Thessalonians; 1 and 2 Timothy; Titus
46-48	Philemon; Hebrews; James; 1 and 2 Peter
49-52	1, 2, and 3 John; Jude; Revelation

APPENDIX 6: A HARMONY OF THE GOSPELS

A Chronological Listing of Scriptures About the Life of Jesus

	MATTHEW	MARK	LUKE	JOHN
From Birth to Twelve Years of Age				
Introduction			1:1-4	1:1-14
Jesus' legal lineage through Joseph	1:1-17			
Jesus' natural lineage through Mary			3:23-38	
John the Baptist's birth announced			1:5-25	
Jesus' birth announced to Mary			1:26-38	
Mary's visit to Elizabeth			1:39-45	
Mary's song of joy and praise			1:46-56	
John the Baptist's birth			1:57-66	
Zechariah's prophetic song			1:67-79	
John the Baptist's early years			1:80	
Jesus' birth announced to Joseph	1:18-25			
Jesus is born in Bethlehem			2:1-7	
Angelic visit to the shepherds			2:8-20	
Circumcision of Jesus			2:21	
Jesus presented in Temple			2:22-38	
Visit of the Magi	2:1-12			
Flight into Egypt	2:13-18			
Return to Nazareth	2:19-23		2:39	
Early growth of Jesus			2:40	
Jesus at age 12 in Jerusalem for Passover			2:41-51	
Jesus' adolescence and early manhood			2:52	
John the Baptist's Ministry				
Beginning of ministry		1:1	3:1-2	
A description and his message	3:1-6	1:2-6	3:3-6	
Warnings and teachings	3:7-10		3:7-14	
His proclamation of Christ	3:11-12	1:7-8	3:15-18	
The Beginning of Jesus' Ministry				
Jesus baptized by John	3:13-17	1:9-11	3:21-23	
Jesus tempted by Satan in wilderness	4:1-11	1:12-13	4:1-13	
John's witness of Jesus as Son of God				1:15-34
Jesus' first followers				1:35-51
Jesus' first miracle—water to wine				2:1-11
Jesus visits Capernaum				2:12
First cleansing of Temple (at Passover)				2:13-25
Nicodemus' visit with Jesus				3:1-21
Jesus must increase, John must decrease				3:22-36
John imprisoned; Jesus to Galilee	4:12	1:14	3:19-20; 4:14	4:1-4
Samaritan woman at well				4:5-42

	MATTHEW	MARK	LUKE	JOHN
Jesus' Ministry in Galilee				
Arrival in Galilee; proclaims gospel	4:17	1:14-15	4:14-15	4:43-45
Child at Capernaum healed				4:46-54
Ministry in Nazareth; Jesus rejected			4:16-30	
Jesus goes to Capernaum	4:13-16		4:31	
Calling of Simon, Andrew, James, John	4:18-22	1:16-20	5:1-11	
Teaches in synagogue, heals demoniac		1:21-28	4:31-37	
Peter's mother-in-law, others healed	8:14-17	1:29-34	4:38-41	
Tour of towns throughout Galilee	4:23-25	1:35-39	4:42-44	
Healing of leper	8:1-4	1:40-45	5:12-16	
Healing of paralytic (hole in roof)	9:1-8	2:1-12	5:17-26	
Call of Matthew, banquet	9:9-13	2:13-17	5:27-32	
Answers objections with illustrations	9:14-17	2:18-22	5:33-39	
Lame man healed in Jerusalem on Sabbath				5:1-9
Attempts to kill Jesus				5:10-18
Jesus teaches He is equal with the Father				5:19-47
Disciples pick grain on the Sabbath	12:1-8	2:23-28	6:1-5	
Healing of man's hand on the Sabbath	12:9-14	3:1-6	6:6-11	
Withdraws to Sea of Galilee, heals many	12:15-21	3:7-12		
Selection of the 12 Disciples and Sermon on the Mount				
Lists of the 12 disciples		3:13-19	6:12-16	
Setting of the sermon	5:1-2		6:17-19	
The blessings	5:3-12		6:20-26	
Salt and light of the world	5:13-16			
The law and righteousness	5:17-20			
Interpreting the law—six contrasts	5:21-48		6:27-36	
Hypocrisy, giving, praying, fasting	6:1-18			
Avarice, judgment, handling the sacred	6:19—7:6		6:37-42	
Application of sermon	7:7-27		6:43-49	
Reaction to sermon	7:28-29			
Increasing Fame and Rejection				
Healing of the centurion's servant	8:5-13		7:1-10	
Widow's son raised from the dead			7:11-17	
John the Baptist's inquiry	11:2-19		7:18-35	
Woes upon Chorazin, Bethsaida, Capernaum	11:20-27			
Invitation to the heavy-laden	11:28-30			
Woman anoints Jesus' feet			7:36-50	
Tour with the 12 and other followers			8:1-3	
Blasphemous accusations against Jesus	12:22-37	3:20-30		
Request for a sign, Jesus' answer	12:38-45			
Natural kinship, spiritual kinship	12:46-50	3:31-35	8:19-21	
The Parables of the Kingdom				
The setting of the parables	13:1-2	4:1-2	8:4	
The parable of the sower and soils	13:3-23	4:3-25	8:5-18	
The parable of sprouting seeds		4:26-29		
The parable of the tares	13:24-30			

	MATTHEW	MARK	LUKE	JOHN
The parable of the mustard seed	13:31-32	4:30-32		
The parable of the leavened loaf	13:33-35	4:33-34		
The parable of the tares explained	13:36-43			
The parable of the treasure in the field	13:44			
The parable of the pearl of great price	13:45-46			
The parable of the fishnet	13:47-50			
The parable of the householder	13:51-52			

Growing Opposition to Jesus' Ministry

	MATTHEW	MARK	LUKE	JOHN
Jesus crosses lake, calms storm	8:18-27	4:35-41	8:22-25	
Gadarene demoniacs, herd of swine	8:28-34	5:1-20	8:26-39	
Jairus' daughter, woman touches Jesus' garment	9:18-26	5:21-43	8:40-56	
More healings, another accusation	9:27-34			
Visit to Nazareth, people respond in unbelief	13:54-58	6:1-6		

End of Galilean Ministry

	MATTHEW	MARK	LUKE	JOHN
Workers needed for the harvest	9:35-38	6:6		
Twelve disciples commissioned	10:1-42	6:7-11	9:1-5	
Disciples sent out	11:1	6:12-13	9:6	
Herod misidentifies Jesus as John the Baptist	14:1-12	6:14-29	9:7-9	
Return of the disciples	6:30	9:10		

Christ's Ministry Extends Beyond Galilee

	MATTHEW	MARK	LUKE	JOHN
Withdrawal across Sea of Galilee	14:13-14	6:31-34	9:10-11	6:1-3
Feeding of 5,000 people	14:15-21	6:35-44	9:12-17	6:4-13
People attempt to make Jesus king	14:22-23	6:45-46		6:14-15
Jesus walks on water	14:24-33	6:47-52		6:16-21
Healings in Gennesaret	14:34-36	6:53-56		
The true bread of life				6:22-59
Some followers defect				6:60-71
Disagreement over ceremonial impurity	15:1-20	7:1-23		
Ministry in Tyre and Sidon	15:21-28	7:24-30		
Healings in Decapolis	15:29-31	7:31-37		
Jesus feeds 4,000 in Decapolis	15:32-38	8:1-9		
Jesus crosses lake to Dalmanutha	15:39	8:10		
Test from Pharisees and Sadducees	16:1-4	8:11-12		
Warning about Pharisees, Sadducees, Herodians	16:5-12	8:13-21		
Heals blind man at Bethsaida		8:22-26		

Jesus' Identity as Messiah Affirmed

	MATTHEW	MARK	LUKE	JOHN
Peter confesses Jesus as the Christ	16:13-20	8:27-30	9:18-21	
Prediction of crucifixion and resurrection	16:21-26	8:31-37	9:22-25	
Coming of Son of Man, judgment	16:27-28	8:38–9:1	9:26-27	
Transfiguration of Jesus	17:1-13	9:2-13	9:28-36	
Healing of demoniac disciples couldn't heal	17:14-20 [21]	9:14-29	9:37-43	
Another prediction of death and resurrection	17:22-23	9:30-32	9:43-45	
Temple tax payment from a fish	17:24-27			
Disciples' dispute over greatness	18:1-5	9:33-37	9:46-48	
Warnings from Jesus	18:6-14	9:38-50	9:49-50	

	Matthew	Mark	Luke	John
Forgiveness toward a sinning believer	18:15-35			
Half-brothers ridicule Jesus				7:1-9
Departure for Jerusalem through Samaria			9:51-56	7:10
Requirements for following Jesus	8:19-22		9:57-62	
Later Judean Ministry of Christ				
People's reactions to teachings and miracles				7:11-31
Pharisees attempt to arrest Jesus				7:32-53
Jesus forgives woman caught in adultery				8:1-11
Conflict between Jesus and Pharisees				8:12-59
The 70 workers sent out			10:1-16	
The 70 workers return			10:17-24	
Parable of the Good Samaritan			10:25-37	
Jesus visits Mary and Martha			10:38-42	
Teaches disciples how to pray			11:1-13	
Blasphemous accusation against Jesus			11:14-36	
Warning about hypocrisy			12:1-12	
Warning against greed			12:13-15	
Parable of the rich fool			12:16-20	
Spiritual riches above earthly wealth			12:21-34	
Warning to be prepared			12:35-48	
Warning about future division			12:49-53	
Warning about signs of the present			12:54-59	
Repent, or perish			13:1-9	
Healing of a woman on the Sabbath			13:10-21	
Healing of a man born blind				9:1-41
Christ as the Good Shepherd and Door				10:1-18
Jews divided about Jesus				10:19-21
Attempt to stone, arrest Jesus				10:22-39
Ministry in and Around Perea				
Leaves Jerusalem, goes to Perea				10:40-42
Question about entering the kingdom			13:22-30	
Jesus' coming death			13:31-35	
Healing of man with dropsy			14:1-24	
Cost of following Jesus			14:25-35	
Parables: lost sheep, lost coin, prodigal			15:1-32	
Parable about the steward, riches			16:1-18	
The rich man and Lazarus			16:19-31	
Lessons to disciples			17:1-10	
Lazarus is sick, dies				11:1-16
Jesus raises Lazarus from the dead				11:17-45
Sanhedrin decides Jesus must die				11:46-53
Jesus withdraws to Ephraim				11:54
Healing of ten lepers			17:11-19	
Foretelling of Son of Man's coming			17:20-37	
Parable of the widow			18:1-8	
Parable of the Pharisee and publican			18:9-14	

	MATTHEW	MARK	LUKE	JOHN
Pharisees ask Jesus about divorce	19:1-12	10:1-12		
Little children, Jesus, the kingdom	19:13-15	10:13-16	18:15-17	
The rich young ruler	19:16-30	10:17-31	18:18-30	
Parable of landowner and laborers	20:1-16			
Prediction of death and resurrection	20:17-19	10:32-34	18:31-34	
Warning against pride: James, John	20:20-28	10:35-45		
Healing of two blind men	20:29-34	10:46-52	18:35-43	
Zacchaeus meets Jesus, is saved			19:1-10	
Parable about delay of kingdom			19:11-27	

Jesus' Last Week

	MATTHEW	MARK	LUKE	JOHN
Arrival at Bethany				11:55–12:1
Mary anoints Jesus	26:6-13	14:3-9		12:2-11
Triumphal entry into Jerusalem	21:1-11, 14-17	11:1-11	19:28-44	12:12-19
Cursing of barren fig tree	21:18-19	11:12-14		
Second cleansing of temple	21:12-13	11:15-18	19:45-48	
Greeks request to see Jesus				12:20-36
Unbelievers depart from Jesus				12:36-50
Withered fig tree, lesson on faith	21:19-22	11:19-25[26]		
Christ's authority challenged	21:23-27	11:27-33	20:1-8	
Parables of two sons and the vineyard	21:28-46	12:1-12	20:9-19	
Parable of the marriage feast	22:1-14			
Question about paying taxes to Caesar	22:15-22	12:13-17	20:20-26	
Sadducees ask about the resurrection	22:23-33	12:18-27	20:27-40	
Scribe asks about greatest commandment	22:34-40	12:28-34		
Christ as David's Son and Lord	22:41-46	12:35-37	20:41-44	
Seven woes against scribes and Pharisees	23:1-36	12:38-40	20:45-47	
Jesus laments over Jerusalem	23:37-39			
The widow's two coins		12:41-44	21:1-4	
The Olivet Discourse: Jesus teaches about the temple and His return	24–25	13	21:5-36	

The Betrayal, Arrest, and Crucifixion of Jesus

	MATTHEW	MARK	LUKE	JOHN
Plot by Sanhedrin to arrest and kill Jesus	26:1-5	14:1-2	21:37–22:2	
Judas agrees to betray Jesus	26:14-16	14:10-11	22:3-6	
Preparation for Passover meal	26:17-19	14:12-16	22:7-13	
Passover meal begins	26:20	14:17	22:14-16	
Jesus washes the disciples' feet				13:1-20
Jesus identifies His betrayer	26:21-25	14:18-21	22:21-23	13:21-30
Disciples argue over greatness			22:24-30	
Jesus predicts Peter's denial			22:31-38	13:31-38
The Lord's Supper established	26:26-29	14:22-25	22:17-20	
Jesus answers disciples' questions				14:1-31
The Vine and the branches				15:1-17
Expecting opposition from the world				15:18–16:4
The Holy Spirit's ministry explained				16:5-15
Jesus prophesies about His resurrection				16:16-22

	MATTHEW	MARK	LUKE	JOHN
Jesus promises answered prayer and peace				16:23-33
Jesus' high-priestly prayer				17
Jesus again predicts Peter's denial	26:30-35	14:26-31	22:39-40	18:1
Jesus' prayers in the Garden of Gethsemane	26:36-46	14:32-42	22:40-46	
Jesus betrayed and arrested, disciples flee	26:47-56	14:43-52	22:47-53	18:2-12
First Jewish trial, before Anna				18:13-24
Second Jewish trial, before Sanhedrin	26:57-68	14:53-65	22:54	
Peter denies Jesus	26:69-75	14:66-72	22:55-65	18:25-27
Third Jewish trial, before Sanhedrin	27:1	15:1	22:66-71	
Judas commits suicide	27:3-10			
First Roman trial, before Pilate	27:2,11-14	15:1-5	23:1-5	18:28-38
Second Roman trial, before Herod Antipas			23:6-12	
Third Roman trial, before Pilate	27:15-26	15:6-15	23:13-25	18:39–19:16
Jesus mocked by Roman soldiers	27:27-30	15:16-19		
Jesus goes to Golgotha	27:31-34	15:20-23	23:26-33	19:17
The crucifixion	27:35-50	15:24-37	23:33-46	19:18-37
Eyewitnesses of Jesus' death	27:51-56	15:38-41	23:45,47-49	
Jesus' body requested	27:57-58	15:42-45	23:50-52	19:38
Jesus' body buried in the tomb	27:59-61	15:46	23:53-54	19:39-42
Soldiers placed to guard the tomb	27:62-66	15:47	23:55-56	

The Resurrection and Ascension of Christ

	MATTHEW	MARK	LUKE	JOHN
The resurrection on the first day of the week	28:2-4			
The tomb found empty by the women	28:1,5-8	16:1-8	24:1-10	20:1
Peter and John go to the empty tomb			24:9-11[12]	20:2-10
Jesus appears to Mary Magdalene		[16:9-11]		20:11-18
Jesus appears to the other women	28:9-10			
The soldiers' report given to Jewish priests	28:11-15			
Jesus and two disciples on road to Emmaus		[16:12-13]	24:13-32	
Two disciples give report to the others			24:33-35	
Appearance to ten disciples, Thomas absent		[16:14]	24:36-49	20:19-23
Appearance to 11 disciples, with Thomas				20:24-31
Appearance to disciples who are fishing				21:1-24
Appearance to 11 disciples in Galilee	28:16-20	[16:15-18]		
Appearance to 500 people—1 Corinthians 15:6				
Appearance to James—1 Corinthians 15:7				
Appearance to all the apostles—1 Corinthians 15:7				
Christ blesses disciples and departs (Acts 1:9-12)		[16:19-20]	24:50-53	
Conclusion				21:25

Appendix 7: Key Words in the New International Version

NASB key words	NIV related words
Genesis	
covenant	oath, treaty
Leviticus	
leprosy	infectious skin disease
Numbers	
blood avenger	avenger of blood
number	listed, listing, count
service	serve, duty, duties, work
Deuteronomy	
fear	revere, revering
heart(s)	yourself, integrity, disheartened, disheartened, mind, way
listen	pay attention, hear, obey
observe	follow, obey, be careful, keep, pay attention to
Joshua	
captured	taken, took
cling	hold fast, ally
command	instruct, tell, word, direct, order
covenant	treaty
fear	be afraid
fight	make war, attack
firm	strong
Israel	Israelites
land	area, border, country, plain, region, territory
possess	acquire, occupy, for your own, take possession
serve	worship
strong	powerful
Judges	
sons of Israel	Israelites
1 Samuel	
evil	disaster, fault, harm, mean, wrong, wrongdoing
inquire	find out
judge	led, leader
sin, sinned	wronged
2 Samuel	
covenant	agreement, compact, sworn
evil	blame, calamity, come to ruin, displeased, guilt, harm, sin, wrong
inquire	find out, pleaded with
king	rule

NASB key words	NIV related words
1 Kings	
according to	as, keeping with, like
command	give orders, told
covenant	treaty
heart	mind, thought, wholeheartedly
pray	declared, called, shouted
sin	commit, wrong
2 Kings	
according to the word of the Lord	as the Lord had said
heart	accord, mind, spirit, wholehearted
high places	shrines
1 Chronicles	
covenant	compact
house	palatial structure
the sons of Judah	the people of Judah
2 Chronicles	
house	temple, palace
seek	consult, inquire
Ezra	
decree	order, authorized, letter
house	temple
Nehemiah	
banquet	dinner
command	regulations
Job	
sons of God	angels
Psalms	
fear	dread
hope	wait for, trust in
prayer	plea
sin	crime, iniquity, malice, wrong
sing	cry out, make music, shout, song
wicked	vile
Proverbs	
instruction	lesson
Ecclesiastes	
directed	turned
discover	comprehend
evil	crimes, misfortune
explain	conclude
labor	efforts
vanity, futile	meaningless

NASB key words	NIV related words
Song of Solomon	
beautiful	delightful, fair
beloved	lover
love	adore
Isaiah	
Lord of hosts	Lord Almighty
Rabshakeh	commander
recompense	retribution
Ezekiel	
iniquity	guilt, doing wrong, evil, wicked
harlot	prostitute, adultery, illicit favors, promiscuity
wrath	anger, fury
heart	courage
covenant	treaty
holy	sacred
offering	special gift
Daniel	
ruler	sovereign
kingdom	sovereign power,
weeks	sevens
Hosea	
harlotry, adultery	unfaithfulness, prostitution
covenant	treaty
return	repent, go back
Amos	
transgressions	sins
Lord God	sovereign Lord
Jonah	
turn	give up
calamity	trouble, destruction
Nahum	
destroy	demolish
sin	transgression
Habakkuk	
proud, haughty	puffed up, arrogant, greedy
Zephaniah	
destruction, desolation	anguish, distress, ruin, wasteland, rubble
in your midst	with you
Haggai	
consider	give careful thought
Lord of hosts	Lord Almighty
the Lord spoke	message of the Lord
all the earth	the whole world, in every land

NASB key words	NIV related words
Zechariah	
burden	oracle
I saw	I had a vision
I lifted up my eyes	I looked up
return	turn
again	further, added
I will dwell in your midst	I will live among you
Lord of hosts	Lord Almighty
Malachi	
Lord of hosts	Lord Almighty
you say	you ask
profane	desecrated
treacherously	broken faith

New Testament
Common differences throughout the New Testament:

Matthew	
finished these words	finished saying these things
Mark	
immediately	at once, quickly, without delay, as soon as, just as, shortly
John	
believe	faith, trust
judge	condemn, verdict, decisions
witness	testify, testimony, speak, spread the word
true	valid, real, right, reliable, surely
works	miracles, things
abide	remain
ask	pray
Acts	
believe	faith, trust
witness	testify, confirmed, bore testimony, showed, martyr
word	preaching, message, statement
Romans	
law	principle
justified	proved right, declared righteous
righteous	justice
wrath	punishment
judge	condemn
Gentiles	nations
reckoned	credit
therefore	then, this is why
flesh	sinful (or natural) man (or nature or selves), unspiritual
choice, chosen	elect
minister	act of worship
weak	failings

NASB key words	NIV related words
1 Corinthians	
wisdom, wise	expert
arrogant	proud, puffs up, pride
now concerning	now for, now about
church	congregation
factions	differences
2 Corinthians	
comfort	encouragement, listen to my appeal
afflicted	hard pressed, harassed, distressed, troubles, hardships, trial, suffer, harm
sorrowful	painful, hurt, grief, sorry
boast	take pride
joy	glad, delighted
work	act of grace
Galatians	
faith	believe
brethren	brothers
Ephesians	
heavenly places	heavenly realms
according to	in accordance with, followed, through, as
former(ly)	at one time, used to, once
grace	benefit
power	strength
walk	live, do
stand firm	take your stand, stand your ground
Philippians	
imprisonment	chains
joy, rejoice	be glad
mind	like-minded, think, attitude, a view of things
Colossians	
all	every, great, everything, full
let no one	do not let anyone
1 Thessalonians	
gospel	message
2 Thessalonians	
glory	honor, majesty
undisciplined	idle
1 Timothy	
endure	put up with
Titus	
doctrine	teachings
deeds	actions, righteous things, do what is good
sensible	self-controlled

NASB key words	NIV related words
Hebrews	
beloved	dear friends
brethren	brothers
better	superior
therefore	for this reason, so, this is why
perfect	clear
covenant	will
James	
say	claims to
works	deeds, actions
brethren	brothers
faith	believe
perfect	mature, finish, complete
judge	be condemned
1 Peter	
chosen	elect
2 Peter	
I am writing	I have written
knowledge	understand, told about
remind	refresh your memory
diligent	make every effort, eager
false	made up
1 John	
know	recognize
abide	remain, continue, be in, live in
truth, true	real
2 John	
abide	continue, live
Jude	
judgment	accusation
Revelation	
overcome	triumph, overpower, conquer
after these things	later, after this
and I saw	I watched, I looked
nations	Gentiles, ages

KEY WORDS IN THE KING JAMES VERSION

NASB key words	KJV related words
Genesis	
commanded	spake

NASB key words	KJV related words
Exodus	
staff	rod
sign	token
test	prove, tempt
grumble	murmur
slave	servant, handmaid
deliver	bring you out
Leviticus	
offering	oblation
atonement	reconcile, reconciliation
holy	glorified, hallowed
restitution	amends, restore
census	sum
Numbers	
grumble	murmur
blood avenger	revenger of blood
Deuteronomy	
watch	take heed
listen	hearken
you shall therefore	therefore shall ye
you shall purge (remove) the evil	put the evil away
the Lord will	the Lord shall
Joshua	
land	country
courageous	good courage
covenant	league
fought	made war
captured	took, take(n)
commanded	charged
cling	cleave
Judges	
sons of Israel	children of Israel
Ruth	
closest relative	near of kin
1 Samuel	
evil	mischief
inquired	asked, counsel
2 Samuel	
inquired	besought
covenant	league, had sworn
evil	displeased, bad, mischief, hurt
1 Kings	
word	saying
word of the Lord	saying of the Lord, mouth of the Lord

NASB key words	KJV related words
2 Kings	
customs	manners
mediums	familiar spirits
spiritists	wizards
idols	graven images
1 Chronicles	
Abraham became the father of Isaac	Abraham begat Issac
the sons of Judah	the children of Judah
inquired	enquired
house	palace
2 Chronicles	
house	palace
cry	shout(ed)
pray	beseech
prayer	supplication
rebellion	rebelled
pride	lifted up
cloud	darkness
Ezra	
guilt	trespass
decree	commanded, commandment, letter
Nehemiah	
remember	neither were mindful, think upon
ordinances	judgments
Esther	
banquet	feast
anger	wrath, indignation
edict	royal commandment
Psalms	
wicked	ungodly
take refuge	put trust
Ecclesiastes	
explain	declare
righteous	just
wickedness	iniquity
Song of Solomon	
wedding	espousals
come (coming)	came, cometh, go up, return
beautiful	fair, fairest
Isaiah	
the oracle concerning	the burden of
nations	Gentiles

NASB key words	KJV related words
Jeremiah	
nations	Gentiles, heathen
listen, hear	hearken
harlot	whoredom
heart	bowels
forsake	leave
calamity	evil
Lamentations	
anger	fury
Ezekiel	
vision	vanity
iniquity	mischief
wrath	indignation
harlot	whore, whores, etc., fornication
Daniel	
man of high esteem	man greatly beloved
Hosea	
harlotry	whoredom
the Lord said	God said
in the last days	in the latter days
Joel	
locust	palmerworm, cankerworm, caterpillar
never again	no more
nations	heathen, Gentiles, a people far off
Amos	
thus says the Lord	thus saith the Lord
thus the Lord God showed me	thus the Lord God shewed unto me
nations	heathen
Obadiah	
nations	heathen
Jonah	
compassion	pity, spare, merciful
relent(s)	repent(est)
appointed	prepared
calamity	evil
Micah	
destroy	desolation, spoiled
Habakkuk	
haughty man	soul which is lifted up
Zephaniah	
that day	some day
in your midst	in the midst of thee

NASB key words	**KJV** related words
all the earth	the whole land, in every land
face of the earth	off the land

Zechariah

what do you see?	what seest thou?
listen	hear
stopped their ears from hearing	would not hear
seventy years	three score and ten

Malachi

fear	dreadful, afraid
divorce	putting away

New Testament
Common differences throughout the New Testament:

Holy Spirit	Holy Ghost
covenant	testament
witness	testimony
many verbs	end in "est," "eth"
your	thy, thine
you	ye
love	charity

Mark

immediately	as soon as, straightway

John

signs	miracles
judge	condemn
witness	record
true (truth, truly)	verily
abide	dwelleth, present

Romans

wrath	vengeance
God gave them over	God gave them up
credited (chapter 4)	counted, reckoned, imputed
flesh	carnal
life	quicken
master	dominion
slave	serve, servants
predestined	predestinate
choice	elect(ion)
authority, ruler	power
judgment	disputation
weaknesses	infirmities

1 Corinthians

divisions	differences
boast	glory

NASB key words	KJV related words
arrogant	puffed up
Immorality	fornication
do you not know	know ye not, do ye not know
now concerning	now as touching
factions	heresies
think(ing)	understanding, thoughts, suppose
now I make known to you	moreover

2 Corinthians

suffering (chapters 8 and 9)	troubled
work	grace

Galatians

freedom	liberty

Ephesians

formerly	in time(s) past, sometimes
strength of his might	power of his might, mighty power
authorities	principalities

Philippians

joy (rejoice)	gladness
mind (attitude)	thinketh
stand firm	stand fast

2 Thessalonians

man of Lawlessness	man of sin
undisciplined	disorderly
example	ensample

1 Timothy

overseers	bishops
slaves	servants
money	filthy lucre

2 Timothy

sacred writings	holy scriptures
suffer (hardships, persecutions)	afflictions, trouble, hardness

Titus

deeds	works
speak	affirm
sensible	sober, discreet

Philemon

appeal	beseech
slave	servant

Hebrews

therefore	wherefore, whereupon

NASB key words	KJV related words
James	
judge	condemnation
1 Peter	
suffering	afflictions
chosen	elect(ed)
precious	great price
imperishable	incorruptible
perishable	corruptible
2 Peter	
remind	remembrance
diligent	endeavor
destroy	perish, dissolved, burned up
mockers	scoffers
1 John	
abide	remain, dwell(eth)
2 John	
teaching	doctrine
abides	dwelleth
Jude	
judgment	accusation
Revelation	
throne	seat
overcame	prevailed
after these things	hereafter, things which shall be hereafter
and I saw	and I beheld
nations	Gentiles
bowl(s)	vial(s)

Books in the
New Inductive Study Series

❧ ❧ ❧ ❧

Teach Me Your Ways
Genesis, Exodus,
Leviticus, Numbers,
Deuteronomy

*Choosing Victory,
Overcoming Defeat*
Joshua, Judges, Ruth

Desiring God's Own Heart
1 & 2 Samuel,
1 Chronicles

Walking Faithfully with God
1 & 2 Kings, 2 Chronicles

*Overcoming Fear
and Discouragement*
Ezra, Nehemiah, Esther

*Trusting God
in Times of Adversity*
Job

*God's Blueprint for
Bible Prophecy*
Daniel

*Discovering the God
of Second Chances*
Jonah, Joel, Amos, Obadiah

*Opening the Windows
of Blessings*
Haggai, Zechariah,
Malachi

The Call to Follow Jesus
Luke

*The Holy Spirit
Unleashed in You*
Acts

*God's Answers for
Relationships and Passions*
1 & 2 Corinthians

*Free from Bondage
God's Way*
Galatians, Ephesians

That I May Know Him
Philippians, Colossians

*Standing Firm in
These Last Days*
1 & 2 Thessalonians

*Walking in Power,
Love, and Discipline*
1 & 2 Timothy, Titus

*Living with Discernment
in the End Times*
1 & 2 Peter, Jude

God's Love Alive in You
1, 2, & 3 John,
Philemon, James

Behold, Jesus Is Coming!
Revelation

Harvest House Books
by Kay Arthur

ⱷⱷⱷⱷ

God, Are You There?
God, Help Me Experience More of You
God, How Can I Live?
How to Study Your Bible
Israel, My Beloved
Lord, Teach Me to Pray in 28 Days
A Marriage Without Regrets
A Marriage Without Regrets Study Guide
Prayers to Bless Your Marriage
Speak to My Heart, God
With an Everlasting Love

Bibles
The New Inductive Study Bible (NASB)

ⱷⱷⱷⱷ

Discover 4 Yourself®
Inductive Bible Studies for Kids
God, What's Your Name?
How to Study Your Bible for Kids
Lord, Teach Me to Pray for Kids
God's Amazing Creation (Genesis 1–2)
Digging Up the Past (Genesis 3–11)
Abraham—God's Brave Explorer (Genesis 11–25)
Extreme Adventures with God (Isaac, Esau, and Jacob)
Joseph—God's Superhero (Genesis 37–50)
Wrong Way, Jonah! (Jonah)
Jesus in the Spotlight (John 1–11)
Jesus—Awesome Power, Awesome Love (John 11–16)
Jesus—To Eternity and Beyond! (John 17–21)
Boy, Have I Got Problems! (James)

Everybody, Everywhere, Anytime, Anyplace, Any Age...
Can Discover the Truth for Themselves

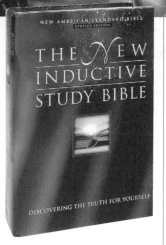

In today's world with its often confusing and mixed messages, where can you turn to find the answer to the challenges you and your family face? Whose word can you trust? Where can you turn when you need answers—about relationships, your children, your future?

The Updated New Inductive Study Bible

Open *this* study Bible and you will soon discover its uniqueness— unlike any other, this study Bible offers no notes, commentaries, or the opinions of others telling you what the Scripture is saying. It is in fact the only study Bible based entirely on the *inductive* study approach, providing you with instructions and the tools for observing what the text really says, interpreting what it means, and applying its principles to your life.

The only study Bible containing the *inductive study method* taught and endorsed by Kay Arthur and Precept Ministries.

• A new *smaller* size makes it easier to carry • individualized instructions for studying *every* book • guides for color marking keywords and themes • *Updated* NASB text • *improved* in-text maps and charts • 24 pages of full-color charts, historical timelines, & maps • self-discovery in its truest form

One Message, The Bible.
One Method, Inductive.

A SIMPLE, PROVEN APPROACH TO LETTING GOD'S WORD CHANGE YOUR LIFE...FOREVER

HARVEST HOUSE PUBLISHERS
EUGENE, OREGON 97402

www.harvesthousepublishers.com

Kay Arthur and her husband, Jack, are the founders of Precept Ministries International. PMI reaches hundreds of thousands of people internationally through various small-group Bible studies for children, teens, and adults. These range from the 40-Minute Bible Studies to Precept Upon Precept Bible studies. Kay's passion to establish people in God's Word extends across the Internet and onto the radio and television program *Precepts for Life*. The best-selling author of more than 100 books and Bible studies, Kay is the active spokeswoman for *The New Inductive Study Bible.*